Assessing Impact

Third Edition

*To educators worldwide who strive to improve their practice
each day so their students achieve their dreams.*

Assessing Impact

Evaluating Professional Learning

Third Edition

Joellen Killion

Foreword by Michael Fullan

A Joint Publication

CORWIN
A SAGE Publishing Company

learningforward
THE PROFESSIONAL LEARNING ASSOCIATION

FOR INFORMATION:

Corwin

A SAGE Company

2455 Teller Road

Thousand Oaks, California 91320

(800) 233-9936

www.corwin.com

SAGE Publications Ltd.

1 Oliver's Yard

55 City Road

London EC1Y 1SP

United Kingdom

SAGE Publications India Pvt. Ltd.

B 1/I 1 Mohan Cooperative Industrial Area

Mathura Road, New Delhi 110 044

India

SAGE Publications Asia-Pacific Pte. Ltd.

3 Church Street

#10-04 Samsung Hub

Singapore 049483

Program Director: Dan Alpert

Associate Editor: Lucas Schleicher

Editorial Assistant: Mia Rodriguez

Production Editor: Amy Schroller

Copy Editor: Terri Lee Paulsen

Typesetter: C&M Digitals (P) Ltd.

Proofreader: Dennis W. Webb

Indexer: Sheila Bodell

Cover Designer: Scott Van Atta

Marketing Manager: Charline Maher

Printed in the United States of America

ISBN: 978-1-5063-9595-1

This book is printed on acid-free paper.

18 19 20 21 10 9 8 7 6 5 4 3 2

Contents

Foreword

I lost count of how many times a state commissioner of education, or a school district superintendent said to me " we have so much professional development going that I can't keep track of it, and I have no idea whatsoever if it is having any impact." Well, your troubles are over (at least on this dimension); Joellen Killion has written the bible on assessing professional learning. *Assessing Impact* is without a question the definitive book on understanding professional learning (PL) and determining its worth.

The book is comprehensive and up to date to the minute—capturing ESSA and the overall purpose of assessing PL in order " to assist school, district, and state leadership in examining ongoing evidence for improvement.". In page after page, Killion demonstrates how to make evaluation and improvement seamless. The twelve chapters (and eight appendixes) are replete with insights, frameworks, tools, case examples, and step-by-step guides for conducting and using evaluations for understanding and improving PL in action.

In education change there is an age-old problem of how to get inside "the black box of implementation"—or as one observer called it "on the risk of appraising non-events." A non-event is something that was supposed to have happened, was carried out superficially, and then evaluated without getting inside what really happened (or didn't happen in actual practice). Such evaluations are impossible to evaluate, but Killion has a solution. She identifies the black box and then provides us the "'glass box" of professional learning: what was supposed to have happened, what actually took place, and how much impact it had. This is a book that is crystal clear about all aspects of a very complicated phenomenon: professional learning in action.

Killion is very clear about "'the theory of change" in terms of three action steps that need to take place and be assessed ranging from assumptions (e.g., collaborative learning of new practices), to implementation (support for implementing certain practices), to actual practice change and its impact on student performance. Every chapter has a valuable rubric to guide action for every step of the way: how to design the evaluation, how to conduct it, and a data interpretation rubric. No detail is missed: how to attribute data, seek permission, manage costs, manage data collection and reporting, avoid pitfalls, organize and display data, interpret data, report and disseminate, and even how to evaluate the evaluation. It is all there in readable detail with case illustrations and displays, and in every place a rubric. You need to figure out how to interpret

what is found? The data collection rubric in Chapter 7 is a gem—as is the data interpretation rubric, and the portrayal of the types of data analysis available. Table 10.2 provides a frame for the possible components of evaluation reports, and so on.

In addition to being comprehensive about a very complicated phenomenon—evaluation of a murky and multifaceted topic like PL—Joellen Killion shows us exactly how the field of PL needs to shift from what it was to what it needs to be in modern times. I especially liked the Table 12.1 comparing the paradigm shift on eleven dimensions of what evaluating used to be and what it needs to be. To take only one of the dimensions: "feared by stakeholders and participants" to "embraced by stakeholders and participants."

In all, *Assessing Impact: Evaluating Professional Learning* not only fills the gap with respect to a critical topic that is much neglected, but it overflows the chasm of poorly or non-conducted treatments of professional learning in action. This is a book brimming with practical and comprehensive ideas on one of the least understood topics in education change: how do we know that professional learning is worth the investment? Read this book and find out.

—Michael Fullan
Professor Emeritus
OISE/University of Toronto

Acknowledgments

Many people have contributed in large and small ways to this third-edition book. The first edition was the result of the vision, passion, and commitment of Hayes Mizell, Learning Forward's Senior Distinguished Fellow and formerly the director of programs for student achievement at the Edna McConnell Clark Foundation. Mizell's leadership and zealous focus on the only prize that matters in professional learning—student achievement—have provided encouragement and resources to assist schools and districts to improve dramatically the quality and impact of their professional learning. He recognized that effective professional learning had a single purpose: to improve student success. After a series of initiatives led by the National Staff Development Council, now Learning Forward, that examined content-specific professional learning funded by the Edna McConnell Clark Foundation, Mizell realized that the efforts to link educator learning with student learning were shallow and limited. He called for action to prepare and support educators with the knowledge, skills, and tools to be proactive in evaluating both the effectiveness and the impact of their professional learning investments and efforts.

I am indebted to the countless individuals who shared sample evaluation tools with me, provided examples of evaluations they conducted, shared their learning about evaluating professional learning, and continue to express frustration with it. It is for those who want to use evidence more effectively to improve both quality and results that I continue to investigate and invest in this work. I am particularly grateful to a small team of districts engaged in a small investigatory study funded by Frontline Research & Learning Institute for their commitment to be my learning partners in this next phase of the work. I want to acknowledge and appreciate my colleague, Linda Munger, who serves as a thinking partner in program design and evaluation. She patiently read every word and commented on many. I trust her expertise and extensive experience in evaluation and have had the professional privilege of working alongside her on multiple initiatives. She provided innumerable insights and suggestions that helped shape this third edition. She shares my passion for facilitating program design and evaluation in schools and districts so that professional learning can achieve its intended outcomes.

I am most grateful to the educators with whom I have shared this book in various professional learning experiences around the world. They have been my wisdom partners in this work, applied the steps, and shared their successes

and challenges with me. I learn more each time I engage with those who care deeply about being able to evaluate their work objectively and rigorously. Thank you for your commitment to be responsible, accountable, ethical, and practical in your effort to strengthen educator and student success.

I am grateful to the leadership team at Corwin for their commitment to advance this next edition. They are investing in their own study about the impact of their work and model the importance of evidence-driven decision making to increase their overall service and support to their clients.

About the Author

Joellen Killion is senior advisor to Learning Forward. Since her retirement from Learning Forward as deputy executive director, Killion focuses on helping school systems and states develop and enact comprehensive professional learning systems that ensure all educators have access to highly effective professional learning that results in student success. She is particularly passionate about the role of coaching as a vehicle for personalizing and differentiating professional learning for teachers, principals, and central office staff. She has led a number of local, state, and national initiatives to improve professional learning, its planning, implementation, and evaluation; served as a consultant to hundreds of schools and school systems; and is the author and coauthor of numerous books and articles.

Introduction

Assessing Impact: Evaluating Professional Learning guides education practitioners to measure the progress and effects of their efforts in professional learning. The necessity for evaluation is urgent and straight-forward logic. The logic for this is simple. Researchers and practitioners agree that the quality of teaching and school leadership are the single greatest factors influencing student success. Professional learning expands and strengthens educators' capacity for teaching and leadership. To increase capacity, education leaders at the state, district, and school levels invest in professional learning. To produce professional learning's intended results for educators and students, education agencies and educators themselves invest in professional learning. To know if the investment in professional learning produces results, educators evaluate it. To make improvements in their efforts to strengthen educator capacity, education leaders engage in evaluation that is practical, ongoing, and meaningful and provides the information they want to improve their efforts.

Evaluation is essential to measure the progress and effects of any professional learning to know if the intended outcomes are achieved and to make adjustments based on **evidence** in an expedient, effective, and equitable way. Emil Posavac notes the natural and essential nature of evaluation: "The practice of evaluating one's own effort is as natural as breathing. Cooks taste their gravy and sauce and basketball players watch to see whether their shots go in. Indeed, it would be most unwise after turning on the hot water to neglect to check the water temperature before stepping into a shower," he states. "At a basic level, program evaluation is nothing more than applying this common-sense practice to settings in which organized efforts, called 'programs,' are devoted to helping people who need education, medical treatment, job training, safe streets, welfare assistance, safety while traveling in airplanes, recreational services, or any of the thousand services provided in a modern society" (2016, p. 1).

In the nearly two decades since the first initiative began and the decade since the publication of the second edition, education decision makers, policy makers, practitioners, evaluators, researchers, and elected officials continue to search for practical, useful, and feasible ways to measure the effects of professional learning. Several well-known randomized control trial studies (Garet et al., 2008; Garet et al., 2010) have failed to show that professional learning

A note about terminology . . .

For the most part, unless a specific source uses the term **professional development**, this text uses **professional learning**. The distinction is to emphasize the difference between the process, experiences, or **activities** to achieve a set of outcomes and the outcomes themselves. *Assessing Impact* intends to focus on results, yet acknowledges that assessing processes provide critical information about how to increase the potential for outcomes. A common mistake in evaluating professional learning or development is to assume that the activities are the outcomes.

results in changes in educator practice and student achievement. Smaller-scale, non-empirical studies and program evaluations find positive effects, yet policy makers at the federal and state levels and private and public funders continue to question the efficacy of professional learning as a viable investment or pathway for substantive improvement of schools. The stakes in terms of accountability for results continue to grow more significant and the need more profound for educators to assume responsibility for evaluating professional learning.

The third edition of this book incorporates changes in federal and state policy related to professional learning. It also reflects the increased accountability for results for investments in professional learning. Federal, state, and local policy makers question the return on their investments in professional learning, particularly since many studies of the effectiveness of professional learning conducted over the last several decades demonstrate the inconclusive results. Educators must do a better job contributing to the body of evidence about professional learning while researchers continue to examine empirically if and how professional learning affects educator practice and student learning. Educators who know from their experience that professional learning is a significant factor in improving educator effectiveness are called on to provide more valid evidence about their efforts both to strengthen their own practice and to increase results.

The **Every Student Succeeds Act (ESSA)**, signed into law in December 2015, defines professional development as

"PROFESSIONAL DEVELOPMENT.—The term 'professional development' means activities that — ""(42) PROFESSIONAL DEVELOPMENT.—The term 'professional development' means activities that—"(A) are an integral part of school and local educational agency strategies for providing educators (including teachers, principals, other school leaders, specialized instructional support personnel, paraprofessionals, and, as applicable, early childhood educators) with the knowledge and skills necessary to enable students to succeed in a well-rounded education and to meet the challenging State academic standards; and

"(B) are sustained (not stand-alone, 1-day, or short term workshops), intensive, collaborative, job-embedded, data-driven, and classroom-focused" (S. 1177-295).

The full definition appears in Appendix A. Following this core definition is an extensive list of additional features of professional development activities intended to guide those responsible for decision-making. At this writing, non-binding federal guidance documents support the implementation of the *Every Student Succeeds Act* and the development of state consolidated plans for the implementation of Title I, II, and V programs.

The revised definition of professional learning in *ESSA* specifies that professional learning is intensive (not a stand-alone, 1-day, or short-term experience),

collaborative, job embedded, data driven, and classroom focused. *ESSA* expands allowable uses of Title II funding to focus on equity and excellence. It clarifies levels of evidence and calls for states to use evidence to select programs with proven or promising results. In addition, *ESSA* requires a plan for continuous improvement of both the plan and its implementation and consultation with a wide variety of stakeholders in the process of plan development (Revised *ESSA* Consolidated Plan Template, 2016).

This edition rests on five guiding principles that collectively provide a rationale for professional learning leaders to engage in rigorous, ongoing evaluation of their efforts. The first is the Data standard of Standards for Professional Learning: Professional learning that increases the effectiveness of every educator and results for all students uses multiple forms and sources of **data** about students, educators, and systems to plan, implement, and evaluate professional learning (Learning Forward, 2011). The second is included in *ESSA*'s definition of professional development. "Professional development . . . may include activities that . . . (xi) as a whole, are regularly evaluated for their impact on increased teacher effectiveness and improved student academic achievement, with the findings of the evaluations used to improve the quality of professional development" (ESSA SEC. 8002 GENERAL PROVISIONS—DEFINITIONS). The third is Principle 6 from *The Learning Educator: A New Vision of Professional Learning*: "Impact: Evaluation strengthens performance and impact" (Hirsh & Killion, 2007, p. 73). The fourth principle, from the PD Redesign Principles, is "Measuring the impact of professional learning provides data that are essential to decision-making and better allocation of resources." And lastly, the principle "What gets measured, gets done." This statement's origin is unclear, yet its meaning is not. An intent to measure progress and results signals the importance of a set of actions and may contribute to increased urgency to act to achieve the outcomes.

This third edition of *Assessing Impact: Evaluating Professional Learning* emphasizes the role of evaluation in continuous improvement, strives to give practitioners more specific and rigorous processes for measuring planning, implementation, effectiveness, and impact of professional learning; acknowledges the continued call for accountability of public funds for professional learning; and encourages states, school systems, and schools to adopt evaluation as a normative practice to enhance data-driven decision-making processes. While much has changed since the reauthorization of the *Elementary and Secondary School Act of 1965* in 2015 in terms of requirements for states regarding the implementation and operation of federally supported, mandated programs in the nine Title areas, what has not changed is the responsibility of educators to be accountable for the success of every student, make informed, data-driven decisions regarding students' education, and engage in continuous improvement to increase equity and excellence in education. The law's purpose is "to ensure that every child achieves" through grants and subgrants to state and local education agencies to

"(1) increase student achievement consistent with the challenging State academic standards;

"(2) improve the quality and effectiveness of teachers, principals, and other school leaders;

"(3) increase the number of teachers, principals, and other school leaders who are effective in improving student academic achievement in schools; and

"(4) provide low-income and minority students greater access to effective teachers, principals, and other school leaders" (*ESSA*, Sec. 2001).

What has not changed in this edition is the clear message that evaluation of professional learning without thoughtful and thorough planning for and resourcing of professional learning is inexcusable and foolhardy, especially if evaluators seek to measure impact. If done with intentionality and rigor, evaluation requires a level of effort and cost that practitioners cannot afford to waste on insufficiently planned and weakly resourced professional learning efforts. The process of evaluating begins then with deliberate and comprehensive planning to ensure clarity of outcomes, evidence-based actions, sufficient resources to sustain professional learning over time, and ongoing formative assessment to adjust practices and meet unexpected challenges to achieve the intended outcomes.

The book encourages education practitioners to engage in evaluation that generates useful information for program improvement and for accountability of effort and investments. Practitioner-based evaluation differs from high-stakes, external evaluation by integrating frequent engagement and review of processes and results to improve their efforts. As such, it will rarely answer the question, How do we know it was the professional learning that caused these results? This question is a question for researchers to answer. Evaluations seek to involve stakeholders in the examination of their practice and its results before, during, and at the end of their efforts. The process is designed to cultivate "evaluation think," a phrase that Joy Frechtling, a member of a national advisory board for the initiative that launched the first edition of *Assessing Impact*, uses to describe how individuals and teams in schools and districts look critically and analytically at their work to discover what is working and what is not in order to redefine their work and to improve results.

PURPOSE OF THIS BOOK

The purpose of this book is to assist state, school system, and school leadership teams to

- plan evaluations of professional learning that provide ongoing evidence for program improvement;
- conduct practitioner-based evaluations that focus on results for educators and students;
- increase the frequency and usefulness of evaluation as a part of program management;
- build the capacity of education leaders and program stakeholders to adopt "evaluation think"; and
- increase the engagement of education stakeholders in decision-making about professional learning.

WHAT THIS BOOK IS AND ISN'T

This book is a guide to assist state, school system, and school leadership teams in planning and implementing evaluations of professional learning. It is designed to facilitate asking the fundamental evaluation questions:

- Does our plan for professional learning meet the criteria for success?
- Is our program ready for evaluation?
- How will we measure progress and results?
- Are we progressing as we intended?
- What is working? Why?
- What is not working? Why?
- What needs to change to increase likelihood of achieving the intended results?
- Did our professional learning efforts produce the intended results?
- What other effects of our efforts are we seeing?

As attributes of effective professional learning are increasingly clear from research (Darling-Hammond, Wei, Andree, Richardson, & Orphanos, 2009; Desimone & Garet, 2015; Desimone, Porter, Garet, Yoon, & Birman, 2002; Garet, Porter, Desimone, Birman, & Yoon, 2001; Learning Forward, 2011; Supovitz, Mayer, & Kahle, 2000; Supovitz & Turner, 2000; Yoon, Duncan, Scarloss, & Shapley, 2007), education practitioners apply these attributes to design more promising professional learning. Yet the application of the attributes will not necessarily produce results. Educators take the next step beyond applying the attributes in designing professional learning to using rigorous measures to evaluate implementation and results of their efforts.

This book is not a program evaluation textbook, a data collection and analysis guide, or a statistics manual. These are topics in which professional evaluators are well-versed and for which there are more scientific sources. This book is designed specifically for professional learning leaders, program or project coordinators, curriculum directors, principals, district and school improvement and leadership teams, or others who want to evaluate their professional learning programs to improve them and to be accountable for their investments and efforts in professional learning and to make informed, data-based decisions.

VALUE FOR EDUCATORS

This book assists practitioners to conduct evaluations of their work. Specifically, it suggests ways to

- design and conduct regular and rigorous evaluations to measure the effectiveness and impact of professional learning on educator practice and student achievement;
- report to policy makers and stakeholders about professional learning;
- assess implementation of professional learning to strengthen its impact;
- design powerful professional learning programs by making their program's theory of change and logic model explicit;

- provide *practical* ways to evaluate professional learning programs; and
- construct an information base for making decisions about professional learning programs.

Perhaps Michael Quinn Patton (1997) has described best what this work also is intended to do:

"Our aim is modest: reasonable estimations of the likelihood that particular activities have contributed in concrete ways to observed effects—emphasis on the word *reasonable*. Not definitive conclusions. Not absolute proof. Evaluation offers reasonable estimations of probabilities and likelihood, enough to provide useful guidance to an uncertain world (Blalock, 1964). I find that policy makers and program decision makers typically understand and appreciate this. Hard-core academics and scientists don't" (p. 217).

Evaluation as Normative Practice

1

Educators in states, school systems, and schools work tirelessly to meet the learning needs of every student. Yet, some students continue to struggle. To achieve their vision of success for every student, educators are increasingly using data to understand and pinpoint opportunities for increasing the effectiveness of their efforts and to make savvy decisions about education programs to implement. Rather than assigning blame elsewhere or shirking their responsibility, they double down on their commitment to be accountable to their **stakeholders**, especially students and their families. They cringe each time they see **results** that disappoint them and acknowledge that the education they are providing is leaving some students behind.

Yet what educators choose to do when they face this situation is perhaps the most crucial decision of all. Rather than grasping at anything available or what is easy and familiar, educators become more deliberate and engage in focused continuous improvement. They use available data to understand where the needs are and their root causes. They investigate evidence-based programs that provide results. They analyze the **context** in which their schools exist to assess the resources, culture, facilities, equipment, and human and social capital that will influence their efforts. Using all this information, they plan thoroughly for implementing **professional learning programs** with high levels of promise. In conjunction with their planning, they simultaneously plan how they will monitor implementation and evaluate their progress and results to address the gaps they have identified. As the professional learning programs are implemented, they review progress, make adjustments, and measure impact on educators and students.

This **backmapping process** (Killion, 1999; Killion & Roy, 2009) for the design, implementation, and **evaluation of professional learning** appears in a variety of forms and by various names. It describes the process for using data to identify needs, understanding context, studying **research** and evidence, planning a program to address needs, implementing the program, monitoring progress, and evaluating effects (see Figure 1.1). This process acknowledges that program selection or planning occurs only after deep analysis of student, educator, and system data. Not only do educators identify where

Figure 1.1 Backmapping Model

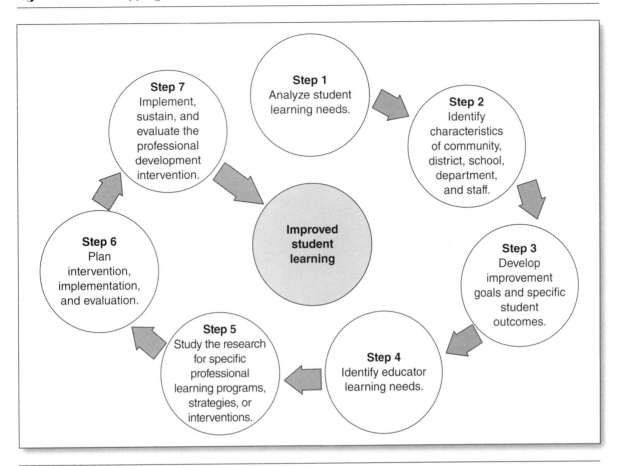

Killion, J. (1999). *What works in the middle: Results-based staff development.* Oxford, OH: National Staff Development Council.

gaps exist in student learning, but they also identify which students are in greatest need, what the most likely root causes are for the existing gaps, and which learning outcomes will eliminate the gaps. They also understand what educator factors and system factors are influencing the results and are in most need of addressing. For example, if most teachers in schools with the highest percentage of students who are underperforming are those with the lowest level of experience, how will program leaders address this factor in designing and implementing professional learning? If teachers have insufficient time for collaboration, a core research-supported component of increasing the quality of teaching within a school, how will the school's leadership team and district leadership team address this potential inhibitor before the program is implemented? Other similar processes such as the cycle of continuous improvement (Killion & Roy, 2009; Learning Forward, n.d.a), Plan-Do-Study-Act (PDSA) (Deming, 1994), or improvement science (Bryk, Gomez, Grunow, & LeMahieu, 2015) focus on shorter cycles of learning, experimentation, and implementation to make ongoing improvements in routine work.

Changes in the *Every Student Succeeds Act* increase state, local education agency, and school leaders' responsibility to evaluate professional learning to improve student academic success, assessment, accountability, school improvement, teacher and leader effectiveness, and use of federal, state, and local

resources. While increasing states' flexibility, the law holds tight on states' accountability to ensure that every student succeeds. It calls for better use of evidence, ongoing commitment to improvement, and engagement of stakeholders. It requires states rather than the federal government to determine criteria and **interventions** for schools in need of improvement and holds the expectation that districts develop evidence-based strategies to address their needs.

Relevant to this book, *ESSA* redefines professional learning to include personalized, job-embedded, ongoing, available to all teachers of all content areas (including administrators and other school staff), collaborative, informed by educator input and data, integrated into school improvement plans, and regularly evaluated. It requires states to use evidence to select programs to address identified needs and to submit a description annually on how their selected activities "improved teacher, principal, or other school leader effectiveness" (S. 1177, Sec. 2104, Ia). This description is a form of evaluation.

As the focus on educator effectiveness increases, the importance of effective professional learning grows as does the need for its evaluation. No longer will **documentation** about participation levels or satisfaction **surveys** serve to substitute for learning and impact. Hayes Mizell (2003) makes this point clear in his article, "Facilitator: 10; Refreshments 8; Evaluation 0." He says, "Workshop satisfaction misses the point. Evaluation means understanding what **participants** learn, when and how they apply the learning, and when and how it benefits students" (p. 10). He calls upon professional learning leaders to invest in their own learning about effective evaluation and how to use it. He notes that there are two overarching reasons for this investment. First, he notes is the continued realignment of resources that often result in reduction of funding for professional learning. Second, he adds, is the increasing pressure to educate all students to high levels, and that this requires ensuring that all educators have the capacity to meet the needs of all students.

Overly simplistic, event-focused perception surveys may produce data, yet they are not the types of data that will enable professional learning leaders to answer their most pressing questions. Data are most useful when they are placed within the context of a systematic investigation of programs and processes. Evaluation—not just data—is increasingly important for reforming schools because evaluation, when thorough, provides state, school system, and school leaders answers to questions about the impact of their efforts. Evaluation, as a critical part of an ongoing improvement process, provides leaders insights into what is working and what is not, and information to make better decisions.

Leaders interested in evaluation sit in every chair in education. A 10th-grade student evaluates the pieces of work in his portfolio to select one which best exhibits his effort to conduct a science lab to solve a problem. A fourth-grade teacher, implementing a new mathematics instructional practice to make student thinking visible, learned in a summer workshop, is evaluating its effectiveness by watching how her weakest students respond when she uses the practice so she can ask her coach for more specific support when they meet next week. The English department at the high school uses evaluation to assess its implementation of a series of lessons on argumentation to understand how to adapt those lessons in the future to address student misconceptions and ensure more students are successful in writing arguments. The middle school

leadership team has implemented a research-based social-emotional skills program, one of the additional criteria beyond student achievement required now in their district for schools in need of improvement, and wants to measure its success with their students and to report to parents, central office, the school board, the state education agency, and the local community foundation that funded the program about their results. The district talent development chief implemented a five-year evaluation of the teacher and principal mentorship program to know if the program is achieving its intended results and is sufficiently resourced. The regional education agency is initiating a program to increase the capacity of paraprofessionals to support literacy instruction in preK and wants to measure its effectiveness.

Evaluation uses data to answer specific questions to create potential for transforming teaching, learning, leadership, and the systems that support them. It is not data alone that transform. Consider this simple analogy. More people are sporting wearables to measure many types of active and passive activities, such as heart rate, distance walked, hours of movement, and sleep patterns, and are logging more and more information such as caloric intake, emotional state, and so on. The apps used even provide daily or weekly reports. Yet it is not these data that will change a person's health, well-being, or activity level. It is interpreting and using the data to make changes where needed, **comparing** last week's to this week's results to know if progress is evident, and to know if one's goals are met. Simply logging caloric intake will not reduce weight, yet logging it, reviewing the data, and acting on the data will have a role in changing behavior. The same is true for professional learning. Knowing that 92 percent of school principals appreciated the district conference day options available to them will not provide information about whether they reflected on how to integrate the new practices, applied their learning on a routine basis, and realized changes in teacher or student learning as a result of their new leadership practices.

Districtwide data management systems make data more readily accessible to educators. As a result, more data conversations are occurring in schools. Data walls display color-coded levels of student performance in a variety of subject areas are frequently visible in schools. Yet, the presence of data alone, however, does little to improve educator practice or student learning. Two missing elements limit the potential of data. Often missing from data conversations is a decision about a planned, purposeful set of actions to address identified needs. *ESSA* requires more careful selection of evidence-based interventions, programs, or practices. Non-regulatory guidance specifies four levels of evidence that states and districts can use for selecting interventions to address school improvement and student learning. The levels are presented in Table 1.1.

Also missing from data conversations is a plan for evaluation. There are several types of evaluations needed to select, implement, and measure outcomes of an intervention. **Planning evaluation** involves data analysis and interpretation to identify the specific problem or needs to address and understand the context or conditions in which an intervention will be implemented. It results in the selection of an evidence-based program to address the identified problem or need. Designing the implementation and outcomes evaluation occurs simultaneously with implementation planning for the selected intervention and results in an evaluation framework; a clear and detailed plan to conduct rigorous, systematic,

Table 1.1 Definition of Levels of Evidence

Level	Description
Strong evidence	Supported by a minimum of one well-designed, well-implemented experimental, randomized control trial study that meets the *What Works Clearinghouse* standards without reservations
Moderate evidence	Supported by a minimum of one well-designed, well-implemented quasi-experimental study that meets the *What Works Clearinghouse* standards with reservations
Promising evidence	Supported by a minimum of one correlational study with statistical controls for selection bias that use analytic methods to compare the intervention group with a non-intervention group
Demonstrated rationale	Supported by a well-specified logic model, based on research or evaluation, that demonstrates that the intervention is likely to improve relevant outcomes

Adapted from U.S. Department of Education. (2016, September 16). *Non-regulatory guidance: Using evidence to strengthen education investments.* Washington, DC: Author. https://www2.ed.gov/policy/elsec/leg/essa/guidanceuseseinvestment.pdf.

and purposeful data gathering; analysis and interpretation; report of **findings** to stakeholders; and use of findings to make improvements. The evaluation framework begins with posing the questions that stakeholders want to answer about the intervention and its use. The framework clarifies what data are needed, from whom, how often, and how much. It specifies how data will be analyzed and interpreted to measure merit, worth, progress, and impact to improve their efforts.

Because many who work in professional learning are action-oriented, they tend to focus on what to do rather than the results they want to achieve. Process becomes more important than results. They tend to think about short-term accomplishments rather than long-term results. They are comfortable reporting what they have done rather than what results they are producing. More effort is allocated to selecting and launching interventions than to implementing and sustaining them. Yet repeatedly professional learning leaders are being held to high **standards** of accountability for their efforts and are asked for evidence of results. The evaluation process described in this book supports these leaders in all phases of evaluation to meet the accountability expectations, specifically for **practitioners** who want to add evaluation to their routine work.

Implementing evaluation as a natural component of all professional learning encourages and supports systematic review, study, and analysis of professional learning to improve outcomes, accountability, equity in access and quality, effectiveness, and efficiency. Evaluation, when it is normative practice, shifts the focus of professional learning leaders from a service orientation (What can we do to meet the unique needs of the education workforce? What is available and when? Who participates? How accessible are the options? How aligned are the learning options with the school system's strategic priorities?) to a results orientation (How are educator practices changing? What supports are increasing changes in practice? What else is changing within the system to

support educator changes in professional practice? How are changes in educator practice influencing student success?)

Leaders of professional learning who integrate evaluation into their normative practice make more informed decisions, respond more quickly to challenges that may interfere with results, use clearly defined outcomes as the primary measure of their success, and keep a laser-like focus on those results. When results are the driver, expectations are clearer and efforts are more aligned. Stephan Bauer, a management consultant, notes, "Results-oriented leaders know how to create systems, build coalitions, motivate employees, monitor performance for effectiveness, and be responsible for results. Organizations and leaders can develop this capacity by constantly asking themselves questions such as:

- What does our organization truly value? How do we prove a consistent commitment to these values in all our work?
- What is our organizational vision for the world? How do we measure progress toward that vision?
- How are we engaging with others toward the realization of our vision in a way that helps us achieve more together than we can individually?
- How do we seek learning, and how does that learning inform how we continually improve our practice and organization?
- How do we engage our staff in conversations about the qualities it takes to lead, and provide them safe space to struggle with the practice of leadership?" (Bauer, 2014).

Evaluation is, as Posavac (2016) says, like breathing. Everyone does it all the time. Yet evaluators approach this work with purpose and intentionality to measure and understand authentic issues that matter most. Donna Mertens and Amy Wilson (2012) state, "Evaluators' ways of thinking are different from ordinary daily decision making, because they engage in a process of figuring out what is needed to address challenges through the systematic collection and use of data" (p. 3). Professional learning leaders who engage in ongoing evaluation as a natural part of their work are results-oriented leaders committed to increasing the success of every member of the education workforce and each student they serve.

QUESTIONS FOR CONSIDERATION

1. How do we currently evaluate professional learning?

2. Who is primarily responsible for evaluating professional learning?

3. What data are we using regularly to examine professional learning?

4. How do we engage stakeholders in decisions about the development, implementation, and evaluation of professional learning?

5. How do we choose interventions for school improvement, professional learning, student learning, or other identified needs?

6. What might be a goal we set for ourselves about improving our use of evaluation so that it is more normative practice?

Professional Learning Program Evaluation Overview

2

This chapter reviews fundamentals about practitioner-driven program evaluation as it relates to professional learning. It includes the definition of evaluation, the difference between evaluation and research, the purposes of evaluation, the difference between programs and **events**, the types of evaluation, and an overview of the evaluation process.

EVALUATION DEFINED

Definitions of evaluation abound. Esteemed scholars in the field offer many definitions that provide a way of thinking about evaluation in general. The following definitions of evaluation from evaluation scholars deserve attention.

Daniel Stufflebeam (2001) asserts that evaluation is "a study designed and conducted to assist some audience to assess an object's merit or worth" (p. 11).

Michael Scriven (1991) says that evaluation is "the process of determining the merit, worth, and value of things, and evaluations are the product of that process" (p. 1).

Michael Quinn Patton (2008) defines program evaluation as "the systematic collection of information about activities, characteristics, and results of programs to make judgment about the program, improve or further develop the program effectiveness, inform decisions about future programming, and/or increase understanding." He specifies that "utilization-focused program evaluation [a specific form of evaluation] is evaluation done for and with specific, intended primary users for specific, intended uses" (p. 39).

Fournier (2005), in the *Encyclopedia of Evaluation*, defines evaluation as "an applied process for collecting and synthesizing evidence that culminates in conclusions about the state of affairs, value, merit, worth, significance, or quality

of a program, product, person, policy, proposal, or plan. Conclusions made in evaluations encompass both an empirical aspect (that something is the case) and a normative aspect (judgment about the value of something). It is the value feature that distinguishes evaluation from other types of inquiry, such as basic science research, clinical epidemiology, investigative journalism, or public polling" (pp. 139–140).

Carol Weiss (1998) suggests that program evaluation is "the systematic assessment of the operation and/or outcomes of a program or policy, compared to a set of explicit or implicit standards, as a means of contributing to the improvement of the program or policy" (p. 4).

To cull across these definitions and for the purpose of this book, evaluation of professional learning, then, is a **systematic, purposeful standards-driven process of studying, reviewing, and analyzing data about a professional learning program gathered from multiple sources to make judgments and informed decisions about the program**. This definition implies that an evaluation results in an individual or team making a reasoned judgment based on the analyzed data. The individual or team uses the judgment to gain insights and deeper understanding and to make decisions about the professional learning program being evaluated. The definition assumes that a reason exists for the evaluation, and decisions will be made as a result of the evaluation. Evaluation calls for rigor in all phases of the work and is guided by a set of standards that, when met, ensure the quality of the process. These standards for program evaluation are set by the Joint Committee on Standards for Educational Evaluation (Yarbrough, Shulha, Hopson, & Caruthers, 2011), the American Evaluation Association (2004), and Learning Forward (2011) and appear in Appendix B.

Key to the definition of program evaluation is the concept of program. Kathryn Newcomer, Harry Hatry, and Joseph Wholey (2015) define program as a "set of resources and activities directed toward one or more common goals, typically under the direction of a single manager or management team" (p. 7). A program may be larger in scale, such as a statewide effort to increase graduation rates, and involve multiple agencies in a coordinated fashion. They may be district focused as in programs designed to improve student performance of mathematics and include curriculum design, formative assessments, professional learning on instructional methods, parent engagement in family math activities, and classroom resources. A preschool program may be upgrading the capacity of paraprofessionals to engage students in literacy-oriented learning experiences aligned to the new preschool curriculum. Programs may also be small in scale such as a team of teachers working together to improve student writing skills. A professional learning program, for the purpose of this book, is a **set of planned and implemented actions, guided by research, evidence, and standards of effective professional learning, accompanied by adequate resources, and directed toward the achievement of defined outcomes related to educator practice and its impact on student learning**.

In each case, regardless of the size of the program, evaluation is a crucial component to understand how the resources and activities implemented influence the outcomes achieved and to make decisions for improving, expanding,

adjusting, or eliminating the program. The scope of the program and its evaluation may vary along several features such as number and frequency of activities, duration, amount and frequency of **data collection**, and number of stakeholders. A team of seventh-grade teachers learning together how to integrate critical thinking routines into their instruction uses data from students to examine the impact of their work monthly and adjust their practice. When school improvement teams engage in evaluation to measure the effects of a schoolwide professional learning program to increase students' use of academic vocabulary, they increase the scope of the activities to achieve results, broaden the data collection over an extended time period, and report to more stakeholders about the effects of their work. They may adjust their activities two or three times a year rather than as frequently as a teaching team. A school system evaluation expands each area even further. It may involve gathering data twice a year and reporting annually on progress and results. In other words, the closer the evaluation process is to its impact, the narrower the scope of the evaluation. Whether the evaluation is large scale or small scale, the evaluation process described in this book is useful.

KEY COMPONENTS OF EVALUATION DEFINITIONS

The following words or phrases are the key components of the definition of evaluation. Each of these terms contributes to a deep understanding of what an evaluation is and its purpose.

Systematic

The term *systematic* suggests that evaluations are orderly, planned, formal, rigorous, objective, and guided by standards for success and quality such as those offered by the Joint Committee on Standards for Educational Evaluation, the American Evaluation Association, and Learning Forward (see Appendix B).

> *Evaluation of professional learning is the systematic, purposeful, standards-driven process of studying, reviewing, analyzing, and interpreting data about a professional learning program gathered from multiple sources to make judgments and informed decisions about the program.*

Standards

Most evaluations measure merit, worth, or impact against predetermined criteria. In addition to the standards for the quality and integrity of evaluation practice, evaluations use standards for professional learning and program outcomes as criteria against which to measure the program's success.

Data

Data take many forms and come from many sources. They may be collected in various ways. "Data are discrete bits of information that becomes evidence through a process of analysis and interpretation" (Killion, 2015, p. 80). Data alone are insufficient to make evaluation useful. It is through the analysis and

interpretation of purposefully collected data that evaluations have usefulness and can inform **decision makers**.

Intended Uses of the Evaluation

Knowing the intended purpose(s) of an evaluation influences many decisions made during the evaluation's planning and implementation. Evaluators and program leaders, therefore, need to identify their audiences and make sure they prioritize the most significant uses of the evaluation before they design it. For example, if a policy maker wants to know if program participation contributes to teacher retention, the evaluator may examine data related to employee retention and engagement in the induction program. If a district HR department wants to improve the program, they might want to collect additional data about which aspects of the program participants perceive to be most beneficial and their recommendations for upgrading the program. They may also want to know what aspects of the program are most costly to examine if other alternatives exist. And, if the purpose of the evaluation is to determine whether students of novice teachers who participate in the induction program receive a high-quality education, a far more complex **evaluation design** is required.

Program

This book is about evaluating professional learning programs rather than *events*. A program implies more than isolated incidents and aligns with the federal definition of professional learning in *ESSA*. A program is a set of purposeful, planned, research- or evidence-based actions and the support system necessary to achieve the identified outcomes. Effective professional learning programs use data to determine the content; occur in collaborative communities; employ multiple, active learning designs; provide implementation support; engage leadership to support learning and create systems of support; include adequate resources; occur over time; and link to educator performance and student learning standards (Learning Forward, 2011). Programs, however, vary widely in scope.

A workshop on classroom management is not a program. Such a workshop is an event or one action included in the set of actions to achieve outcomes for educator learning and student success. Program planners would likely derive the need for a classroom management workshop from identified student achievement needs, such as poor performance, and investigate further to discover that insufficient engagement and lost instructional time may be root causes. To turn the workshop into a professional learning program, it would be incorporated into a comprehensive plan of actions designed to develop educator **knowledge**, **attitudes**, **skills**, **aspirations**, and **behaviors** that would include classroom demonstrations, visits to peer classrooms, planned classroom-based support with ongoing coaching, opportunities to review and reflect on practice, and collaboration among peers to assess and evaluate the effects of their practice on students using defined criteria. Since much of what has been

provided as professional learning has not been considered a program, its results have been mixed. For those who want to evaluate professional learning, they must first have a professional learning program to evaluate. It is only in the context of a full professional learning program that data emerging from individual events contribute to understanding how a program is progressing toward its defined outcomes.

Evaluation Versus Research

Many educators confuse evaluation with research. Both are a part of a larger class of social science inquiry. Both are guided by questions, data collection and analysis, and findings reported to stakeholders. Many education **decision** and **policy makers** completed courses in research methodology; few took courses in evaluation. Because they may not fully understand the distinction, decision and policy makers often assume that evaluation and research are the same. A frequent example of this confusion is a local school board member asking the question: How do you know it was professional learning that caused the changes in student achievement and not something else? This type of question is one a researcher can answer under certain conditions and with an appropriate research methodology. Evaluators can answer other questions: Did the professional learning contribute to educator practice and student achievement? What changes occurred in educator practices? What actions of the program had the greatest impact on changing educator practice? Which educator practices were most significant in influencing student results? What conditions contributed to and interfered with the program's success? While there are many similarities in processes, methods, and tools used in both research and evaluation, the purposes are different (see Table 2.1).

An examination of the purposes of evaluation and research may be helpful in understanding the distinction so that educators can draw appropriate conclusions and appropriately use evaluation findings. Education practitioners will benefit from applying the eight-step evaluation process outlined in this book to guide their work as evaluators rather than trying to conduct research or present their evaluation findings as if they were research.

Carol Weiss (1998, p. 47) notes that evaluations are political in nature: "Evaluations are conducted on social programs—most important, on social programs in the public domain," she notes. "Social programs are manifest responses to priority individual and community needs and are themselves 'the creatures of political decisions.' They are proposed, defined, debated, enacted, and funded through political processes, and in implementation they remain subject to pressures—both supportive and hostile" (p. 47). Evaluation, she contends, "makes implicit political statements about such issues as the problematic nature of some programs and the unchangeability of others" (p. 48). Because professional learning programs are situated within a context that influences the choice of the intervention, its implementation, and most likely its results, evaluators consider carefully how to increase objectivity in their work to provide honest, reliable evaluations that will be useful.

Table 2.1   Difference Between Program Evaluation and Research

	Program Evaluation	*Research*
Purpose	Determines whether a particular program has merit, worth, value, and impact (e.g., did it achieve its outcomes? Was it perceived to be worthwhile? Did the activities occur as planned?) The focus is usually on the effectiveness, results, and improvement related to the program.	Explores the interaction among variables, adds to the general or field-specific knowledge base about a particular phenomenon, tests a theory, and advances that field.
Grounded in	Uses a theory of change and logic model.	Uses theory and literature review to design and apply intervention for study.
Focus	Focuses on program description, clearly defined outcomes, and data about results of a particular program that occurs within its natural contexts; variations are studied and noted especially in terms of how those variations impact results.	Looks at results produced by groups in which a particular program does and/or does not occur; program is implemented in carefully controlled contexts to minimize variations beyond the existence of the program between treatment and control or comparison groups.
Use of Findings	Identifies how effective the program is and informs decisions about program improvement, continuation, discontinuation, expansion, and so on for the same context and population.	Generalizes the results to develop theory and inform practice in other contexts and populations.
Dissemination of Findings	Reports findings and proposed next actions to decision makers, including policy makers, stakeholders, participants, and program managers.	Reports findings to field for critique of design, validity, and reliability and shares intervention for implementation in other settings.

Evaluation Versus Assessment

Another term frequently confused with *evaluation* is *assessment*. While assessment may be a part of evaluation, evaluation is not always a part of assessment. Assessment is an objective measurement based on data for improving something, whereas evaluation is objective measurement based on data or evidence, and standards or criteria for success for judging or valuing something. When planning professional learning programs, planners determine the standards of success when they develop the program's goals and outcomes. These standards become the criteria against which a program is judged as successful. In the case of evaluation, assessments may focus on the processes of a

program to improve them during the program's operation. The program's evaluation is done at the end of the program or at significant points in the program's history to judge the program's success against established criteria. Assessment is formative in nature while evaluation is summative. Assessment is for diagnostic purposes while evaluation judges the degree to which specific outcomes are achieved.

While conducting an evaluation of an aspiring administrator program within a district, the district steering committee may conduct both an assessment and a periodic evaluation. The annual assessment may be based on a program completion survey or **interview** of participants about what they appreciated about the program, the significant experiences they had in the program, and their perceptions of the program's impact on their desire to become an administrator. These data gathered annually provide the steering committee with an assessment so they can make annual adjustments to the program to improve it before the next cohort begins.

Periodically the steering committee or the school board may call for an evaluation of the program. The designated evaluator gathers all the assessment data from the previous years to use in the evaluation, and adds other data to be able to make a judgment about the program's overall impact, whether it meets the program's goals, and whether it is valued by the district and the participants. Some additional data the evaluator collects might include the number of participants who move into and remain in an administrative position; a comparison of performance appraisals of administrators, new to the role in the past five years who completed the program and those who did not participate in the program; a comparison of the school performance data with principals who completed the program and those who did not complete the program; and a comparison of scores on a 360-degree survey of supervisors, supervisees, and peers of new administrators in the past five years who completed the program with those who did not.

Assessment is appropriate for continuous improvement. Multiple assessments of a program may occur prior to or as a part of an evaluation of a program. Evaluation, however, is essential before any significant decision about a program is made. Assessments are useful for continuous improvement if small adjustments are to be made along the way; however, if a decision about continuation, discontinuation, expansion, or reduction in the program, its operation, or funding is needed, evaluation is essential to ensure that the program meets its outcomes and the standards it is intended to meet. It would, for instance, be unfair to determine if a student is able to write and support an argument if the only evidence available is the student's ability to identify supporting evidence in a text or even a draft argument. It is in the

---

Key Terms

Merit: The intrinsic value of a program; how it is perceived by those it intends to help based on established criteria

Worth: The extrinsic value of a program to those outside the program, such as the larger community or society

Value: The political or social contextual criteria influencing decisions about merit or worth; what one person, organization, or entity perceives as valuable may not be perceived as valuable to another one

Impact: The effect of a program on its participants and their **clients**; for example, teacher professional practice and student learning

student's finished product, measured against the standards set in a **rubric** for exemplary performance, that final evaluation is made.

Evaluation then serves the purpose of judging merit, worth, value, and impact of a program based on established standards and sufficient data or evidence. This book acknowledges that most educators have a strong interest in continuous improvement and use it frequently, yet may not evaluate as often. Frequency of use does not diminish the necessity of being able to conduct evaluations of professional learning to make informed decisions about it.

PURPOSES OF EVALUATION

Evaluation serves a variety of purposes, and an evaluation's purpose influences decisions about how the evaluation is designed and implemented. Several scenarios involving evaluation of professional learning are described below.

1. The high school science collaborative learning team is shifting to blended instruction and wants to know if what they are learning and applying in their classroom is positively influencing student science achievement.

2. A school improvement team is implementing a professional learning program as a part of the school improvement plan and wants to measure the impact of the program on teaching, school culture, and student learning.

3. The mathematics curriculum team works with the district math curriculum coordinator to revise the mathematics curriculum and select new instructional materials to implement the revised curriculum. They plan and implement extensive teacher professional learning to ensure that teachers have the mathematics content and the content-specific instructional processes to implement the new curriculum. They want to conduct an impact evaluation of the curriculum-related professional learning on teacher classroom practice and student achievement.

4. A district committee responsible for implementing the *College, Career, and Civics Social Studies Framework* across the district is strengthening social studies instruction. Teachers engage in extensive training and school-based support in using new instructional strategies. Teachers, principals, parents, and the district social studies coordinator want to know how to determine whether the approach improves student achievement in social studies.

5. A superintendent proposes a significant increase in the professional learning budget to provide small grants for individual schools to address the district's strategic priority on personalization and deeper learning. He engages the members of the school board in conversation about what they want to know about the return on their investment to demonstrate his intent to hold schools accountable for the investment in professional learning.

6. A school improvement team is examining several professional learning programs aimed at increasing students' active engagement in learning. They want to learn more about the types of evaluations that were conducted on the three programs they are considering.

7. The district improvement team wants to know whether schools' use of professional learning resources is effective. The teacher leaders who serve as chairs of schools' professional learning committees ask clarifying questions about what they specifically want to know and what evidence the schools are required to provide, and seek guidance in how to go about collecting and providing the requested evidence.

8. A state professional learning supervisor is required to provide an annual impact report on the use of Title I and Title II funds to the state school board and to the U.S. Department of Education as a component of the state's report on its comprehensive plan.

9. A director of teaching and learning is facing a budget cut and, with the district's professional learning advisory team, is preparing a recommendation to the superintendent about which professional learning program to fully fund and which to reduce. She wants the recommendation to be data informed.

10. A district leadership team wants to ask its school board and community to support changing the teacher workday to include weekly 90-minute, student-free blocks for teachers to engage in professional learning teams. To solidify the rationale, the district committee wants to provide a plan for assessing the impact of the allocated time.

The overarching purpose of evaluation is to conduct qualitative inquiry, a process of making meaning and understanding how things work to be able to assess their value, merit, worth, and impact to improve them. Patton (2015) summarizes seven **contributions** evaluation makes. It illuminates meaning; studies how things work; captures stories to understand perspectives and experiences; understands how systems work and how they influence people; understands context and its impact on experience; identifies unanticipated consequences; and makes comparisons to find trends and themes. For those in education, particularly public education, the purposes for evaluating professional learning depend on the key stakeholder requesting the evaluation. Table 2.2 summaries common **uses**, **users**, and purposes of evaluation of professional learning.

Clarity of purpose in evaluation facilitates decision making during the evaluation's planning and implementation phases. Yet, occasionally in evaluation planning, various stakeholders have different and sometimes competing purposes for the evaluation. The varying interests and demands can be challenging within a single evaluation and may necessitate multiple evaluations, some occurring simultaneously or nested together in a more sophisticated design. While evaluations can be designed to accommodate multiple purposes, they become more complex. Even though an evaluation may have more than one

Table 2.2   Intended Uses, Users, and Purposes of Evaluation

Intended Uses of Evaluation	Intended Users	Purposes of Evaluation
Determining merit, worth, value, and impact	Program directors, policy makers, decision makers, and stakeholders	To determine merit, worth, and impact of a program; to determine the overall effectiveness of a program and make decisions about its adjustment, expansion, continuation, or discontinuation; to compare a program with other programs
Facilitating improvements	Program directors, such as professional learning leaders or curriculum coordinators, principals, school improvement teams, or professional learning communities	To make improvements to an existing program; to determine a program's strengths and weaknesses; to identify unexpected benefits and barriers; to determine progress toward the intended outcomes; to identify and solve unanticipated problems; to assess participants' progress toward intended outcomes
Generating knowledge	Program developers, such as professional learning leaders and curriculum coordinators	To add to the body of knowledge about the program's effectiveness; to share experiences with programs with others; to identify patterns of best practices or principles of effectiveness across programs; to understand how a program's components or actions interact
Providing accountability	Policy makers and decision makers, such as boards of education, superintendents, program managers, principals, program funders, state education agency, and local education agency staff	To assess compliance with intended purposes and mandated processes; to provide evidence of fiscal responsibility; to provide evidence of public accountability for resources; to submit annual descriptions on how selected interventions improved effectiveness of teachers, principals, other school leaders, and other employees and affect their primary clients

purpose, just one should be identified as the primary purpose. When an evaluation is to serve more than one purpose, specific aspects of the evaluation will need to be customized and appropriately sequenced to address various needs and interests. Newcomer and colleagues note that the "evaluation's purpose and major subordinate purposes must mesh at least in part—and certainly not directly conflict with—the interests of key stakeholders; otherwise the evaluation process is unlikely to get off the ground, and even if it does the process and its findings will be misused and ignored" (2015, p. 46).

For example, most school systems provide professional learning to staff to improve performance. This may be the work of a single department or several departments or even be outsourced to individual schools and divisions. The superintendent and school board want to know if they are fiscally responsible for investments in professional learning and are asking if the professional learning available to staff is producing results. School systems and even schools often have several professional learning programs operating simultaneously, all under the umbrella of a comprehensive, cohesive system-based professional learning program. Individual program managers may have other purposes for evaluating their programs, such as measuring their impact on educator practice and student success, and evaluating the perceived value of the program rather than fiscal accountability. One component of an overall professional learning program in a school system is an induction program designed to address the specific developmental needs of new teachers, teacher leaders, principals, and other employees. The school system's comprehensive professional learning program most likely includes other programs, some of which may be required by federal, state, or local regulation or law, to meet the needs of other employees or to address other goals such as a customer service program for support staff who interact frequently with the public or a new program to meet the literacy needs of preschool, second language learners.

To answer the superintendent's and school board's question, professional learning leaders need to first determine what is being evaluated—the comprehensive professional learning program, its individual programs, some of the individual programs, the operation of the professional learning system, the performance of the director of professional learning, or something else. The evaluator or evaluation team defines the purpose or purposes of the evaluation by establishing the specific **constructs** to evaluate and the criteria for measuring merit, worth, value, or impact. These decisions are often political in nature because they are made based on the need for an evaluation, its purpose, and stakeholder interests and needs. Occasionally evaluators negotiate with stakeholders to either narrow or broaden the purpose of an evaluation to increase the usability of an evaluation. Because the specific outcomes of the collection of professional learning programs available differ, an impact evaluation will require various outcome measures and multiple smaller impact evaluations to provide evidence of impact across multiple programs. It is possible to conduct a merit, perceived value, efficiency, or effectiveness evaluation across multiple programs, without an impact evaluation, if there are common criteria that apply to all programs. For instance, school system leaders might be interested in knowing the quality of its overall professional learning program. They might use an instrument such as the *Standards Assessment Inventory* (Learning Forward, 2012) to measure teacher perception of the effectiveness of professional learning based on the *Standards for Professional Learning*. This measure, however, is not an impact evaluation. An impact evaluation of professional learning is one that measures changes in educator behavior and their effect on students or other clients.

TYPES OF EVALUATION

Evaluations may occur at different phases of a program's development and implementation. The most common types of evaluations in terms of when they occur are planning, formative or implementation, and summative or end of a program.

Planning Evaluations

Planning evaluations, those conducted before a professional learning program is designed, help identify the social conditions and needs that a program should address. Using this information, those leading professional learning can make better decisions about the types of interventions that are more likely to achieve results. If the needs are not clear and aligned to student learning outcomes and educator performance outcomes, and if the context and conditions are unknown, professional learning is difficult to design. For instance, a school that continues to experience low student achievement results in reading, yet whose staff has had extensive training in literacy, most likely does not need more training, assuming the training was aligned to the student outcomes and curriculum. What might be more appropriate is extensive classroom-based support for implementation of the learning and opportunities for extending or personalizing learning for staff who want more specifics about literacy instruction and opportunities for staff to meet in collaborative learning teams to plan for integration of the new practices, to examine their practice and its impact on students, to visit each other's classrooms, and to identify collectively necessary refinements in instruction to meet the needs of all students. The caution for all professional learning leaders is to be sure they identify real, evidence-based needs and their root causes rather than perceived needs or preferences.

An Example: Listening to Teachers' Needs

The district professional learning leadership team analyzed student reading performance on the statewide assessment. Tenth graders' scores were consistently well below the state average. Principals and the reading consultant in the district discussed the need to provide training to teachers on reading in the content areas. They envisioned providing eight total hours of training in sessions scheduled throughout one school year. The program would follow a "training of trainers" model. Under the proposed plan, each school's literacy coordinator would take the lead in training fellow staff members at his or her schools and then be available to provide follow-up support to interested teachers.

When all the school literacy coordinators met to plan the training, several of them expressed doubt that teachers would implement the

strategies they planned to teach. One even said that teachers were unwilling to incorporate reading strategies into their instructional lessons because they believed that it would take time away from their course content. Together with the reading consultant, the literacy coordinators expressed a concern that most teachers perceived that they did not share responsibility for student reading performance, and thus were not open to learn how to improve students' reading performance. They also worried that teachers might believe that if students had not learned to read by the time they reached 10th grade they were unlikely to learn within their content-area courses and would need interventions from a reading specialist. The group continued to guess about the perceived discontent among teachers until one of the literacy coordinators suggested that they ask some teachers. By conducting focus groups at each high school, the reading coordinators discovered that teachers did expect students "to read independently for comprehension" by the time they got to high school and were finding that students' inability to read was interfering with their academic and dispositional success. They also learned that many teachers were eager to tackle the challenge because they saw a tremendous benefit for them as well as their students.

Literacy coordinators also learned that teachers needed less help with reading comprehension strategies and more help with understanding and assessing students' reading deficiencies and how to intervene within the context of their individual courses. They wanted guidance in making appropriate instructional decisions that would lead to student success regardless of their reading levels. They also wanted resources with different levels of text complexity for student use. Coordinators realized that their initial plan would likely have been met with resistance and even failure. Taking time early on to understand teacher needs by engaging teachers in informal focus groups to listen to their concerns, the district team could remodel their plan for professional learning, shifting to a coaching and consulting model rather than a training model, and supplement it with resources for student use before it was implemented.

Formative Evaluations

While planning evaluations are done prior to designing a program, **formative evaluations** are conducted during a program. They provide information about how a professional learning program is working. This type of evaluation information is essential to improving programs, preventing and managing problems related to implementation, and ensuring that the program is fully functioning, thereby increasing the likelihood of achieving the intended outcomes. Evaluators can also use formative evaluations to help explain how the program works and how it contributes to the results it achieves. To replicate a program, strengthen it, and tell the story of the professional learning, program managers seek to understand and explain how the program's activities lead to results.

An Example: Making Adjustments to Improve Outcomes

The district science coordinator launched a professional learning program to develop middle-grade teachers' content knowledge to implement the district's new science curriculum based on the Next Generation Science standards. The change had been approved by the board of education for full implementation during the following school year. She wanted to help teachers be prepared to use the curriculum when the school year started.

First, teachers completed three 2-hour workshops on the standards and curriculum online at their own pace within a two-month period. The coordinator visited schools several weeks after the teachers completed the workshops for follow-up conversations, to answer questions, and to explore challenges teachers anticipated with the curriculum. She discovered that several teachers had tried parts of one of the sample units she provided in the workshops. While the coordinator was pleased that teachers had so quickly tried the units, she realized that they were not aligned to the existing curriculum and that no teachers mentioned developing their own units based on the new standards.

During the visits. she observed and interviewed teachers as a part of her formative evaluation of the professional learning she started. She gathered the information she needed to make some significant changes in her initial plan, which included only the online workshops. Her visits helped her realize that one of two things was likely to happen when the new standards and curriculum were launched: Teachers would run out of model units and revert to their old units, or teachers would demand that she provide more units. She discovered she left out a crucial component of her professional learning plan—helping teachers use the standards and curriculum to design units to teach them. She realized that she could address this gap by inviting a small group of teachers from multiple schools to come together to examine how to use the new curriculum and standards to design units. She could also engage a group of more expert teachers in developing more units to share as models. Now that she realized these missing elements, she could work to integrate additional actions into her plan to help teachers understand how to use the standards and curriculum for instruction, develop units, critique each other's units, revise existing units that somewhat aligned with the new standards, and help teachers find appropriate instructional materials to integrate into the new units. Her revised plan also provided an opportunity for some teachers to field test and revise units before the next year's full implementation. Her informal, yet informative, formative evaluation helped her identify several problems related to her plan. Fortunately she had time to revise and adjust before implementation and without negatively impacting student achievement in the next school year. She also could differentiate how teachers experience the added professional learning.

Summative Evaluations

Summative evaluations are perhaps the most familiar. Typically, a summative evaluation provides information on achievement of the program's outcomes or overall impact, and it may include information that might be

useful for improving the program. Summative evaluations are done at the end of a program or at a particularly important benchmark point, such as the end of a year of implementation for a multiyear professional learning program. If a program is three years long, a summative evaluation would obviously be conducted at the end of the three years. If the program continues beyond its three years, ongoing evaluation might be done every three to five years to determine whether the program continues to impact both educator and student learning. Sometimes programs culminate with the end of a funding cycle. When conducted at that point, summative evaluations provide information about the program's success and may or may not serve as a basis for decisions about continuation of the program or justification for future funding. Sometimes summative evaluations are conducted only to meet funders' requirements and have little or no influence on a program's future unless a program continues beyond the external funding cycle.

Increasingly, programs with a specified duration, such as five years, incorporate annual formative evaluations to provide information to program managers to make improvements and occasionally to determine continued funding. In general, policy makers may be more interested in summative evaluations ("what are the results?") and less interested in formative or planning evaluations ("how are we getting the results?"). Summative evaluations may have less value or usefulness to program stakeholders, who may be more interested in understanding how what they have done influences the outcomes.

An Example: Impact of Project-Based Learning

A team of high school teachers received a district innovation grant to implement project-based learning in several science and social studies courses. The district required that extensive professional learning for staff be a component of the innovation. The district had been considering moving toward deeper learning in the high school and decided to offer several grants to teachers willing to experiment with a variety of related innovations. The district wants to understand what each innovation would take to be successful, whether one approach was more effective than another, whether it was possible to have multiple approaches within a single school, and whether a focus on deeper learning had a positive or negative impact on student academic success, teacher grading and assessment practices, and students' postsecondary experiences. The teachers worked with the district's research and evaluation, curriculum, and professional learning departments to develop a specific plan for implementing project-based learning and the evaluation that would take place over the next two years. The evaluation team helped the high school steering committee identify different types of data to collect to answer as many of the district's questions as possible, yet made it clear that some questions, such as the impact on students' postsecondary experiences, would not be able to be answered in the short period of funding for this innovation.

Planning, formative, and summative evaluations have distinct purposes. Planning and formative evaluations can provide essential information to program stakeholders and inform ongoing improvements. Summative evaluations typically lead to decisions regarding program continuation, adaptation, or discontinuation. Professional learning directors will sometimes want to conduct all three types of evaluations for one program. In other cases, they will select just one or two types of evaluations to conduct. Table 2.3 is useful for determining the type or types of evaluation needed and how to complete each.

Although the three types employ many of the same evaluation tools and strategies, their purposes and timing are different. Effective uses of the three types vary from case to case. Using evaluation to improve professional learning before, during, and after its design and implementation can sometimes strengthen a program, increase its chances of achieving its intended results, and maintain stakeholders' commitment to engaging in evaluation as they collaborate to make the needed improvements.

Table 2.3 Types of Evaluation

Type of Evaluation	Processes and Action Steps Needed
Planning Evaluations	Uses collaborative processes to • determine overall needs and problem to be solved; • determine which stakeholders to include in the program planning and as its participants; • assess participant needs, characteristics, and working conditions; • identify and address conditions and context that are likely to support and potentially inhibit the program's success; • clarify outcomes; and • assess stakeholders' reaction to the intended program plan.
Formative Evaluations	Uses collaborative processes to • assess using data whether the program is being implemented as designed; • construct understanding of what is working, not working, and why; • assess progress toward outcomes; • identify positive or negative unintended consequences; and • study data in relationship to identified benchmarks to inform revisions, improvements, or adjustments to program design.
Summative Evaluations	Uses systematic evaluation processes to • collect data upon which to base judgments about the program's merit, value, worth, and impact; and • provide a summary judgment about the program's performance and impact.

STEPS IN THE EVALUATION PROCESS

Planning and conducting evaluations is a linear process in which the steps are highly interrelated. The success of one step depends on the success of the previous step. While some recursiveness is involved, much of the work is sequential. For example, the evaluator would have difficulty in determining how to collect data unless he has already decided what data to collect. The evaluation process outlined in this book has eight steps (see Table 2.4). Each step will be briefly described here. Subsequent chapters contain in-depth discussions of each step.

Getting Ready to Start the Evaluation Process

Until a professional learning program is designed, it cannot be evaluated. If professional learning leaders want to commission an evaluation of their program, they first make sure that their professional learning program is ready to be evaluated. "Designed" programs include outcomes, planned actions to achieve those goals, and the resources necessary to implement the plan. Designed professional learning programs meet the *Standards for Professional Learning* (Learning Forward, 2011), district or state standards for professional learning, or another set of rigorous standards for the quality of professional learning.

Step One: Assess Evaluability

Now the evaluation process can begin. The evaluator or evaluation team seeks to understand the professional learning program to be evaluated if she has not been a part of the program planning process. If, for some reason, the professional learning program is insufficiently designed, the evaluator helps them do so. In some cases, the program exists but has not been clearly defined. Based on their understanding of the program, the evaluator and program leaders together determine whether the program is "evaluable" (i.e., ready to be evaluated). This simply means asking, "Can this evaluation even take place?"

The evaluator examines the program's design to determine whether it is complete, sufficient, feasible, and logical. This involves examining the program's outcomes, standards, and indicators of success; theory of change; and **logic model**—all critical to conducting a successful evaluation. Evaluation planning depends on program planning, and in ideal situations, they are done simultaneously. Chapter 4 covers assessing evaluability in depth.

Step Two: Formulate Evaluation Questions

Formulating good **evaluation questions** depends on first identifying all the intended users of the evaluation, their needs and expectations, the purposes of the evaluation, and the program's outcomes. Clear purposes will help to shape decisions about the overall design of the evaluation and guide the development of evaluation questions and the selection of an evaluation methodology.

Once the users and purposes are clarified, the evaluator formulates the questions the evaluation seeks to answer. These questions will direct the scope and methodology of the evaluation (the framework). Creating good evaluation questions requires thoughtful attention and may benefit from collaboration among the evaluator, those who commissioned the evaluation, the program manager or other professional learning leaders, and other stakeholders. With mutually agreed-upon evaluation questions, the framework for the evaluation can be developed. Chapter 5 focuses on formulating evaluation questions.

Step Three: Construct the Evaluation Framework

Multiple methodologies exist for conducting evaluations. Evaluators of professional learning programs tend to adopt either qualitative or descriptive methodologies. Because of their sophistication, other methodologies might require support from someone with deep expertise in evaluation. **External evaluators** or technical assistance providers may be tapped for support in the design and implementation of the evaluation, if necessary. The evaluation team selects an evaluation methodology that aligns with the questions to be answered (i.e., reasonable and feasible) and that will provide the evidence needed to answer the questions. A thorough discussion of how to construct the framework is presented in Chapter 6.

Step Four: Collect Data

Once the evaluation framework is ready, the evaluator collects data using the collection methods identified within that framework. The data-collection methods align with the type of data required to answer the evaluation questions. Multiple sources of data can strengthen an evaluation study particularly if they provide multiple perspectives on the same construct. Carefully designed data-collection tools and well-trained data collectors will facilitate this often labor-intensive process. In this crucial step, the evaluator manages the data-collection process, making sure consistent and careful processes result in accuracy. Chapter 7 presents information about managing data collection and selecting appropriate scoring processes.

Step Five: Organize, Analyze, and Display Data

Organizing, analyzing, and displaying data include summarizing, collating, synthesizing, displaying, and analyzing data to examine patterns, trends, **outliers**, and anomalies. Creating visual displays or infographics to display data facilitates the process of forming conclusions based on the data and subsequent interpretation and reporting. Chapter 8 is a more detailed discussion of these processes. Some of the processes may be technical and may require the evaluator to tap the expertise of someone who is skilled in statistical analysis. Nevertheless, those practitioners skilled in using spreadsheets and computing descriptive statistics will be able to perform most data analyses.

Step Six: Interpret Data

Interpreting data is the process of examining the analyzed data and responding to the evaluation questions, based on the strength of the data. The interpretive process, detailed in Chapter 9, requires the evaluator, program participants, and others included in this phase of the work to form judgments that are based on the analysis of the data and make recommendations about the program. Because interpreting data is a process of making meaning, engaging a wide range of stakeholders in this step enhances the meaning-making process. This phase often uses preestablished criteria against which the analyzed data are compared to determine the merit, worth, value, or impact of the professional learning program.

Step Seven: Report, Disseminate, and Use Evaluation Results

Reporting, disseminating, and using the evaluation results involves preparing both written and oral reports of the evaluation results, sharing the reports, and using the results to make informed decisions about the professional learning program. The evaluator may prepare multiple reports for dissemination to different audiences to address their specific interests in the evaluation. For some, a very comprehensive technical report is best, while for others a brief executive summary will be appropriate. Using visual displays or infographics to share data and to allow the audience to see how the data supported the findings increases readers' ability to understand the report. Evaluators support stakeholders in sharing the evaluation results with the appropriate audiences, including stakeholders and professional learning program participants. Various presentation formats for dissemination are discussed in Chapter 10. Once the evaluator prepares and disseminates reports, the evaluation process continues as stakeholders and other decision makers use the evaluation results to make informed decisions about the program's future and about other professional learning programs, if applicable.

Step Eight: Evaluate the Evaluation

A step not often included in evaluations is **meta-evaluation** of the evaluation. Both evaluators and stakeholders benefit from assessing the quality of the evaluation, procedures used to conduct the evaluation, and the perceived value of the evaluation. This might be done informally or formally. Improving the skills of the evaluator or evaluation team, design of the evaluation, dissemination of findings, or evidence collected are some reasons for evaluating the evaluation. This process benefits both the evaluator, by providing an opportunity to reflect on his or her work, and the stakeholders, by ensuring an opportunity for them to express their views about the usefulness of the evaluation. Both purposes can lead to improved evaluation practices. Chapter 11 lends insight into this last step of the evaluation process and will encourage practitioners to "finish what they start."

Table 2.4   Steps in the Evaluation Process

Planning phase	
• Assess evaluability	Is the program sufficiently designed and ready for evaluation?
• Formulate evaluation questions	What questions do we want to answer in this evaluation?
• Construct the framework	What is the plan for the evaluation?
Conducting phase	
• Collect data	What data are we collecting, how, and from whom or what?
• Organize, analyze, and display data	How are the data organized, analyzed and displayed in order to make meaning of them?
• Interpret analyzed data	What do these analyzed data mean?
Report phase	
• Disseminate and use the findings	To whom are we disseminating the findings and how? How will we use the findings?
• Evaluate the evaluation	How well did we conduct the evaluation? What did we learn about the evaluation process to improve future evaluations? What did we learn to strengthen our evaluation skills?

Evaluating
Professional Learning

3

EFFECTIVE PROFESSIONAL LEARNING

Three fundamental conditions are necessary for effective professional learning. If the conditions are not in place, further planning and design work should precede the evaluation. If the conditions are not completely addressed in the planning phase of the program and stakeholders opt to continue with evaluation, the evaluator may decide to conduct only a formative evaluation rather than a full summative evaluation. The absence of any condition has the potential for a significant negative impact on the outcomes of the professional learning.

Condition 1: The professional learning program is data driven, research or evidence based, and well designed to meet standards for effective professional learning.

What contributes to professional learning that influences educator practice and student learning is no longer a mystery. Research over the last several decades and attention to the development of standards for professional learning (Learning Forward, 2011) make it clear what constitutes effectiveness. There is no longer a need for guesswork nor for inadequacy in the design and implementation of professional learning. Professional learning for educators must rest within a comprehensive system of professional learning that establishes the vision, standards, roles and responsibilities, resources, assessment, and evaluation (Killion, 2013). Such a system should exist at the state and district levels to ensure that every member of the education workforce has equitable access to effective professional learning aligned directly to his performance standards and to his clients' performance standards. For teachers, clients include peers and students. For administrators, clients include teachers, peers, and students.

Professional learning leaders use data about students, educators, and systems to design effective, standards-based, data-driven, and research- or evidence-based professional learning programs. They use student data and analyses of root causes to understand the needs or problems to address. They establish outcomes for students based on the identified needs. Next, they examine educators' learning needs in relationship to student outcomes and establish outcomes for educators that identify the necessary changes in knowledge, attitudes, skills, aspirations, and behaviors to lead to student success. They examine attributes of the system including the context, culture, and structures in which the professional learning will occur because the ecosystem influences success and often must be improved for professional learning to have its full impact. They study research and evidence to determine what types of professional learning have contributed to achieving similar outcomes in similar contexts. With this information, they develop a theory of change, a logic model, or both that define the program's planned, sustained actions to achieve the outcomes. They allocate appropriate resources to implement the planned actions. With these elements in place, they may begin to plan both the formative and summative evaluation. When professional learning programs are grounded in data that define the needs and root causes, they are likely to take advantage of critical opportunities for learning and support to fill gaps.

Condition 2: The education agency seeking to evaluate professional learning has the capacity, including fiscal and human capital, to implement both the program and the evaluation with fidelity to their designs.

A plan for a professional learning program or its evaluation is not equivalent to a program's implementation or evaluation of that program. Without capacity to put the plans in action, neither the professional learning nor its evaluation is likely to succeed. Capacity means human, fiscal, time, technology, and material and leadership advocacy. Both professional learning and its evaluation require these resources and advocacy.

Some worry that redirecting any resources to an evaluation drains resources from the professional learning program and deprives participants of services. On the contrary, evaluation adds value because it provides valuable information to improve decision making and make better use of resources. Evaluation provides program stakeholders with essential information about what works and what does not work so they can strengthen their program operation. For example, if teachers know that their application of new learning is missing a critical component, they are better able to adjust their efforts early in the process. Principals who learn that they are not reinforcing the use of the new practices in conversations with teachers can refine their practice of supporting teachers and focus on integrating more attention to the topic in both learning walks, interactions with teachers one-on-one and in meetings of facilitators of learning teams. District leaders who find that recent requests to schools unrelated to the professional learning priority are sending mixed messages to school staff about what is

important and can modify their demands on school staff so they are able to focus on the priority areas.

Typically, the more complex an evaluation design, the costlier it is in terms of fiscal and human resources. Yet even low-cost evaluations are valuable because they can produce useful information. When decision and policy makers want more rigorous evaluation, such as a program's impact on student learning, they must be ready to invest the resources and leadership advocacy to support it so that the evaluation is reliable, valid, and valuable. In an era of accountability, the cost of evaluation is a requisite part of any fiscal planning.

Newcomer, Hatry, and Wholey (2015) identify some typical evaluation costs that include (1) the lead evaluator who plans and conducts the evaluation; (2) engagement of stakeholders who serve as a part of the evaluation team; (3) participants in professional learning who contribute data to the evaluation; (4) staff and support staff who coordinate, collect, manage, and organize data, and prepare reports and disseminate the findings; (5) costs for compensating or replacing services, if necessary, to support participation in the evaluation; (6) materials and supplies; and (7) technology resources. They also acknowledge that evaluation may cost potential loss of goodwill among participants who feel burdened by the extra workload associated with engaging in the evaluation. Another potential cost is the time the policy and decision makers invest in reviewing the evaluation report and making decisions based on it. Most of these costs can be considered business as usual in a learning organization committed to continuous improvement.

Evaluation is a value-added process. When an evaluation is designed thoughtfully, it can become a part of the intervention itself. For example, when reviewing literature about professional learning in K–12 writing to design the program and its evaluation, an evaluator noted the importance of teacher collaboration in learning communities for achieving improved results for students. To apply this finding, and practice and increase the amount of collaboration among program participants, the evaluator selected data-collection methods that reinforced collaboration such as focused groups and collaborative work products rather than those that were individually oriented such as a survey or interview. The evaluator engaged teachers in conducting collaborative classroom walk-throughs to observe student and teacher behaviors during writers' workshop and used scoring conferences to assess several samples of student work at different times during the evaluation.

Not only were these experiences rich opportunities for data collection, but they also modeled structures for teacher collaboration with a focus on student achievement. The evaluation design, in this case, extended the professional learning intervention and might have contributed to the impact of the program. The decisions the evaluator makes may also positively influence participant ownership and commitment to the program and the usefulness of the evaluation. In addition, the evaluation results may be more understandable and useful to all stakeholders. When focused on carefully crafted questions that reflect stakeholder priorities, evaluations are perceived as valuable tools and normative practice for continuous improvement.

There are many options for evaluation designs, some of which are costlier than others, so it is important to weigh the need for a complex design and its projected cost against the perceived value of an evaluation. When evaluations are designed to address specific questions intended users want to answer, the evaluation is an investment rather than a cost. Involving the users in decisions about the evaluation is critical.

Condition 3: Key stakeholders in education agencies intend to use the evaluation results to make decisions about the program.

Justifying the costs of evaluation requires that the investment be for a worthwhile, utilization-focused evaluation designed for a specific audience (users) and for specific purposes (uses). When evaluations are constructed for identified purposes and for identified stakeholders, the perceived value of the evaluation increases, as do stakeholders' understanding of and interest in the evaluation, especially if they have been actively involved in planning the design of the evaluation and the eventual use of the results (Patton, 2008). The value of evaluations can be determined by three factors: the reliability and validity of the evidence; the credibility of the evaluation to those who commissioned it and who plan to use it; and the usefulness of the findings in decision making (Patton, 2015). In **describing utilization-focused evaluation** methodology, Patton (2005) comments that "intended users are more likely to use evaluations if they understand and feel ownership of the evaluation process and findings [and that] [t]hey are more likely to understand and feel ownership if they've been actively involved. By actively involving primary intended users, the evaluator is preparing the groundwork for use" (p. 423).

The intent to use evaluation findings demonstrates and sustains interest in both the program and its evaluation. The evaluation itself sends a message about the importance of the program and has the potential to increase participants' perceived commitment to the program. It may also increase participants' interest in and effort exerted toward the program. The expression, "What gets measured, gets done," is an apt adage of the interrelationship that exists among evaluation and stakeholder and participant interest and effort.

Before an evaluation is conducted, the evaluator determines who the primary stakeholders of the evaluation are and who will be the primary users, and what will be the primary uses of the evaluation. In addition, the evaluator and professional learning leaders determine the degree to which their program meets the conditions described and make necessary adjustments prior to launching the program or its evaluation.

ANALYZING EVALUATION APPROACHES: UNDERSTANDING "GAPS" AND "BOXES"

A major challenge in the evaluation of professional learning is the frequent use of overly simplistic methodology for evaluation. This often occurs when inexperienced evaluators assume that available data are an adequate representation

or substitute for other data—for example, assuming that a survey of participant reactions to a learning experience is a viable substitute for a measure of participant learning or implementation of learning. Implementation or impact evaluations of professional learning require examining, analyzing, and measuring a series of interrelated changes that work together to produce the intended outcomes. This series might be considered a pathway or sequence of learning that begins with an educator's decision to participate in the program and continue through full, deep, and consistent application in the workplace and eventual changes in clients. Providing information or documentation about the duration of participation, the number of coaching visits, or a description of the content will not suffice as a measure of acquisition or application of learning, nor the impact of changed practice on clients. These approximations of outcomes are insufficient to make strong **claims** about the program's impact.

Stephan Katz and Lisa Ain Dack (2013) define learning as "permanent change in thinking or behavior" (p. 3). The pathway to learning that leads to a change in professional practice, way of thinking, and results for clients (think students for teachers or teachers for administrators) cannot be reduced to merely providing information. Professional learning that changes practice, thinking, and results for clients requires multiple, interconnected actions carefully designed to achieve the desired outcomes. To determine if professional learning alters educator practice and results for their clients, evaluators must gather evidence along the pathway of activities designed to achieve those ends.

Yet, in some professional learning, the pathway to the outcomes is underdeveloped. It is riddled with holes or missing entire sections. Gaps in the pathway negatively influence the potential for professional learning to succeed. The gaps may occur anywhere from the initial planning phase to the expected completion. They may rest in the culture of the environment in which the learning occurs or is implemented. They may be in the commitment of educators to engage in continuous learning and improvement. They may be in the lack of resources, leaders' advocacy for professional learning, clarity of outcomes or expectations, or sufficient implementation support to achieve high levels of professional practice with integrity, fidelity, and consistency.

When gaps occur in professional learning, the evaluation is also likely to fall short because evaluators will have fewer opportunities to gather data along the pathway. The absence of data may result in weak or faulty findings or conclusions, insufficiently supported with evidence, about the relationship between the program's action and the outcomes. There is another problem that may arise. The program may be well designed and include adequate actions sequenced logically and sufficient resources to achieve the outcome, yet its evaluation may be weak. Weak evaluations have poor designs, collect insufficient evidence to support claims, skip data collection about critical actions along the pathway to demonstrate relationships, or use approximations rather than authentic representations of the intended changes.

Black-Box and Glass-Box Approaches to Evaluation

When shortcomings occur either in the program design or in the evaluation, the "black-box" appears. It is an opaque or empty space that fails to articulate

sufficiently how a program works. It provides inadequate opportunities to collect evidence about the changes occurring within the program to make valid claims about the connections between the actions to outputs and outcomes. "Glass-box" program designs or evaluations, in contrast, reveal the transformative process that a program initiates. It delineates, through clear, sequenced actions and evidence of their intended outputs and outcomes, the interactions that occur among the actions and the outputs and outcomes.

In a **black-box evaluation**, the evaluator has incomplete or insufficient data about the effects of the program's actions, and, if the desired results are achieved, may make an assumption that the program contributed to or influenced the results. Because there is insufficient evidence, stakeholders may question the validity of the evaluation and be left to guess about the effects of the activities. This kind of evaluation fails to help stakeholders understand how the program contributed to the outcomes. It keeps stakeholders in the dark about the interrelationships among the inputs; what is needed to make the professional learning program work; the program activities; the outputs, **documents**, tools, and processes created within the operation of the program that might add value to other programs; and the outcomes—the intended changes occurring for both educators and students. See Figure 3.1 for a depiction of a black-box program.

For example, consider the following evaluation. The input: Teachers participate in a 25-hour workshop in reading strategies for underperforming readers. The outcome: Student scores in reading on a standardized state achievement test increase. Because black-box evaluations fail to shed light on how a program's activities and inputs interact to produce outputs and outcomes, practitioners are justified in questioning the link between professional learning and student achievement.

Black-box evaluations only use data about inputs or the occurrence of the activities as substitutes for changes in knowledge, attitude, skills, aspiration, or behaviors. The inputs might be the budget expenditure for the professional learning consultant and books given to teachers. They may also be the stipend to teacher leaders who provided peer coaching. Data about the occurrence of a professional learning activity might include attendance rosters, dates, times, and materials from professional learning sessions; coaching **logs**; or principal walkthrough logs. With only these types of data, evaluators may form inaccurate

Figure 3.1 A Sample Black-Box Evaluation

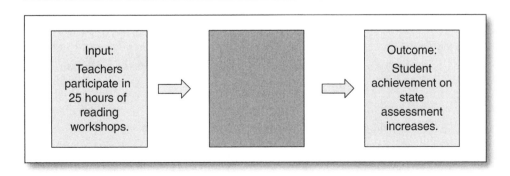

conclusions about the impact of professional learning. With insufficient data, conclusions that changes in student learning resulted from changes in educator practice resulting from professional learning are unsubstantiated, causing stakeholders to question the credibility of the evaluation.

Several examples of black-box evaluations will illuminate the challenges they present. One example is a school leadership team that uses documentation about staff participation in professional learning as a substitute for implementation and suggests that the increase in student achievement at the end of the school year is associated with the 92 percent of the staff participation in professional learning that took place at the beginning of the school year. Another example links data about inputs, such as placing coaches in schools, with student academic success. In this black-box evaluation, stakeholders might mistakenly conclude that investing in coaching improves student success without any data or evidence about the work of the coach, the interactions between coaches and teachers, the coach's impact on teaching practices, or changes in teacher practice.

Heuy Chen (1990) indicates that black-box evaluations such as these are "characterized by a primary focus on the overall relationship between the inputs and the outputs of a program without concern for the transformation processes in the middle" (p. 18). Chen continues to suggest that such evaluations will offer a "gross assessment of whether or not a program works but fail to identify the underlying causal mechanisms that generate treatment effect, thus failing to pinpoint the deficiencies of the program for future program improvement or development" (p. 18). While an effort to use documentation about program activities to affect educator practice or student learning may provide stakeholders some information about a professional learning program, it is inadequate to draw conclusions about any relationship among them. Black-box evaluations lack credibility with the policy makers who know too well their limitations. Black-box evaluations cannot help program leaders or stakeholders improve either the program results or program efficiency.

Another problem associated with black-box evaluations is the inability to explain or examine the potential influence of extraneous factors that occur during the program. Schools, districts, and communities are complex systems with innumerable factors influencing student learning. Black-box evaluations by their very nature are insensitive to unanticipated contextual or organizational factors that may influence results. As such, these evaluations are unable to consider how the professional learning program interacts with its context or how unanticipated events might influence the program and its results. Black-box evaluations, because they fail to examine all aspects of the program and the interim changes that occur within it, provide insufficient information for stakeholders to replicate the program in the future and achieve similar results.

Glass-box evaluations, on the other hand, illuminate how a professional learning program's components interact to produce results. Because they measure changes that occur throughout the program, they provide useful information to program directors and stakeholders, such as whether the program activities generate the anticipated changes, which if any activities may be more effective, and if discrepancies in implementation occur. A glass-box evaluation

may help program directors understand how the program is being implemented and highlight any inconsistencies, problems, gaps, or redundancies that might interfere with the program's success. When evaluators measure the effects of each activity along the program's pathway, program leaders and stakeholders use the information to make appropriate adjustments en route to strengthen the program's success. Figure 3.2 depicts a glass-box design with inputs to the program on the left, actions that occur during the program in the center, and outcomes of the program on the right.

Glass-box evaluations provide data to help program directors and stakeholders know what happened and why. They use the data to make informed modifications rather than respond to squeaky wheels or rely on hunches, opinions, or guesses. Rather than basing decisions on intuitions and preferences, well-designed, comprehensive professional learning programs coupled with a glass-box evaluation leave little to chance. Figure 3.3 illustrates the design of a glass-box evaluation for a program and the explicit pathway of the necessary actions within a professional learning program, organized in a logic model (described in more detail in the next chapter) to increase proficiency in reading. This pathway informs the design of a glass-box evaluation. In a glass-box evaluation, an evaluator gathers data along the pathway of the changes that occur as a result of the program's actions to demonstrate how the actions are interconnected and influence the outcomes.

This information assures the evaluator that the professional learning program is sufficiently designed and that the program is ready for evaluation. To better understand and delineate the relationships among the inputs, activities, outputs, and outcomes, professional learning leaders make their program theory of change explicit and test it. Evaluations can help stakeholders discover and test their program theories, the planned actions based on a set of assumptions, and how their programs work so that they can improve the program on an ongoing basis and use the program's design as a model for subsequent programs. Chen (1990) defines program theories as "a specification of what must be done to achieve the desired goals, what other important impacts may also be anticipated,

Figure 3.2   Glass-Box Evaluation

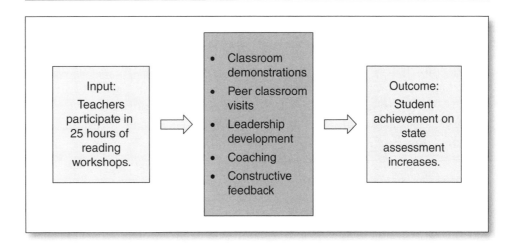

Figure 3.3   Sample Glass-Box Evaluation

Inputs (resources allocated for program operation)	Professional learning plan components (sometimes called activities)	Outputs (products, documents, or services created)	Outcomes (changes that occur in program participants and their clients)		
			Initial changes in teachers	Intermediate changes in teachers	Student outcome
• Literacy coaches in every school • Training for literacy coaches • Extended literacy blocks • Leveled classroom books • Time for meeting with the coach individually and as a team	• Summer workshop for all teachers continued through the school year with monthly sessions • Biweekly individual or team coaching • Construction, implementation, scoring, and analysis of formative assessments • Data dialogues on formative assessment data and other benchmark and year-end data • Principal training on supporting literacy instruction • Feedback process with individual teachers	• Coach logs • Data dialogue protocols • Data wall • Formative assessments • Instructional units • Classroom maps for use of space during literacy instruction • Sample anchor charts	• Increased knowledge about causes of reading deficiencies and multiple interventions to address them • Increased skills to diagnose and intervene pedagogically • Sense of urgency to improve literacy skills • Ability to design mini-lessons to address student skill gaps • Skills to confer with students	• Routine implementation of instructional practices in the classroom to address student learning gaps in literacy • Selection and use of appropriate reading intervention strategies • Commitment to meet the needs of all students • Engagement in cycle of continuous improvement • Routine use of pedagogical practices aligned with the program • Use of ongoing student assessment	• 25% increase in student reading proficient for below-level readers • All students meet third-grade reading goal by the end of third grade

and how these goals and impacts would be generated" (p. 43). A more complete discussion of a program theory of change is included in Chapter 4.

Both stakeholders and the evaluator will have a deeper understanding of the program and its component actions when they specify the underlying theory about how professional learning is expected to influence the client. By testing their theories against what really occurs, program designers can find out whether their theories hold true and, if they do not, they will be in a better position to adjust them. In the case of educators, those clients are often students and their success is frequently defined as academic achievement, yet there are other forms of success such as social, emotional, behavioral, or civic. Educators seek all types of success for their students, and evaluations of the impact of professional learning may include success indicators beyond academic achievement.

The distance between educator learning and student learning may seem great, yet it is not far at all. Glass-box evaluations illuminate the transformation processes and afford many benefits and opportunities. They

- provide useful insights for improving the professional learning;
- clarify the core, essential components of the professional learning program necessary to produce results;
- increase understanding of the conditions necessary for success;
- help implementers understand how the context interacts with activities;
- illuminate program limitations;
- prevent program deterioration;
- add to the knowledge base about professional learning;
- aid replication and adaptation of successful programs; and
- justify continued financial support for successful professional learning and its evaluation.

An evaluation that provides information to strengthen a program's design, implementation, or results is advantageous, even if it is more complex and resource intensive. The benefits justify the resources required for ongoing evaluations of both new and well-established professional learning programs. The usefulness of evaluation findings for making improvements in a program design, efficiency, effectiveness, and results, and informing decision making about the program, determine an evaluation's quality and value. Evaluators seek to support claims that professional learning did or did not contribute to the measured outcomes. Practitioner-evaluators are less concerned with isolating the effects of professional learning because they understand that, in schools and districts, the dynamic and interdependent nature of the many components of the education system are all interrelated and influential in student learning. Schools and classrooms are complex environments that do not lend themselves easily to randomized control trial (RCT) studies that meet the highest level of evidence for inclusion without question in the *What Works Clearinghouse.*

Researchers more than evaluators are concerned with isolating effects of a program through rigorous experimental and quasi-experimental methodologies to determine causal relationships between professional learning and student success. Evaluators frequently turn to descriptive or comparative studies to make decisions about a program's effectiveness and impact in natural contexts. Practitioner-evaluators recognize that many **variables**, not easily controlled, influence student success and that political, ethical, and logistical considerations of randomization make it difficult to use RCT design in evaluation studies. While the use of RCT design within evaluation allows evaluators to conclude with relative certainty that professional learning causes the results achieved, evaluators of professional learning are more interested in discovering and reporting the changes that did occur—how the context, inputs, and activities interacted to produce the results achieved. In other words, their emphasis is more on improvement rather than research, and they consider evaluation as a process of continuous improvement.

MEASURES OF STUDENT SUCCESS

A challenge in the evaluation of professional learning is the availability of reliable and valid data, particularly about changes in educator practice and student success. Most policy and decision makers consider student achievement data from high-stakes assessments the most significant measures of the effects of professional learning, yet those data may not be sufficiently sensitive or related to the professional learning outcomes for educators or students. To evaluate professional learning's impact on student academic success, the measure of achievement must align with the standards, curriculum, pedagogy, and the content of the educators' professional learning. It is only when there is tight alignment that evaluators can draw conclusions about the relationship between educator learning and student learning. When such alignment does not exist, the evaluation loses reliability and validity. For convenience, many evaluators choose readily available **data sources** of student achievement without considering the degree to which the measures of achievement match both the written and taught curriculum as well as the content of professional learning. This mismatch between the learning and practice outcomes for educators and the measures of student achievement complicate an evaluation of professional learning.

Some measures of student achievement may not be sensitive enough to account for differences in student achievement. Norm-referenced, standardized **tests**, for example, are psychometrically very reliable, yet they are designed to assess a student's acquisition of commonly accepted content rather than the specific curriculum adopted by a district or the content aligned with the classroom. For this reason, inferences related to student academic success or program effectiveness may be invalid because they are not a good measure of students' application of learning (Guskey, 2000; Popham, 2001).

The **case study** that follows provides a specific example of the challenge associated with selecting appropriate measures of student achievement.

A Case Study: Mathematics Achievement

In response to the new state mathematics standards that incorporated mathematical practices, school district leaders recognized the need to revise its curriculum as well as prepare educators to implement and support the new curriculum and pedagogy. The district's math coordinating team designed an extensive, three-year professional learning program planned to expand and cultivate the capacity of the educators who were essential to full implementation—principals, coaches, and teachers. The professional learning for the math coaches emphasized supporting change and building collaborative teams of teachers to work together to achieve consistency and quality across classrooms in math instruction and to support one another in the necessary changes. Principal professional learning focused on supervising and supporting changes in math pedagogy and building the culture and structures necessary for the sweeping changes ahead. Teacher professional learning emphasized mathematics content knowledge, pedagogical skills and practices to implement the curriculum, and sufficient and differentiated support over multiple years to ensure deep and sustained

implementation. The school board, when it approved the financial support for the professional learning program, requested an evaluation to measure the impact of their investment on both teaching and student learning.

The district measured students' math achievement annually in Grades 3–8 using the state's annual test. Analysis of the subskills measured in the test revealed that only 40 percent of the new curriculum was included. While both state and district leaders were aware of a need for a new statewide assessment in mathematics, this change was years away. State officials felt obligated to initiate implementation of the curriculum and, to compensate, they removed sanctions for poor performance until the new test was ready for deployment.

When planning the evaluation, the evaluation team discussed the discrepancy between the existing measure of student achievement and the new curriculum. They proposed to the board that district leaders develop and implement two new benchmark assessments annually for each grade to compensate for the shortcomings of the current state assessment. The board agreed to the new assessments, yet district leaders did not complete the benchmark new assessments until the end of the second year of the professional learning program.

After two consecutive years with no evidence of change in students' performance on the mathematics state test, a parent group began to question the new mathematics curriculum, the pedagogy they were observing in their students' work, and the investment in professional learning. The math coordinator and the math coordinating team recognized the challenge the assessment discrepancy created and vowed to implement the benchmark assessments during the third year of the professional learning program.

At the end of the third school year, after analyzing collected data, the district's assessment and evaluation coordinator reported on the effectiveness of the curriculum and the professional learning program. The new state test implemented during this third year indicated that the district's students in all grades performed at the state mean; however, there was no way to measure an increase in math performance since this was a baseline year. The alternative measures of student performance in mathematics indicated that the students' ability to understand advanced concepts such as statistics and probability, algebraic reasoning, and problem solving improved significantly from fall to spring. Other data collected indicated that (1) teachers had a greater comfort with mathematics instructional practices; (2) principals logged significantly more evidence of math practices by the end of year 3 than at the end of year 2; (3) students reported higher levels of engagement in classroom activities; (4) more female and minority students enrolled in advanced mathematics classes at the end of the three years than prior to the program's implementation; and (5) more students completed algebra in eighth grade. All findings served as supporting evidence of the success of the curriculum and the professional learning program. Because of the changes in the student assessments, the board authorized an additional year of evaluation to validate the results.

Analysis of the Case

This case study raises several issues related to evaluating professional learning. Two years of no results had undoubtedly caused alarm and raised

legitimate questions about both the curriculum and the quality of professional learning. While educators could rationalize the mismatch among the curriculum, pedagogy, and student results, this was difficult for parents to understand. And even though teachers, coaches, and principals understood the assessment mismatch, it was still disappointing to them to recognize that the student data did not reflect their hard work and persistence to make the necessary changes. They were grateful that surveys, principal walk-throughs, and coach perceptions provided evidence of their change in practice, yet those data did not hold significant weight for the school board. In similar circumstances, many school boards and district decision makers might have ended the mathematics program or revised the curriculum and reverted to more comfortable and familiar ways of teaching and learning math or even implement another new program rather than address the apparent inconsistency between the measure of achievement and the expected results.

Challenges similar to the mismatch between **program outcomes** and measures of student or educator success are not likely to disappear. States that responded to the U.S. Department of Education requirements to incorporate student growth as a factor in measuring teacher effectiveness will continue to question the validity of such measures, especially as the requirement has been lifted in new *Every Student Succeeds Act (ESSA)* requirements. *ESSA* now requires districts to identify at least one nonacademic indicator as a component of measuring and monitoring schools in need of improvement. Over the years, assessment specialists have contributed to making measures of student academic success more fair, valid, and reliable. The same level of rigor does not yet exist in many measures of nonacademic factors. States will need to be vigilant in selecting or developing measures of nonacademic indicators with the same degree of validity and reliability before they can be used to measure the effectiveness of schools, educators, or intervention programs.

Assess Evaluability

4

Planning Phase

- Assess evaluability
- Formulate evaluation questions
- Construct the evaluation framework

Conducting Phase

- Collect data
- Organize, analyze, and display data
- Interpret data

Reporting Phase

- Report, disseminate, and use evaluation results
- Evaluate the evaluation

The inadequacy of a professional learning program is a major contributor to challenges evident in evaluations of professional learning. When the program is insufficient in scope or power, it is unlikely to produce the expected results, especially results for students.

The first step of the evaluation process is assessing evaluability. In this step, the evaluator seeks to answer several questions:

1. Is this program conceptually and logically sufficient and feasible? In other words, does it seem likely that it has the potential to produce the results it intends?

2. Is the theory of change clearly articulated?

3. Are the outcomes specific and clear?

4. Are the indicators and measures of success explicit?

5. Are the activities and resources substantive enough to produce the changes?

6. Is there logic in the relationship among the inputs, the activities, the outputs, and outcomes?

7. Will this evaluation be useful to all stakeholders, especially primary ones?

Evaluability is the degree to which a proposed program for professional learning is ready for evaluation because it clearly articulates what the program seeks to achieve and what will occur within the program to achieve those outcomes. The program's components or activities and resources specified within

its plan are sufficient to produce the planned outcomes. An evaluator is making a decision about the program's efficacy, its capacity to produce the intended results. Applying the questions above to the case study that follows offers an opportunity to assess the evaluability of a professional learning program. The program at Barron High School is typical of professional learning programs and highlights the problems that occur when professional learning has design flaws and is not evaluable.

A Case Study: Critical Thinking

Barron High School wants (1) to improve students' achievement by developing students' capacity to construct and support arguments and (2) to build a collaborative culture among staff. This critical thinking process is applicable to English, social studies, and science curriculum, and it can strengthen staff consistency in instructional quality and collaboration across departments. The plan for professional learning includes engaging teachers in developing the knowledge and skills to share a consistent understanding about argumentation, types of support for arguments, and how to teach and assess argumentation. The plan called for teachers to work together in teams to develop a rubric to assess student performance in argumentation across the grade levels and subjects, and design and implement at least three interdisciplinary units during the school year, each culminating with a performance assessment involving student application of argumentation and each emphasizing a different one the three disciplines (see Figure 4.1).

The professional learning program had multiple components. Teachers participated in 18 hours of training designed to develop common knowledge and skills in teaching and assessing argumentation and integrating curriculum. They had time within the training to work in interdisciplinary teams to design at least one interdisciplinary unit that they would agree to teach within one month after the training. After their implementation of the first unit and before their credit was awarded, teachers were asked to work together to revise the unit, write an assessment of the unit, and submit samples of student work from the unit. Immediately after the training, curriculum consultants who provided the training on argumentation offered to assist any team in the development or implementation of its unit and to observe as teachers were teaching the unit. Teacher teams were expected to submit their two additional units

Figure 4.1   Map of Interdisciplinary Professional Learning Program at Barron High School

Teacher training:	Unit development:	Unit implementation:	Student engagement:	Student learning:
Teachers develop knowledge and skills related to argumentation and the teaching and assessment of argumentation.	Teachers develop interdisciplinary units to teach and a rubric for assessing argumentation.	Teachers use units in their classrooms.	Students complete learning tasks within the unit.	Students demonstrate the ability to construct and support arguments on end-of-unit assessment.

within 90 days of completing the course, with an expectation that the remaining units would be implemented prior to the end of the school year.

The evaluation team, consisting of a professor of research and evaluation and two graduate students from a local university, developed two surveys to administer to staff and students. The staff survey gathers data about their unit development and implementation, their understanding and integration of argumentation within their units, their perceptions of students' level of critical thinking related to argumentation, and their views about the degree of collaboration across departments. Staff completed the survey during a staff meeting near the end of the school year to increase the likelihood of having a high response rate and to allow ample time for teachers to implement the units. Students completed their survey near the end of the school year in English classes because 75 percent of the students were enrolled in English. Other students were notified that they could complete a survey in the counseling office. The survey asked students for their views about how cross-department assignments and performance tasks and consistency in instruction about argumentation had influenced their understanding of and performance in argumentation assignments. Evaluators intended to gather student performance data on the end-of-unit performance task to analyze trends across the three tasks.

The findings of the surveys were as follows. The mean number of interdisciplinary units taught by all teachers in the school was 1. The range was 0–3. Teachers reported limited collaboration with colleagues in other departments. Students indicated that they had very little knowledge about argumentation, and most (more than 60%) were unable to articulate how the interdisciplinary consistency contributed to their depth of understanding with argumentation. Thirty percent of the students scored proficient on the performance task at the end of the first common unit; 20 percent were advanced; and 50 percent were below proficient. Because only three of the 32 total English, social studies, and science teachers implemented two additional interdisciplinary units, evaluators **disaggregated** student performance task scores for the 94 students who participated in three interdisciplinary units on argumentation to compare student performance on the second and third units with that of the first unit. Performance steadily progressed upward with 62 percent of the students proficient on the second unit and 22 percent advanced. On the third performance task 72 percent of the students were proficient and 25 percent advanced. Most teachers expressed limited collaboration with peers beyond the training and mostly felt the common assignments and performance task hampered their instruction and limited their content. The three teachers who implemented all three units were outliers in a positive direction on nearly all aspects of the teacher survey, as were their students.

Case Study Review

There are several flaws in this situation in both the design of the professional learning program and in the design of the evaluation. These include (1) the evidence of need for a focus on argumentation across core disciplines, (2) staff engagement and expectations related to the identified need, (3) administrative support for and expectations of implementation of the professional

learning, (4) the adequacy of the training and support, (5) the implementation of a single unit by the majority of staff rather than the intended three units planned, (6) staff commitment to the intended goals of the program and full participation, (7) the design of the student and staff surveys, (8) the possible exclusion of a number of students, (9) the use of the common performance task as a measure of student achievement, and (10) the feasibility of implementing three interdisciplinary units within one school year.

What might be the starting point for considering this program is its overall efficacy to produce the results. Considering the questions below will clarify how the design of the professional learning might have contributed to the limited results of this professional learning.

- How was the need for this professional learning program determined and to what degree were teachers involved in the process?
- How committed were teachers to address the problem, participate in the training, and apply their learning in practice?
- How reasonable is it to expect that interdisciplinary units, no matter how well planned or how many, would increase student achievement in argumentation?
- What research supported the selection of interdisciplinary approach as the most feasible way to improve student learning in argumentation?
- Is it reasonable to expect that 18 hours of training accompanied by the expectation to design, teach, and report on one interdisciplinary unit would produce more than one interdisciplinary unit or impact students' ability to apply argumentation in performance tasks?
- If the planned activities included having teachers design and teach three interdisciplinary units, where in the plan was there support for completing that portion of the plan? What was the role of the administrators in supporting the goal for three units and three performance tasks for students?
- Where in the plan was time built in to allow teachers to collaborate, especially across disciplines?
- What systems and supports were put into place to assist teachers who wanted or needed additional supports?
- What role did the school's principal play in conveying the importance of this intervention?
- How did department chairpersons assist their staff members in meeting the program expectations?
- What resources did the curriculum consultants provide teachers to facilitate the design of additional units?
- How did teachers experience the feedback process to review and reflect on their first unit before they received credit?

The point of this case is simply this: It is futile to expect results for students from a professional learning program that is unlikely to produce them. Evaluation cannot compensate for a professional learning program that is poorly conceived and constructed. Perhaps Chen (1990) said it best: "Current

problems and limitations of program evaluation lie more with lack of adequate conceptual framework of the program than with methodological weakness" (p. 293). Evaluation of ill-conceived professional learning programs wastes limited human and fiscal resources and educator goodwill and effort. In these cases, evaluations sanction programs with gaps in their conceptual frameworks by appearing to condone mediocrity. Wasted evaluations rob students and educators of powerful opportunities to learn at high levels. And when evaluations attempt to assess programs with fuzzy outcomes, faulty conceptual frameworks, or illogical, poorly structured activities, the evaluation may be difficult to design and of questionable integrity. Professional learning that is not based on an identified problem defined through analysis of student, educator, and system data, is poorly planned, and which is not focused on what educators need to learn to help students achieve identified learning goals may impede student success by taking attention away from the high-priority needs.

Professional learning to change practice and thinking takes time, extended support, clarity of expectations, monitoring, and sufficient resources. Professional learning that changes professional practice and opportunities for student learning requires persistence, diligence, resources, advocacy, leadership, and hard work. Too often new practices are implemented only occasionally rather than at a deep and sustained level because the professional learning plan fails to integrate implementation monitoring and sustained support. If implementation support is lacking, then it is safe to assume that only a small portion of learners will use the information regularly to solve problems associated with their practice.

Joyce and Showers (1995), in their seminal research study about the methodologies and outcomes of professional learning, found that only 5–10 percent of participants used their new learning when there was merely presentation of theory. These numbers increased slightly to 10–15 percent when demonstration and low-risk practice were added to the instructional methodology. Only when ongoing support was added in the form of coaching, study groups, and so forth did the percentage of participants using their new learning increase to 85–90 percent. If the design of the professional learning program fails to include ongoing support in the form of coaching or study groups, then the results will be few.

CONDUCTING THE EVALUABILITY ASSESSMENT

One way to circumvent the problems associated with evaluating poorly designed professional learning programs is to begin with an **evaluability assessment**. This process assists both the evaluator and the program planner in knowing whether the program can be evaluated by examining the program need and design, clarity of outcomes and indicators of success, logic and sufficiency of activities, adequacy of resources, planned benchmark assessments, and intention to modify and adjust periodically. If Chen's statement is accurate—that the problem of evaluation rests largely with the program's conceptual design—then

it makes sense that the evaluator and program developers and stakeholders join hands at an early stage to define the **program goals** with clarity, its resources with completeness, and its activities with logical sequence.

The goals of the evaluability assessment are to ensure that

1. program goals, outcomes, important side effects, and priority information needs are well defined;

2. program goals and outcomes are plausible and reasonable;

3. relevant data can be obtained; and

4. the intended users of the evaluation results have agreed on how they will use the information (Wholey, 2015).

Evaluators have both an obligation and responsibility to facilitate program planning to ensure that the plan meets the evaluability criteria prior to implementation. Program planners concomitantly have an obligation and responsibility to engage the evaluator or an evaluation lens in program planning to ensure that a program is evaluable.

The steps of evaluability assessment are as follows: (1) establish need and rationale for the program; (2) examine the program's goals, outcomes, and standards for success; (3) examine the program's theory of change and/or its logic model; and (4) adjust the program design based on the assessment. This is an iterative process; depending on the outcome of the first three steps, the fourth step involves making program design adjustments and repeating the first three steps. The remainder of this chapter is intended not only to help evaluators know what to look for in their evaluability assessment but also to help program directors develop these essential program components.

Program Need and Rationale

Professional learning programs are grounded in identified needs that emerge from analysis of student, educator, and system data. Research, evidence, and data guide the design of the content and process of the professional learning to respond to the identified problems. If student performance in reading comprehension, for example, is persistently low, program planners use data to identify where the leverage is for addressing this problem. If the leverage point is instruction and educator practice, professional learning is likely the appropriate intervention. If the problem is inadequate resources, then adding resources is the appropriate intervention. This book assumes that when professional learning is the planned intervention, sufficient needs analyses based on data indicate that the practice of educators, if improved, will have a positive impact on student success.

When the evaluator meets with program planners to conduct an evaluability assessment, she asks program planners to provide their analyses of student, educator, and system data and explain how they identified the need and potential causes. They also provide the research or evidence base for the professional learning planned. Should the program planners not have sufficient evidence of either,

the evaluator will probe with questions such as the ones below to engage program planners in developing greater specificity and certainty in their program design.

- What evidence or data provide a basis for the problem identified?
- What is the breadth, depth, and urgency of the problem?
- What evidence or research provides support for selecting professional learning as the appropriate or high-impact intervention?
- What evidence supports that this planned professional learning is sufficient to achieve the intended outcomes?
- Which educators are the primary participants for this professional learning intervention? Who supports them and will benefit from professional learning for their supporting responsibilities?
- What aspects of educator practice, if changed, will have the greatest impact on the problem identified?

The evaluator, if he finds that the problem is insufficiently defined or supported with evidence may suggest a program need and planning problem evaluation, one that examines the current state using data, stakeholder perception, and context analyses to determine the problem and then support program planners in a study of research- and evidence-based interventions to refine or redesign the program before implementation. When taking this step, the evaluator assists program planners in understanding the potential consequences of designing programs for ill-defined needs or implementing poorly developed programs and expecting positive results. While the steps may delay implementation, the delay and revisions increase the potential for positive results from the professional learning program.

Program Goals, Outcomes, and Standards for Success

Many professional learning programs begin with unclear or fuzzy goals or outcomes that focus on implementation rather than results. Carol Weiss (1998) suggests that "part of the explanation [for fuzzy goals] probably lies in practitioners' concentration on concrete matters of program functioning and their pragmatic mode of operation. They often have an intuitive rather than an analytical approach to program development. But there is also a sense in which ambiguity serves a useful function; it may mask underlying divergences in intent. Support from many quarters, inside and outside the program agency, is required to get a program off the ground, and the glittering generalities that pass for goal statements are meant to satisfy a variety of interests and perspectives" (p. 52).

Regardless of the reason for them, unclear goals or outcomes or even unreasonable ones have the potential to create gaps in actions and impede goal and outcome attainment. Clarifying the goals and outcomes of the professional learning program is a critical function in designing the program because they determine everything. Sometimes the terms *goals* and *outcomes* are confusing. A *goal* is a statement of a desired state toward which a program is directed, what the overall purpose of the program is. Goals inspire people to engage in the program. An ultimate or long-term goal is one that "typically take a long time to achieve; furthermore, their achievement is contingent on

many factors," states Chen (2015, p. 106). In education, ultimate goals may be to prepare students to be college and career ready or to be responsible global citizens. These are long-term goals. A short-term goal is one that is more specific and measurable in a reasonable period, sometimes beyond the scope of a program. "Short-term goals easily provide the 'measuring sticks;' with which program staff can see their successes and be motivated to press on with their work" (pp. 106–107). In professional learning, the ultimate goal is student success. The short-term goals are defined as performance in a certain discipline or level of performance overall.

A common point of confusion in planning professional learning occurs in developing goals, outcomes, and activities. Outcomes operationalize goals in defined, measurable ways. The examples below in Table 4.1 offer some clarification.

Table 4.1 Goal, Outcomes, Standards for Success, and Activities

Goal	Outcomes	Standard for Success	Activities/Program Components
Students graduate college and career ready.	**Students:** Students achieve proficiency on the end-of-course algebra exam at the end of eighth grade.	90% of students	• Use data from student benchmark assessments to plan instruction • Use flexible grouping for students during instruction • Design and implement reteaching and extension experiences for students based on data
	Teachers: Teachers implement mathematical practices and differentiation within math instruction.	All teachers use appropriate math practices and differentiation in the design, implementation, and assessment of math units of instruction.	• Provide training for teachers in math practices and UDL • Provide collaborative learning time facilitated by math coach to develop understanding of and strategies for implementing math practices • Design multiple approaches to differentiating instruction through Universal Design for Learning (UDL) • Observe demonstration lessons by math coach • Engage in team and individual coaching
	Math coaches: Math coaches facilitate teacher planning and support implementation.	All math coaches use math practices and UDL as the focus for instructional planning with teams and in individual coaching sessions.	• Engage math coaches in training on math practices and UDL • Coach math coaches in facilitating team planning using math practices and UDL • Meet with coach supervisor to identify challenges and acquire strategies to address them • Meet with math coordinator to clarify content and instructional methods related to applying math practices and UDL

Goals shape the overarching reason for the program and reflect the identified problem to solve. Outcomes specify the changes that are needed to achieve the goal. Program evaluations focus on measuring outcome attainment because goal attainment might be too remote to assess. If the program described above is three years in length, it will not be possible to know if eighth-grade completion of algebra influenced college or career readiness at graduation, four years hence. Outcomes are stated in terms that can be measured, and the standards of success establish the criteria against which success is measured. Chen (2015) suggests, "Outcomes provide tangible yardsticks for measuring the accountability variables that funding agencies and/or public may scrutinize" (p. 107). In the example above, if only some teachers are routinely implementing math practices and UDL, the program will be only partially successful. The activities are the means to achieve the outcomes and become the components that make up the program. They describe what the program does to achieve the defined changes.

Some districts and schools use SMART goals, a combination of goals and objectives. SMART goals identify results as

- **S**pecific
- **M**easurable
- **A**chievable
- **R**esults-oriented
- **T**ime-bound

Smart goals are often substitutes for outcomes because they define the specific change required to achieve a broader, yet unstated goal. Sample SMART goals are below.

- By 2020, all eighth-grade students will pass the algebra end-of-course examination at proficiency level or above.
- At the end of the school year, 90 percent of all students in Grades 3–8 will demonstrate the ability to read and comprehend grade-appropriate text by scoring at the proficiency level or above on the state reading test.

Involving an evaluator in the early stages of program planning will help program directors "begin with the end in mind." A comprehensive plan for a program of professional learning will logically and conceptually connect the identified needs with the desired results. The plan will specify the activities planned to move participants from the need to the intended results, the outcomes, and eventually the goal. Evaluators experienced in designing evaluation will be invaluable to developers in the planning stage.

Program planners often confuse outcomes and activities because they fail to gain clarity on the specific changes they want to achieve. As a result, they substitute their actions in place of outcomes. Janice Bradley, Linda Munger, and Shirley Hord (2015) surmise, "Beginning a change project without knowing

where one is going creates confusion—uncertainty and doubt about what to do differently to see changes in educator practices and improvement in student results. When educators focus on activities first, they assume that changes and improvements will result. However, without a clear image of the desired outcomes, educators' frustration occurs year after year when educator practices and students' learning do not change or improve" (p. 46).

When developing outcomes for educators to operationalize goals and to gain clarity about the types of changes needed to achieve them, planners might use the KASAB framework to clarify the needed changes in both educator practice and student learning. KASAB stands for Knowledge, Attitudes, Skills, Aspirations, and Behaviors. Table 4.2 defines each and provides an example.

KASABs are distinct from one another, and acquisition of one does not necessarily mean that others have been achieved. Here's an example. An adult female has a goal of physical wellness. Her specific outcomes are to have a healthy body mass index, normal blood pressure and glucose level, cardiovascular capacity, and healthy weight as recommended by the National Wellness Institute. In relationship to the outcomes on body mass, weight, and glucose level, she acknowledges that weight loss is in order. She can name and describe eight different weight loss programs (Knowledge); she has a positive attitude about wanting to be physically fit and is committed to improving her all-around health (Attitude); she has tried several weight loss programs before

Table 4.2 Types of Changes in Teachers and Students

Type of Change	Teachers	Students
Knowledge: Conceptual understanding of information, theories, principles, and research	Teachers understand mathematical concepts they are responsible for teaching.	Students have a deeper understanding of key mathematical concepts measured on criterion-referenced tests.
Attitude: Beliefs about the value of information or strategies	Teachers believe students' competence in mathematics is important to their success, both within and beyond school.	Students enjoy mathematics.
Skills: The ability or capacity to use strategies and processes to apply knowledge	Teachers know how to employ a variety of instructional strategies to help students visualize mathematical concepts.	Students demonstrate their understanding of math on classroom performance tasks.
Aspiration: Desires, or internal motivation, to engage in a practice	Teachers have a genuine desire for their students to understand and perform well in mathematics.	Students want to advance their understanding of mathematics and aspire to advanced work in mathematics.
Behavior: Consistent application of knowledge and skills driven by attitudes and aspiration	Teachers consistently employ inquiry-based instructional practices in mathematics to help students acquire a deep understanding of math concepts.	Students regularly apply mathematical reasoning to solving problems in math and other areas of their curriculum.

with success (Skills) so she knows how to lose weight; she has a significant social event in the near future and wants to look her best (Aspiration); and she finds it difficult to exercise (Behavior). The absence of the last component of KASAB will make it difficult for her to achieve her overall goal and perhaps her outcomes. All five components are interdependent and work together, with behavior often serving as the measure of the first four. Steven Katz and Lisa Ain Dack (2013) define learning as permanent change in behavior and thinking. In this case, behavior and attitude are the signals of learning, and knowledge, skills, and aspirations may be enablers yet are often prerequisites to changes in behavior and attitude. When program developers attend to the full scope of the KASABs in professional learning, they are more likely to achieve deep change in educators that will be sustained over time and impact student learning.

KASAB helps program developers, as well as evaluators who work with program stakeholders, clarify the intended outcomes of a program. Programs may have various actors who are instrumental in contributing to the outcome and goal attainment. For example, a program can expect changes for students, teachers, teacher leaders, coaches, principals, central office personnel, parents and community members, or others involved in the educational process. A frequent failure of professional learning programs is focusing too narrowly on a single actor group without considering the changes necessary in other actors to support them. In this way, it is possible to consider the primary actors as those who are directly influencing the success of students and the secondary actors who influence or support the primary actors. For example, in most professional learning programs related to student success, teachers are often the primary actors because their instructional behaviors directly influence student learning. Principals, coaches, and teacher leaders, along with district curriculum or professional learning staff, may be secondary actors since they provide the conditions and support teachers need to implement new instructional practices. Without attending to changes in the secondary actors' practices, the primary actors may not have adequate support for full, consistent, and accurate implementation.

Another reference for developing outcomes is the levels of training evaluation developed by Claude Bennett (1975, 1979, 1982), Thomas Guskey (2000), Donald Kirkpatrick (1998a, 1998b; Kirkpatrick & Kirkpatrick, 2006; Kirkpatrick & Kirkpatrick, 2016), and Jack Phillips (1997). The levels delineate tiered effect of training on participants and their clients, and as such may help specify the outcomes of professional learning. The early levels focus on immediate responses to training, satisfaction, and acquisition of knowledge and skill, while the latter stages focus on effects on clients and return on investment. Table 4.3 describes each level. Evaluators may evaluate merit at levels 1 and 2. They may evaluate worth at levels 3–6 and impact only at levels 5 and 6.

Clear outcomes make program design and evaluation easier. In the case of the levels of training evaluation, it is necessary to align the program outcomes with the appropriate type of evaluation. A poorly designed evaluation resulting from substituting, for example, participant satisfaction for the level of learning or implementation will lead to invalid conclusions from the evaluation.

Table 4.3 Levels of Training Evaluation

Levels 1–6	Sample Evaluation Questions	Value of Information	Frequency of Use	Difficulty of Assessment
1. Measuring participants' response to the learning experience	Were participants satisfied with the learning experience? (A measure of intrinsic value)	Least valuable	Frequent	Easy
2. Measuring participants' acquisition of learning	What did participants learn? (A measure of intrinsic value)			
3. Measuring organizational support and change	How has the culture of the school changed? (A measure of extrinsic value if criteria are established)			
4. Measuring the first level of effectiveness (i.e., participants' application of learning)	How often are participants implementing the new practices? (A measure of intrinsic value and potentially extrinsic value if criteria are established)			
5. Measuring the second level of effectiveness (i.e., impact on participants' clients, e.g., teachers, students)	Has student achievement increased? (A measure of extrinsic value if criteria are established)			
6. Calculating return on investment	What is the fiscal return on stakeholders' investment? (A measure of extrinsic value if criteria are established)	Most valuable	Infrequent	Difficult

Conversely, the evaluation of a poorly conceived program with unclear outcomes not only will be difficult but also will be likely to produce limited results.

After setting goals and outcomes for a professional learning program, it is also necessary to set standards, or criteria, against which to measure a program's success. Some evaluators may choose not to do this and to judge the success of the program without explicit criteria. If an outcome is to raise student achievement, specifying the level of increase that is acceptable or desirable makes the judgment more objective and specific. A 1 percent increase is not the same as a 10 percent increase, yet both are increases. If teachers implement an instructional practice once, they are not likely to get sustained change in their own practice or in student learning. What if the professional learning program focused on teachers' mathematics instruction and student achievement occurred in science? Will that suggest that the program was successful? If achievement occurs in science and not in mathematics, will that indicate

success? Program planners often work in collaboration with stakeholders to establish criteria for the program's success or impact.

Using past performance as a starting point is one way to begin a conversation about a standard. If the percentage of students achieving proficiency in reading at grade level has increased an average of 2 percent for each of the last three years, and if a new literacy professional learning program focused on reader's workshop is being implemented to increase reading achievement, it is reasonable to expect an increase greater than 2 percent. Examining typical growth in other districts that have implemented a similar program or the research on the program might provide the necessary information to determine the standard for success. Planners may set a 4 percent growth rate for the first year of implementation and 6 percent for each subsequent year. Identifying multiple standards for success over time, such as this, is another way to set standards for acceptable performance. Expanding the indicators to include outcomes for teachers as well as students may be another way of setting standards.

Program stakeholders and directors sometimes choose to scaffold expected impact over several years. For example, they might expect a modest student achievement gain the first year, increase it the second year, and raise it again the third year. This process acknowledges the well-documented "implementation dip" that occurs with new programs; in the dip during the early implementation stages, scores may fall slightly before they grow dramatically (Fullan, 2001). In the case of the literacy professional learning program, the student achievement gain may be set at 3 percent and measures of teacher efficacy with the workshop approach and their use of reader's workshop set at 90 percent in the first year. In the second year, once teachers are more comfortable using reader's workshop and have developed the baseline skills to do so, and rearranged their classroom instruction and physical space to accommodate readers workshop, the standards for student achievement may increase to a 5 percent gain and 100 percent of teachers implementing reader's workshop measured through self-report data. In the third year, the standards may increase to a 10 percent gain in student achievement and 100 percent of teachers implementing reader's workshop as observed by coaches and principals. Scaffolding standards for success over time provides program directors clear indicators of where they expect to be after a specific benchmark and allows them to review formative assessment data to adjust in the program before the final evaluation.

External standards, such as those established by state departments of education as a part of their school improvement and accountability measures, or comparison standards, such as performance within bands of similar school systems, may become the standards to set if they are related to the professional learning program's content. Any number of factors can be the basis for establishing standards for success of a professional learning program. Keeping at least one indicator of student success as an indicator reminds program participants about the intended outcome and impact of educator learning on students and reinforces the link between educator practice and student success.

Whether to set a standard high rather than low may be a difficult decision. A standard for success that is low may not be compelling to participants or convey a sense of urgency and significance for the changes the program intends. A standard that is too high may be debilitating. Program directors are hesitant to acknowledge that they failed to meet their goals, yet when those goals are significant—stretch goals—it will be easier to acknowledge falling short.

As a part of the evaluability assessment, evaluators determine whether the standard of success for program outcomes is feasible and can be supported. They might also inquire about the engagement of stakeholders in the decision making. Involving program stakeholders in establishing standards for acceptable performance increases their understanding of the program's purpose, generates support for the program, and informs them of the program's expectations.

EXAMINE THE PROGRAM'S THEORY OF CHANGE

Developing a theory of change assists program developers, coordinators, and providers in articulating comprehensively what the professional learning program is and how it is expected to produce the intended results. A program's theory of change delineates the causal processes through which change happens as a result of a program's strategies or actions. It links how program developers believe change happens with their choice of actions. Dana Taplin and Heléne Clark (2012) describe theory of change both as a product and process: "A theory of change is a rigorous yet participatory process whereby groups and stakeholders in a planning process articulate their long-term goals and identify the conditions they believe have to unfold for those goals to be met. These conditions are modeled as desired outcomes, arranged graphically in a causal framework. A theory of change describes the types of interventions (a single program or coordinated initiative) that bring about the outcomes depicted in the outcomes framework map. Each intervention is tied to an outcome in the causal framework, revealing the often complex web of activity required to bring about change. The framework provides a working model against which to test hypotheses and assumptions about what actions will best produce the outcomes in the model" (p. 1). Chen (2005) states that program developers design programs based on implicit or explicit assumptions about what is needed to address the identified problem. Later he adds that a program's theory of change "can be viewed, then, as a configuration of the prescriptive and descriptive assumptions held by stakeholders and thus underlying the program stakeholders create" (2015, p. 66). The theory of change then describes what must occur in what sequence for the outcomes to be achieved.

Some evaluation and research scholars describe the logic model as a graphic depiction of a program's theory of change, yet Funnell and Rogers (2011) and Patton (2015) differentiate a theory of change and logic model. A program's

theory, Funnell and Rogers note, is comprised of both a **theory of change** and a **theory of action**. The theory of change "is about the central processes or drives by which change comes about for individuals, groups, or communities—for example the psychological processes, social processes, physical processes, and economic processes. . . . the theory of action explains how programs or other interventions are constructed to activate these theories of change" (p. xix). Patton (2015) adds that distinguishing a theory of change from a logic model is useful: "The only criterion for a logic model is that it be, well *logical*, that it, it portrays a reasonable, defensible, and sequential order from inputs through activities to outputs, outcomes, and impacts. A theory of change, in contrast, bears the burden of specifying and explaining assumed, hypothesized, or tested causal linkages. Logic models are first and foremost *descriptive*, that is, describing the steps of a program from intake through completion. A well conceptualized theory-of-change model is *explanatory* and *predictive*" (pp. 200–201; emphasis in original).

A theory of change has several core components. One is the program's rationale, which explains what actions are included and the sequence of the actions and their interrelationship to achieve the program's goals and outcomes. Another core component is the set of underlying assumptions upon which the program is based. These assumptions explain why certain actions or strategies are included and sequenced as they are. The assumptions reflect previous successful practices, research, or other evidence that supports the plausibility and efficacy of the program to achieve its outcomes. Identifying the assumptions behind the design of a program encourages program designers to ask why they believe the actions included will bring about the results they seek. The program's actions, a third component, articulate what the program provides in terms of actions to achieve the goals and outcomes.

John McLaughlin and Gretchen Jordan (2015) suggest that the value of establishing and testing a program's theory of change is establishing and testing the often implicit hypothesis that if the right resources are transformed into the right activities for the right people, then these are expected to lead to the results the program was designed to achieve" (p. 69). They also add that the program's theory of change allows "the evaluator and others to see how it is supposed to work or thought to be working from multiple perspectives" (p. 70). A program's theory of change specifies how a program's goals and outcomes are logically related to its inputs (resources) and activities. The theory of change is a comprehensive representation of how the program is intended to work. Patton (1997) describes it as a "straightforward articulation of what is supposed to happen in the process that is intended to achieve desired outcomes" (p. 223). A program's theory of change specifies the goals and the activities—the series of actions that are likely to lead to the attainment of both the short-term outcomes and the long-term goals (the results).

Figure 4.2 provides a sample of a high-level theory of change for teacher professional learning. It includes the actions and their corresponding assumptions.

Figure 4.2 A Simple Theory of Change for Professional Learning

---

Action 1: Teachers engage in collaborative, standards-based professional learning.

Assumptions:

1. Professional learning is effective in changing educator knowledge, attitudes, skills, aspirations, and behaviors when it meets the standards of effective professional learning.

2. Teachers, when they collaborate with peers, benefit from others' experiences, are supported in application of learning, engage in problem-solving with trusted peers, and are more comfortable with change when they can see others experience similar challenges and successes.

3. Peers serve as motivators for increased effectiveness.

Action 2: Teachers receive support to change instructional practices.

1. Teachers, when more confident about the changes expected, are more likely to implement them.

2. Teachers appreciate being within a community of other professionals while implementing change to benefit from others' experiences.

3. Teachers are more likely to implement change when they have support.

4. Teachers are more likely to implement change when they know the changes are expected and likely to be successful.

Action 3: Teacher change in practice alters students' opportunity to learn and influences their performance.

1. Teachers change classroom instruction when they learn new instructional practices.

2. Positive student response in terms of engagement and academic success motivates teachers to implement the new instructional practices.

3. Teachers persist in implementing new instructional practices when they receive positive reinforcement or acknowledgment from supervisors and peers.

This simple theory of change includes the theory of action—the delineated and sequenced actions that describe how to improve student performance. It also includes the theory of change—the explanation and prediction about this program's approach to improving student performance.

Overarching Theories of Change

The field of professional learning has proposed several commonly accepted theories of change. Some of these theories have emerged from research and successful practice related to human learning and change and organizational or school improvement. These theoretical and practical approaches to improving educator and student learning can assist program developers as they design their programs.

One theory of change is Bennett's Hierarchy, conceived by Claude Bennett (1979, 1982) to support the evaluation of cooperative extension programs.

Patton (2008) describes the application of the hierarchy, a chain of interrelated program events, to education-oriented interventions.

1. Inputs (resources must be assembled to get the program started.

2. Activities are undertaken with available resources.

3. Program participants (clients, students, beneficiaries) engage in program activities.

4. Participants react to what they experience.

5. As a result of what they experience, changes in knowledge, attitudes, and skills occur (if the program is effective).

6. Behavior and practice change follow knowledge and attitude change.

7. Overall community impacts result as individual changes accumulate and aggregate—both intended and unintended impacts (pp. 355–356).

Another theory of change draws on research by Joyce and Showers (2002). They identified four components of training that relate to a participant's ability to apply new information to solve real-life problems. These components are presentation of theory, demonstration, low-risk practice, and study groups, coaching, or other forms of follow-up (Joyce & Showers, 2002). If a program developer were designing a professional learning program with the goal of developing and transferring new instructional or leadership practices, she might choose to use this research to construct the both the theory of change and theory of action for the program so that it incorporates knowledge, skill building, and ongoing support as essential components.

If, however, she believes that people move through stages of concern and various levels of use before they can focus on the consequences of their work and collaborate with others, she might use the research that emerged from the Concerns-Based Adoption Model (Hall & Hord, 2014) to design the program. In this way, she would ensure that the program incorporates ways to address stages of concern (from awareness to refocusing) and to move participants through levels of use, from nonuse to routine use.

The levels of evaluation (discussed earlier) are another potential theory of change. Program managers may view the levels as a sequence of actions: Teachers enjoy their learning, acquire knowledge and skills, and apply them as prerequisites to student learning increasing. Adopting this theory of change assumes that educators will follow this process: First, they engage in learning experiences that they enjoy or find valuable. Second, they increase their understanding, as demonstrated by an increase in knowledge and skills. Third, they have the necessary organizational context to implement the new practices. Fourth, they apply their learning in the classroom. Lastly, their actions produce changes for students.

A more detailed theory of change for a professional learning program in reading might be illustrated in Figure 4.3 as a cycle of actions grounded in the following assumptions.

Figure 4.3 Theory of Change for Professional Learning Program to Improve Student Reading Performance

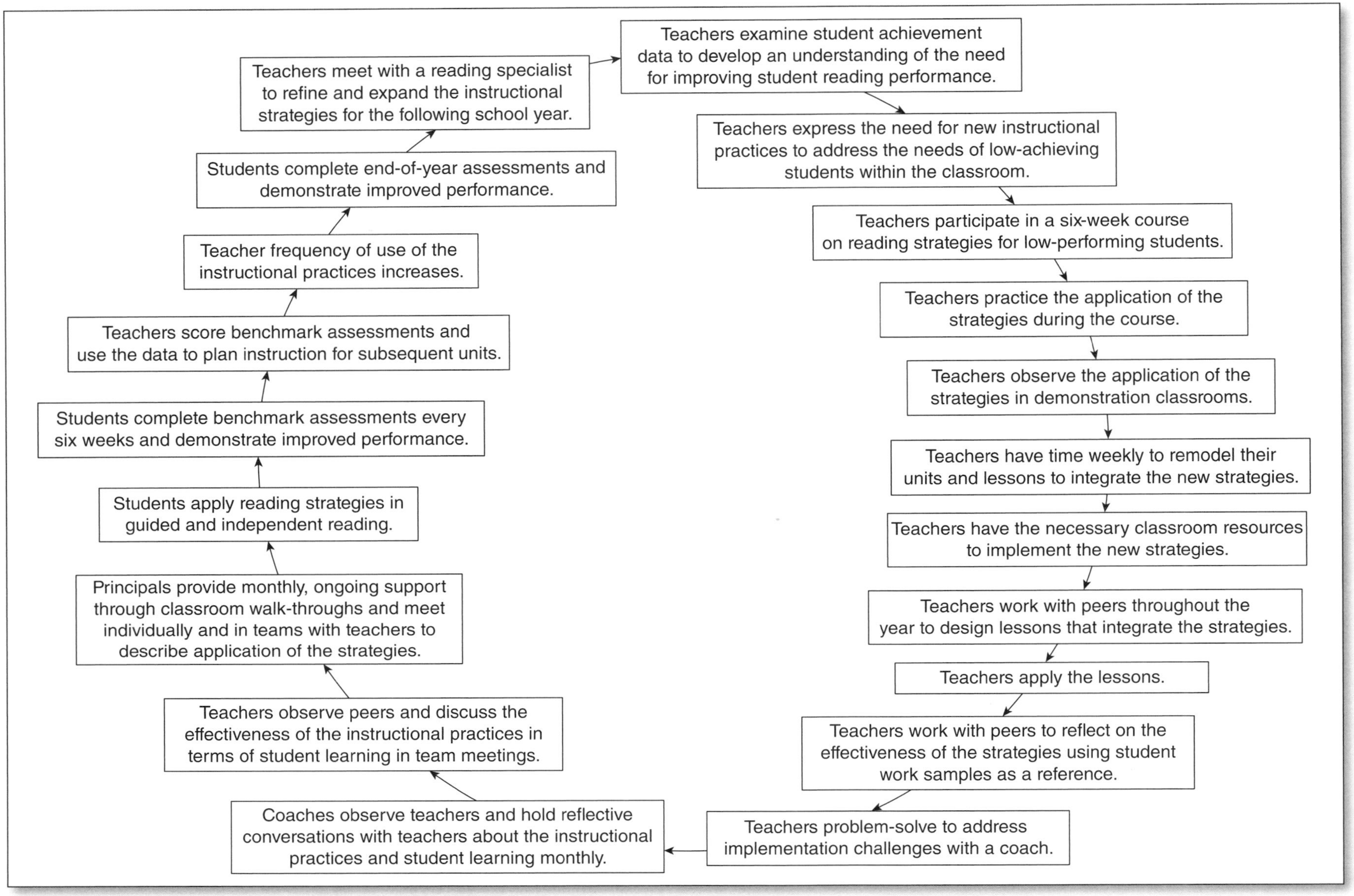

The theory of change depicted in Figure 4.3 is based on these assumptions:

- Student need serves as a motivator for changing teacher practice.
- Teachers' understanding of and skillfulness in instructional strategies precedes their use of them.
- To use new instructional strategies, teachers have the appropriate material, human, and time resources.
- The availability of support reinforces the expectation to implement new learning.
- Success builds with an increase in practice and support.
- The opportunity to collaborate with peers both energizes and motivates teachers to change practice.
- Classroom-based coaching supports teachers as they apply new practices.
- Consistency and accuracy in implementation of new practices emerge over time.
- Student success motivates teachers to sustain new practices.
- Student achievement comes from consistently applied, research-based instructional practices delivered by teachers who have in-depth understanding of content and content-specific instructional strategies.

It is possible to address the problem of low performance in reading through alternative approaches. Other theories of change might involve student tutoring or extended instructional time. The choice depends on the identified need and perceived root cause. The measure of good theories of change, according to Connell and Kubisch (1998) and Connell and Klem (2000), is fourfold: (1) they are plausible—evidence and common sense suggest that the specified activities will lead to the desired results; (2) they are doable—the initiative has adequate financial, technical, political, institutional, and human resources to implement the strategies; (3) they are testable—the pathways of change are specific and complete enough, with measurable indicators and specified preconditions for tracking the progress in a credible and useful way; and (4) they are meaningful—stakeholders perceive that the results are important and that the magnitude of change the program will bring about is worthwhile.

Why Articulate a Program's Theory of Change?

Clearly articulating a program's theory of change is beneficial for several reasons. It clarifies what the program is and creates a common understanding among all stakeholders. Both program directors and participants will have a big picture of the scope of the program and their respective responsibilities related to it. They will also understand the results the program intends to achieve. When the program's theory of change is fully developed, many implementation problems are eliminated from the planning stages. The theory of change will identify the sequence of activities that will logically lead to the desired results. If

any of the activities cannot be fully supported or implemented with available resources or do not achieve their **intermediate outcomes**, then program developers must seriously consider whether the overall program is likely to produce the intended results. In this case, program developers may need to discontinue plans for an evaluation until all essential components of the program are planned. Attainment of the intended results will depend upon implementation of the entire program plan.

A program's theory of change informs the evaluation of a program. The evaluator will be able to work with the program stakeholders to establish what they want to learn as the program is implemented. With a theory of change articulating how the program results are achieved, the evaluator can better determine which activities of the program are necessary and opportune for data collection to establish the relationships among actions and outcomes. The evaluator is in a better position to focus on the components that may need closer examination to determine their contribution to the program's results.

Program designers may alter or refine the program's theory of change as the program evaluation occurs to best reflect what occurs throughout the program and to better depict the causal assumptions of the program. Once the program is implemented and evaluated, its theory of change can be adapted and inform the design of future initiatives.

A program's theory of change can be beneficial to the field of professional learning by providing models for others to consider in their design efforts. Since each situation is unique, program designers alter theories of change to adapt to the context of each innovation, yet having a pool of possible theories of change contributes to conceptual understanding about professional learning and prevents the need to reinvent the wheel with the development of each new professional learning initiative.

EXAMINE THE PROGRAM'S LOGIC MODEL

As noted, *theory of change* and *logic model* are often used interchangeably. In this book, a theory of change is distinguished from a logic model. A *theory of change* identifies rationale for the chain of causal actions that predicts and explains how the program works to achieve the intended results. It is a strategic picture of how the program actions will produce results. A *logic model* uses the theory of change to depict the operation of a program by delineating several key components of an action or operational plan, including

1. the program resources or inputs;

2. the actions or strategies program designers plan to use to produce the results (theory of change);

3. the outputs each action produces, if any;

4. the outcomes of the actions, both short and long term;

5. the goal of the program; and

6. the context of the program.

A logic model has three parts: the program structure, outcomes, and the context. The first three—inputs, activities, and outputs—constitute the program's structure, that is, what the program is. The program structure is what the program directors control, although the program structure may be altered by unexpected context factors. The initial and intermediate outcomes and goals are the components of the outcomes. These are the program's expected results. The outcomes are what the program intends to produce. The context is the environment, political, social, fiscal, or relational factors that influence the success of a program.

Inputs

The inputs include the resources, personnel, facilities, equipment, and so on used to accomplish the program's activities. Inputs are essential to consider early in the program's design because program activities may be limited by available resources. One common reason professional learning interventions fail to produce results for students is that they have inadequate resources to deliver what is necessary to promote educator learning and support the implementation of that learning.

Activities/Components

Activities include the services a program provides to accomplish its goals; activities may be the focus of formative or process evaluations. After implementation, some program activities may be found to be more beneficial than others, and program developers may alter their theory of change to reflect that. Activities may appear to be discrete events, but they are not. They are implemented with coherence with the intention of working together to produce results for adults and students.

Outputs

Outputs are the products program managers and/or participants produce. They serve as documentation of the completion of an activity or series of activities.

Initial Outcomes

Initial outcomes are early changes in participants' knowledge, attitudes, and skills. They are a part of the first level of effect of a program, (E^1). These changes have little inherent value in themselves yet are important because they lead to the intermediate outcomes and desired results.

Intermediate Outcomes

Intermediate outcomes are behavior and aspiration changes participants make during or after their involvement with the program. They are also a part of the first level of effectiveness (E^1); these benefits can be defined in terms of changes in aspirations or behaviors that result from the changes in knowledge, attitudes, and skills.

Results (Goals)

The results, or goals, are the intended, desired impact on participants' clients, the second level of impact (E^2). For teachers their clients are students' and their learning. For nearly all professional learning, improved results for students is the ultimate goal of the program.

Context

Context includes the conditions under which the program operates, including the external factors that might influence its success; characteristics of the program participants or staff; or other social, economic, or political factors that may intentionally or unintentionally influence the program's results. When a long-serving superintendent who is a strong advocate for a program suddenly leaves a school district and no other champion for the program exists, the environmental conditions in which the program exists changes. If the district receives grant funds to hire additional coaches, the conditions change. If the school board suddenly learns of a reduction in state or federal funding affecting implementation of the program, the conditions change.

A logic model serves to guide the evaluation design because it identifies both the initial and intermediate outcomes of the actions contained in the theory of change. These initial and intermediate outcomes serve as benchmarks of the program's progress toward its goals. Figure 4.4 is a diagram of a logic model framework. Table 4.4 is a detailed portion of the logic model for the reading professional learning program described in Table 4.3. It delineates the specific resources, outputs, outcomes, and intended results of the program activities and serves as a tool for monitoring program implementation and progress and conducting formative and summative evaluations.

Figure 4.4 Logic Model Framework

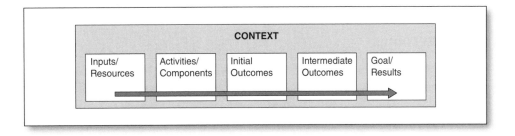

Table 4.4 Logic Model for Reading Professional Learning

GOAL: Students will become proficient, lifelong readers who read both for learning and enjoyment.

Inputs/Resources	Activities/ Components	Outputs	Initial Outcomes	Intermediate Outcomes	Intended Results
Full-time literacy coaches for each low-performing school and halftime coaches for middle- and high-performing schools.	• Principals hire literacy coaches. • Coaches complete coaching preparation program.	• Coach contracts • Coaching preparation syllabus and materials • Attendance rosters • Coach logs	• Coaches develop knowledge and skills for coaching teachers.	• Teachers identify and solve implementation challenges within their own classrooms.	**Year 1:** 60% of the students score proficient or above on the state reading test in Grades 3–8. Students read at least 30 minutes a week for pleasure. **Year 2:** 80% of the students score proficient or above on the state reading test in Grades 3–8. Students read at least 60 minutes a week for pleasure. **Year 3:** 100% of the students score proficient or above on the state reading test in Grades 3–8. Students read at least 60 minutes per week for pleasure. Students identify reading as a lifelong tool for learning and enjoyment.
Human, fiscal, time, and material resources and physical space and equipment for teacher training and follow-up support	• Central office staff develops and implements a six-week course for teachers. • Schools acquire classroom resources to implement reading strategies. • Teachers observe demonstration classrooms. • Literacy coaches provide monthly coaching to all teachers. • Principals conduct monthly walk throughs. • Teacher meet in collaboration to redesign units and lessons, perform core assessments, and problem-solve implementation issues.	• Course syllabus and materials • Teacher observation records • Teacher units and lessons integrating reading strategies • Coach logs • Student tasks integrating reading strategies • Change in school-day schedule to create uninterrupted time for reading instruction	• Teacher knowledge about the reading process and skills for teaching reading to under-performing students increases. • Teacher efficacy in teaching under-performing readers increases. • Teachers access new classroom resources. Teachers use new classroom resources in guided reading.	• Teachers accurately and consistently apply new reading instructional strategies in their classrooms with support from coaches. • Students use classroom resources for independent and guided reading.	

(Continued)

(Continued)

Inputs/Resources	Activities/ Components	Outputs	Initial Outcomes	Intermediate Outcomes	Intended Results
Ongoing assessment of student progress.	• Teachers collect and report student progress data every six weeks and at the end of the year.	• Benchmark assessments • Student performance scores on benchmark and end-of-year assessments	• Teachers, principals, and literacy coaches use student progress data to identify necessary adaptations in instruction.	• Teachers use assessment data to adapt instruction based on student learning needs. • Teachers and coaches use student data to design instructional interventions for those students who need extra assistance.	
Human and fiscal resources to provide principal training in conducting walk-throughs to observe for reading strategies.	• Central office staff designs and implements training for principals. • Principals complete training. • Principals conduct monthly walk-throughs in each classroom.	• Course syllabus and materials • Principal walk-through guides	• Principals develop knowledge and skills for conducting walk-throughs and reporting their observations to teachers. • Principals gain familiarity with new reading instructional strategies.	• Teachers' use of instructional strategies and review of student progress data increases with principal support.	
Additional reading materials for all schools.	• Reading materials are selected and purchased.	• Materials are accessible to students and teachers in classrooms.	• Students and teachers use new reading materials.	• New reading materials are used in classrooms.	
High-quality instruction for students.	• Teachers apply reading strategies they learned in their classrooms.	• Teachers implement lesson and unit plans with student formative assessments, rubrics, and anchor papers.	• Students learn strategies for improving their reading performance.	• Students apply the new strategies in reading for both learning and pleasure.	

Driving and restraining internal and external context forces: competence and availability of staff for coaching roles; sustained funding for program operation; shift in federal, state, and local priorities; change in school and district leadership; stability of teaching workforce; shifts in community priorities and support; level of commitment of educators; and competing curricular or instructional programs

Developing a Theory of Change and Logic Model

McLaughlin and Jordan (2015) encourage program developers to consider logic models as a developmental process that benefits from stakeholder engagement. They acknowledge that developing logic models takes time and is often a process that program developers frequently try to take shortcuts when creating. Often the program's theory of change and logic model emerge concomitantly, although one can precede the other. The steps recommended for developing a logic model are described below (McLaughlin & Jordan, 2015).

Conduct Research and Gather Relevant Data

This step is described as Condition 1 in Chapter 3. It is the process of analyzing student, educator, and system data to understand the current condition. It is also a process of conducting research review to identify what others have done to solve similar problems in similar contexts. Considering how the school or district has handled other initiatives involving professional learning will support the development of this program's logic model.

Determine the Program Needs and Context

A design team that typically includes the program director, representative stakeholders, and the evaluator begins with using the data to develop a clear understanding of the program needs, the problem to be addressed by the program, and its potential root causes. Clarifying the problem, the context, and the limitations will help the design team be more focused and realistic in the design of the program.

Align With Program's Theory of Change

Sometimes a program director, together with a stakeholder team and the evaluator, will develop a tentative theory of change they want to assess and modify as the program is implemented and depict this draft in a logic model. The theory of change and logic model should hold consistency so that the theory of change reflects the rationale and the logic model reflects the operation. It is important to note that both the logic model and theory of change may be adapted during the program's implementation as the program itself is adjusted to reflect what occurs or added activities, inputs, or outputs.

Determine What Is Known or Common Practice

One way to develop a logic model for a program is to begin with what exists and what is known about the inputs or resources, initial and intermediate outcomes, and results. By sketching those out first on a large piece of chart paper, the design team will see the gaps.

Generate Elements

Sometimes the design team examines the components of the logic model and brainstorms elements that would fall into each category. For example, what are all the possible resources we might need? What are all the activities we could do?

This process might uncover possibilities that would not normally be considered in a more linear process. Thinking beyond what has always been done is not always easy to do, so engaging stakeholders who are not typically a part of program planning and using brainstorming might be ways to generate new possibilities.

Create Logical Sequence

Then, using a flowchart, the design team maps the logical sequence of the elements, linking those that go together. For example, if one of the activities is to provide classroom coaching, a necessary resource is classroom coaches. The diagram helps stakeholders understand the underlying assumptions and connections among various components of the program. Logic models can get messy at this point. Sometimes it is necessary to focus on the high-level actions rather than the more minute ones. Perhaps segmenting out the logic model to display the outputs and outcomes from one action or a subset of actions might help with the complexity of the diagram.

Verify the Model

Those who create the program's theory of change and logic model will want to share their draft with stakeholders for their reaction and input. The broader the perspectives of stakeholders who review the model, the more likely the model will address all stakeholders' needs and be successful in guiding the program to achieve its intended results. Key questions to ask stakeholders might include the following:

- Is the logic model logical?
- What seems to be missing in the inputs or activities?
- Are the inputs and activities sufficient to produce the outcomes?
- Are the inputs and activities feasible and plausible based on what you know about this context?
- What context factors might influence the success of this program that have not been listed?

ASSESSING THE PROFESSIONAL LEARNING PROGRAM'S EVALUABILITY

One of the evaluator's tasks is assessing the program's evaluability before proceeding with developing an evaluation plan. After working with the stakeholders to clarify the theory of change and logic model, the evaluator might use the rubric in Table 4.5 to assess the program's design and determine that it is ready to be evaluated.

If, after a careful assessment of evaluability of a professional learning program, both the evaluator and the program stakeholders agree that the professional learning program is well conceived, logically planned, and likely to produce the intended results and the evaluation is warranted, the next step is to design the evaluation questions and framework. To decide that a program is not

evaluable and the evaluation is not warranted at this point should not be considered a sign that the program planning has been ineffective. In fact, it is better to postpone an evaluation until further planning can address the gap in the program's plan. It is also better to postpone the evaluation if it seems likely that the conditions for success are not present.

The flaws or deficiencies typically indicate that further clarification of the program is necessary before initiating the evaluation, and that further clarification may be a simple matter of more detail. Addressing the deficiencies at this stage would ensure that the program is successful, that evaluation produces the most useful information, and that any investment in the program and evaluation is well spent.

Table 4.5   Evaluability Assessment Rubric

Area	Not Ready to Implement or Evaluate	Revise Before Program Implementation and Evaluation Design	Ready to Evaluate
Goals	Program goals are fuzzy or unclear.	Program goals state the desired results in vague terms and/or are means-focused only.	Program goals state clearly the desired result in specific terms and are focused on changes in educator and/or student results.
Outcomes	Outcomes are stated in imprecise terms or as activities.	Outcomes identify some of the changes needed to produce the results.	Outcomes specify the specific changes desired and expected for both program participants and their clients.
Standard of Success	Standard of success is expressed in terms of completion of activities or with no specific or measurable indicator of success.	Standard of success is measurable and specific, yet is set too low or too high, resulting in a standard that is either uninspiring or unreasonable.	Standard of success is challenging, motivating, reasonable, measurable, and specific.
Theory of Change	Theory of change is missing or provides insufficient rationale for the program's design.	Theory of change identifies key actions without underlying assumptions, the actions are insufficient to produce the desired results, or the assumptions offer little explanation or rationale about the selection of actions.	Theory of change identifies the key actions of the program in a causal process and is accompanied by the underlying assumptions that explain why the actions are included and how they will produce the expected results.
Logic Model	The logic model is missing or fails to display the logic in the program's design.	The logic model is missing a few components or the components are not aligned with one another. The display of the logic model is difficult to understand.	The logic model clearly delineates the inputs necessary to conduct each activity, the outputs from the activities, the initial and intermediate outcomes the actions are expected to produce, the desired or intended result (goal), and the context factors that may influence the program's success. The model's display is clear and understandable.

Planning Phase

- Assess evaluability
- Formulate evaluation questions
- Construct the evaluation framework

Conducting Phase

- Collect data
- Organize, analyze, and display data
- Interpret data

Reporting Phase

- Report, disseminate, and use evaluation results
- Evaluate the evaluation

Formulate Evaluation Questions

5

Thoughtfully crafted evaluation questions give structure and focus to the overall evaluation and guide the design of the evaluation framework. Evaluation questions specify what information the intended users hope to gain from the evaluation. Knowing the intended use of the information helps the evaluator make critical decisions about the evaluation framework. Well-defined evaluation questions facilitate both design of the evaluation and use of the findings.

At this stage, the evaluator seeks to answer several key questions:

1. What questions does the evaluation seek to answer?

2. Are the questions aligned with the professional learning program's goals, outcomes, and activities?

3. Do the questions reflect the priority interests of key stakeholders and the intended uses of the evaluation?

4. Are the questions clear and understood by key stakeholders?

5. Do the questions guide decisions about the evaluation's design, data collection, and analysis?

6. Can the questions be answered?

7. Do the questions accurately reflect the understood purpose of the evaluation?

TYPES OF EVALUATION QUESTIONS

Preparing focused evaluation questions will prevent problems during the evaluation. Too many questions may distract from what is most important, may place an added burden on the evaluator or the informants and those who provide the data, and may cause problems with data analysis (Weiss, 1998). "Matching evaluation questions to a client's [stakeholder] information needs can be a tricky task," state Kathryn Newcomer, Harry Hatry, and Joseph Wholey (2015). "When there is more than one client, as is frequently the case, there may be multiple information needs, and one evaluation may not be able to answer all the questions raised. This is frequently a problem for nonprofit service providers, who may need to address multiple evaluation questions for multiple funders" (p. 25). In an evaluation, stakeholders typically desire the answers to more questions than can be answered.

This is particularly true when there are many intended users who are searching for information for very different purposes. For example, a professional learning director may want to know whether the program design is working; principals may want to know whether the program is being implemented correctly in classrooms; school board members may want to know what impact the program is having on student learning; teachers may want to know how the program affects their teaching decisions; others in the field of professional learning or those responsible for developing programs themselves may want to know what worked and why. Each of these uses suggests the need for a different evaluation question. Table 5.1 shows such differences in focus. Each question is distinct, and the evaluation may require that different data be collected and analyzed to answer them. Stafford Hood, Rodney Hopson, and Karen Kirkhart (2015) emphasize the importance of considering the cultural appropriateness of questions, "for contexts in which direct questions are culturally inappropriate, this stage identifies what it is that stakeholders seek to learn about the program or community. Both the focus and wording of questions or statements of intention are critical here in order to set the evaluation on the right path" (p. 292). They recommend that the formulation of the evaluation questions involves critical dialogue among stakeholders and between the evaluator and stakeholders so that meaning is clear and reflects the needs of stakeholders, the nuances of language or orthography is responsive to the community and participants, and the required evidence or data to answer the questions are considered credible by stakeholders.

Evaluation questions fall into several categories, and they parallel the purposes of evaluations. The categories—program need, program design, program process, program impact, and social justice and human rights—offer evaluators a way to help stakeholders clarify what they want to learn from an evaluation.

Table 5.1 provides a list of possible evaluation questions corresponding to each purpose of evaluation. It delineates the typical user or stakeholder interested in each purpose of evaluation.

Table 5.1 Sample Evaluation Questions Aligned With Evaluation Purpose

Purpose of Evaluation	Intended Users	Type of Evaluation Question	Possible Evaluation Questions
Program need	Professional learning director Program director District steering committee	Problem/need to address	What is the problem that needs addressing? Who is most affected by this problem? What is the magnitude or scope of the problem? Who has the greatest leverage in addressing it? What gaps exist in students' performance? What evidence or data supports these gaps? What are the most feasible/high-leverage root causes? What do educators need to learn and do to address student performance gaps? What evidence or data supports these needs? What conditions exist that will influence the success of this program? What are the characteristics of the participants? How will their characteristics be integrated into the plan? Whose needs are high priority? What evidence or data supports the highest-priority needs? What services do participants perceive are needed to address this need?
Program plan	Professional learning director Program director District steering committee Implementation team	Program plan	Who is being served by this program? Are the participants and clients served those with the greatest need? Are the activities the best possible ones for this situation? Are the activities supported with data or evidence? Are the planned activities reasonable for the program participants? To be successful in their role, how are program staff prepared? Have sufficient inputs or resources been allocated to support full implementation of the plan? What assumptions are being made about the plan's design, participants, activities, and their relationship? Is the plan logical, feasible, and plausible? Are the outcomes plausible based on the inputs and activities? Does the plan fit the context? Have stakeholders reviewed the plan and expressed comfort with it?

(Continued)

Table 5.1   (Continued)

Purpose of Evaluation	Intended Users	Type of Evaluation Question	Possible Evaluation Questions
Program implementation	Principal School improvement team District steering committee Implementation team	Program implementation	Are inputs available as planned?
			Were inputs used as planned?
			What additional inputs were added?
			What prompted changes in the inputs/resources?
			What unexpected problems interfered with the availability of inputs? How have they been addressed?
			Have the activities been completed as planned?
			Have participants engaged in activities as planned?
			Are the participants with highest-priority needs engaging in activities as planned?
			Are the program activities being implemented with fidelity?
			What unanticipated problems are occurring with implementation?
			How frequently and accurately are new behaviors being implemented?
			What activities do participants report to be the most influential in changes in their knowledge, attitudes, skills, aspirations, and behaviors?
			Are there particular participants who are not engaging at the intended level?
			What unexpected problems interfered with the implementation of the activities? How have they been addressed?
			What aspects of the program are most salient in producing intended results?
			Have needs emerged that the plan did not anticipate or address?
Program impact on participants (E[1])	Teachers Teacher leaders School improvement team Principals Program participants Implementation team	Program impact	What changes are evident in participant knowledge, attitudes, skills, aspirations, and behaviors related to the professional learning program?
			How frequently and accurately are new behaviors being implemented?
			What changes are evident in teachers' content-specific lessons and units?
			How are student classroom experiences changing?
			How are student learning tasks, assessments, or engagement in learning changing?
			How is level of implementation influencing behavior changes?
			Are the activities producing the intended outcomes?
			How did the context influence the achievement of outcomes?
			How did positive and negative unanticipated effects influence the achievement of outcomes?
			Will these activities produce similar educator outcomes in a different context?
			What contributed to the program's outcomes?
			Are the intended outcomes achieved?

Purpose of Evaluation	Intended Users	Type of Evaluation Question	Possible Evaluation Questions
Program impact on clients (E²)	School board members Key program decision makers Policy makers Program participants	Impact	How is student performance on various measures of indicators of success changing?
			What are the most and least significant changes in client knowledge, attitudes, skills, aspirations, and behaviors?
			How is level of implementation influencing behavior changes?
			Are the activities producing the intended outcomes?
			How did the context influence the achievement of outcomes?
			How did positive and negative unanticipated effects influence the achievement of outcomes? Why or why not?
			Do the outcomes have a beneficial or detrimental impact on clients of participants?
			Will these activities produce similar client outcomes in different contexts? Why or why not?
			What contributed to the program's outcomes?
			Are the intended outcomes achieved?
Social justice and human rights	Decision makers Policy makers Program director Program participants External audiences	Program plan, implementation, and impact	Does the program meet the needs of all participants and their clients equitably, especially those who are traditionally underserved?
			Were inputs equitably distributed?
			Were activities equitably distributed?
			Was the program's burden equitably distributed?
			Was implementation fair?
			Which participant group by race, ethnicity, gender, sexual orientation, religion, or socioeconomic status benefited most/least from participation?
			Which client group by race, ethnicity, gender, sexual orientation, religion, or socioeconomic status benefited most/least from participant engagement?

Program Need

Before planning any professional learning program or improvement effort, leaders, stakeholders, and providers conduct a program needs evaluation to assess the context and characteristics of the environment and the participants. This initial activity is part of the planning evaluation; it often yields details about the evident problem or need, their root causes, characteristics about environment or context in which the program will operate, and characteristics about the program participants who are expected to make the changes. This information is useful to inform planning decisions so that they are more focused and aligned to the unique characteristics of the individuals, school, or district. Without this type of information, program planners might miss the mark completely. Conducting a thorough needs assessment that gathers data about clients, participants, and the context allows professional learning leaders to make specific recommendations for program activities and resources to stakeholders.

Program Plan

Evaluations related to the program plan focus on the program's theory of change, its perceived logic, and its potential to produce results. It does this by examining the relationship among the inputs, activities, outputs, and outcomes for their feasibility and plausibility of the program's efficacy. Discussed extensively in Chapter 4, "Assess Evaluability," this form of evaluation increases the likelihood that the planned resources and activities will lead to the initial and intermediate outcomes as well as the program's intended results. Before they implement a program fully or even conduct a pilot study, evaluators can conduct a program plan evaluation with stakeholder input. In this process, minor or major revisions can be made either before any implementation takes place or before implementation moves to full scale.

Program Implementation

Program implementation evaluations, or formative evaluations, focus on implementation and the operation of the program and can improve or strengthen a program's design. Knowing the extent to which a program's activities are carried out with fidelity to the design is important for several reasons. First, program directors will want to know whether the program plan or design is working and, if not, how to improve it. Second, to determine whether the program has merit or worth, it will first be necessary to know whether the program is implemented as designed. Third, if there are gaps in the program plan that require adjustments to the program's design, it will be important to know how the gaps are identified and addressed. Lastly, it is important to observe if any activity is not completed or implemented as planned or does not reach its intended participants. These changes may influence attainment of outcomes, so it is crucial to note them.

Those involved with professional learning efforts often form conclusions about a program's effectiveness without substantial information about the status of the program's implementation. Uninformed conclusions can lead to the elimination of a program that may have tremendous potential to achieve its outcomes had it not encountered implementation problems. Numerous educational innovations have been abandoned without adequate implementation support or without adequate evaluation of their implementation phase.

Some program evaluations merely monitor implementation. This form of monitoring is a systematic documentation about program activities and inputs, and it allows the evaluator to make judgments about the operation of the program but not about the effects of the program. This distinction is essential. Program implementation evaluations are designed to assess whether the program is operating as planned or intended. If done well, they can contribute useful information to guide ongoing implementation and to improve the quality and operation of the program.

Program Impact

An evaluation that focuses on outcomes seeks to answer questions about the impact or effects of the program at one or two levels. The levels measure

what has changed as a result of the program. Changes can occur in knowledge, attitudes, skills, aspiration, and/or behaviors of the program participants or in their circumstances or context. This level is Effectiveness[1].The second level of impact, Effectiveness[2], focuses on what changed for clients of the program participants. These outcomes may occur if the program is sufficiently strong and if there are clearly stated outcomes related to clients of participants. Questions regarding program impact or effect are directly related to the program goals and outcomes, not the outputs. If goals or outcomes change during a program's implementation as a result of the formative evaluation, program designers modify the evaluation's questions and framework to reflect those changes. The amount or type of data may also change, or the time frame for collecting data may change, for example. When unanticipated outcomes emerge from the program implementation, the evaluator adjusts the evaluation questions and framework as needed to gather evidence about the new outcomes.

In evaluations of educator professional learning, stakeholders typically want to measure changes in educators' and students' knowledge, attitudes, skills, aspirations, and behaviors and examine the interrelationship among them. The hypothesis is that changes in educators lead to changes in student opportunity to learn, and that in turn leads to changes in student learning (Desimone, 2009; Learning Forward, 2011; Timperley & Alton-Lee, 2008). For many school districts, the stated purpose or mission of professional learning is to change student success through changes in educator performance. Yet, some consider changes in educators or schools the best measure of the success of professional learning. While measuring changes in educator practice is a part of a comprehensive impact evaluation, it does not guarantee that the changes will lead to an increase in student success. If the goal of the professional learning program is to focus on educator practice only, effectiveness[1] measures will be the final measure; however, the most authentic measure of the impact of professional learning and the reason school systems invest in professional learning is to strengthen educator practice so that students achieve at higher levels.

A danger in impact evaluations, or outcome evaluations, is the tendency to suggest a causal link between the program and its intended outcome. Evaluators must be cautious about implying causality when the evaluation design does not support a conclusion of causality. To establish causality requires rigorous experimental or quasi-experimental evaluation design that is often not feasible in schools. Rather than focusing on whether professional learning *caused* an increase in student achievement, evaluators can help professional learning leaders and policy makers understand how professional learning *contributes* to student achievement. Conclusions of causation are only possible when the evaluation design justifies them (i.e., either randomized control trial or quasi-experimental using matched comparison study validates the conclusion). On the other hand, conclusions about contributions can be made from descriptive evaluation design or other forms of comparison studies.

Lens to Guide Social Justice or Human Rights

Programs are both political and social entities that reflect the values of a community. "Evaluators work in diverse cultural, contextual, and complex

communities," according to Hood, Hopson, and Kirkhart (2015), and the programs being evaluated and their evaluations are "set within an increasing global demand for monitoring and evaluation of public programs and the requirements by governments and international organizations to use evaluations, especially in settings and communities that have traditionally been underserved, underrepresented, or marginalized" (pp. 281–282). The purpose of evaluations that seek to answer questions about social justice or human rights is to "create accurate, valid, and culturally-grounded understanding of the evaluand" (p. 286), that is, what is being evaluated, and occurs not in a separate process of evaluation for this purpose alone, but with thoughtful, deliberate attention to the evaluation process through the lens of social justice and human rights.

Serving Interests of Multiple Stakeholders

In complex systems such as educational institutions, a combination of initiatives or efforts work together to produce results. In systems, each initiative influences the capacity of others to succeed. Understanding any one initiative and its influence within a system offers the potential to understand other initiatives that are influenced by it and in turn influence it. The dynamic nature of systems means that there are often multiple stakeholders with multiple interests for every program evaluation. If the coaching program is being evaluated in the district, not only will principals, coaches, teachers, and the curriculum department have interests in the evaluation and what questions it is answering, but those working in the talent development office will also be interested in the evaluation results. The results of this evaluation are likely to influence how coaches are selected, prepared, supervised, and deployed.

Whole system reform efforts orchestrated through strategic plans, in reality, incorporate multiple reforms at a single time. Some leaders in the district may want to know which of these reforms *alone* caused an increase in student achievement. Yet, the district designed a multi-prong strategic reform that recognized the contribution each change could make to the overall improvement effort. So, answering this question is impossible unless each initiative is implemented singly for sufficient duration to know its effects; it also suggests that any one alone, not all working in tandem, can produce the intended changes. Some might wonder if it is important to know whether one initiative caused the change; or if it were eventually known to be the cause, would the other initiatives be considered irrelevant? Is it possible to have a change in an instructional framework without high-quality professional learning and sufficient resources to support implementation and expect significant results? If a school or district has significantly strengthened its professional learning program, some of the following changes are likely to occur concomitantly: There is more time for collaborative professional learning, more financial and human resources for professional learning, or new expectations for curriculum, assessment, and instruction. Evaluators and stakeholders can help policy and decision makers understand the dynamic, interrelated, and complex nature of multiple initiatives working seamlessly together to produce results for students and help them shape questions that are feasible and useful to the evaluation design.

The questions guiding the evaluation of professional learning, then, should focus on what is useful and possible to know. Evaluators of professional learning require the "ability to ask good questions and a basic understanding about how to find valid answers. Good evaluations provide information that is appropriate, sound, and sufficiently reliable to use in making thoughtful and responsible decisions about professional development processes and effects" (Guskey, 2000, p. 2).

A Case Study: One-to-One Technology

As a part of the implementation of a one-to-one technology initiative, a small district wanted to improve student success by increasing teachers' classroom use of technology to personalize learning. Building on the research of the effects of one-to-one technology by Ben Harper and Natalie Millman (2016), the district invested in purchasing tablets for each student. The district adopted the principles of personalized learning: choice for demonstrating learning, mastery-based assessment, co-planning learning, voice and choice, varied strategies, flexible pacing, and just-in-time direct instruction. The district's goal was to increase student achievement, motivation, engagement, and interest by increasing teachers' capacity to alter the learning environment, learning experiences, and instructional practices through the integration of one-to-one technology tools.

Below are the proposed evaluation questions. They represent some of many diverse questions that could be answered, yet are the ones considered most important to answer early in the implementation and throughout to make ongoing adjustments and to report on the value of the investment.

> Consider what additional questions other stakeholders might want answers to.
>
> - School board
> - Parents
> - Teachers
> - Students
> - Community members
> - Local businesses
> - Superintendent
> - Principals

Program Needs

How was the need for this program identified?

How many teachers supported the implementation of the 1:1 technology initiative?

To what extent are current teaching practices addressing student motivation, engagement, differentiation, and personalization?

What do teachers, principals, and central office personnel need to learn and do to be able to implement this program?

Program Design

Do the planned professional learning experiences meet the standards for effective professional learning (see Appendix C)?

Does the program plan demonstrate feasibility, plausibility, and efficacy?

Are the program activities logically sequenced to achieve desired outcomes?

Are the inputs sufficient to implement all aspects of the program?

Program Process

Is the program being implemented as designed?

How many teachers and principals are participating in the professional learning experiences?

Are teachers implementing the practices in their classrooms?

Are teachers seeking and receiving follow-up support?

Are resource materials readily available to teachers?

How are principals and central office staff supporting program implementation?

What teaching practices are changing?

How are student learning opportunities changing?

Program Impact

Is student success increasing?

Are all the outcomes achieved?

Is the program producing any unanticipated results?

Social Justice and Human Rights

Does the program address the needs of all students equitably, especially those who are traditionally underserved?

How are families engaged in understanding the student and family responsibilities related to the technology provided to students?

What opportunities are provided to accommodate for students' use of technology outside the school if students do not have access to the conditions for effective use?

Case Study Review

The list of evaluation questions is extensive. Most evaluators would ask stakeholders to prioritize the questions and the purpose(s) for the evaluation before planning an evaluation or engage in a multi-tiered evaluation, one that occurs over time to answer the majority of the questions. To expect that a single evaluation could potentially address so many questions is ambitious, costly, and time-consuming. By clarifying the purpose of the evaluation and the interests of the stakeholders, an evaluator will use the outcomes to generate questions whose answers will meet the stakeholders' needs.

CHARACTERISTICS OF GOOD QUESTIONS

Good evaluation questions have several characteristics:

Reasonable: Can the questions be answered within the scope of the evaluation resources available, including the evaluator and staff time, skill, and the budget?

Appropriate: Do the questions align with the program's goal, outcomes, and design?

Answerable: Can data be collected to construct answers to the questions? Sometimes the information needed to answer an evaluation question can only be answered through approximations rather than authentic data. For example, if it is unreasonable to gather actual data about implementation through classroom **observation**, approximation data such as teacher perceptions of implementation can substitute. Authentic data are stronger than approximation data.

Measurable or observable indicators of program success or performance: Do the questions reflect evident standards and indicators of success to guide the evaluator in knowing what success looks like or provide a standard against which to judge success?

Means for measuring the outcome: Do the questions clarify the means for measuring success?

When evaluation questions accurately reflect the program goals, outcomes, purpose of the evaluation, its planned use, and meet the criteria above, the evaluation design can proceed.

EXAMPLES AND COMMENTARY

Sample program goals and formative and summative evaluation questions appear below with brief commentary about how each meets the criteria of being reasonable, appropriate, answerable, and specific about the standard and the measure. For these examples, the goals specify the desired results for students and the outcomes specify the changes desired for educators. In some programs, there will be outcomes about student changes as well as educator changes.

Example One

Program goal: Increase student achievement in reading by 10 percent on the state reading and math tests in three years.

Program outcome: Increase teachers' knowledge and skills related to reader's workshop to increase differentiation in instruction and assessment and student engagement in the reading process.

Formative evaluation question: Did teachers benefit from the training program offered at the beginning of the school year to implement reader's workshop?

The question is *reasonable* and even *answerable.* The evaluator could ask teacher participants to identify how they benefitted. It is not, however, appropriate as a question. If the program outcome is to increase teachers' knowledge and skills related to reader's workshop, this question is too vague; it does not specify the specific benefits that the program outcome intends to achieve. It also does not suggest a standard of success or a way to measure whether teachers benefit.

Recommended version: Did teachers report that they gain the baseline knowledge and skills related to reader's workshop during the training program to implement it in their classrooms?

Reasonable: The question can be answered by the evaluator with a reasonable time investment.

Appropriate: The question reflects the outcome.

Answerable: The question can be answered through surveys, interviews, **focus groups**, or demonstrations of practice to gather either approximation or authentic data.

Measurable or observable indicators of program success or performance: The standard of success is baseline knowledge and skill to implement reader's workshop.

Means for measuring the outcome: The question indicates that teachers will "report" about their knowledge and skills.

Example Two

Program goal: Increase performance of all students on state science standards in the next five years.

Program goal in measurable terms: Increase students' performance on the engineering design standard in the next five years by at least 10 percent, including by 14 percent for the groups of female and underrepresented students.

Summative evaluation question: Did the performance of all students on the fourth- through eighth-grade state science assessments in engineering design increase by at least 10 percent, and by 14 percent for the groups of female and underrepresented students?

This question meets the criteria. It is *reasonable and answerable* because data from the state assessment currently exist and are likely to be available in five years. District officials will require only minimum effort to analyze the data for increase and to disaggregate for the designated student groups on the specific items that measure the engineering design standard. It is *appropriate* because it aligns with the program's intended outcome; it provides *measurable or observable indicator of success*; a specific standard of success is provided; *it specifies the measure,* the state's fourth- and eighth-grade science assessment.

Example Three

Program goal: Increase students' civic engagement in their community.

Program outcome: Implement classroom-based learning opportunities to promote and support student civic engagement within the community.

Formative evaluation question: Did teachers learn strategies for designing classroom-based learning opportunities to promote and support civic engagement within the community?

The question is *reasonable*. It can be answered with moderate effort and cost. The question is not appropriate though. It focuses on acquisition of strategies, and the outcome focuses on teachers' implementation of learning opportunities. While it is likely that acquisition of strategies precedes the design and implementation of the learning opportunities, the question does not match the program outcome or the goal. It is *answerable*; however the answers rest in the unit serving as an approximation of teachers' implementation of strategies. The question *does not specify the standard*. It suggests that there are some specific strategies teacher can use to design and implement the learning opportunities, yet those are unclear and need to be identified. The question suggests that the *specific measure* of acquisition will be the design of a unit that integrates the strategies.

Recommended version: Did teachers apply within the design of a new or revised unit, which meets the acceptable criteria of an effective unit, at least five strategies they acquired for designing classroom-based learning opportunities to support and promote civic engagement?

Reasonable: The question can be answered by the evaluator with a moderate time investment. The evaluator will review the units and apply the criteria.

Appropriate: The question aligns with the outcome.

Answerable: The question can be answered through unit analysis. The evaluator will review the units and apply the criteria.

Measurable or observable indicators of program success or performance: The unit criteria establish the indicator of success as does the integration of five different strategies.

Means for measuring the outcome: The analysis of the teacher-designed or revised unit is the means for measuring the outcome.

Example Four

Program goal: Increase student success in social studies by 5 percent annually for the next three years.

Program outcome: Full implementation of new C3 social studies curriculum.

Formative evaluation question: How well is the new middle school social studies curriculum implemented as measured by the implementation rubric?

This question *may or may not be reasonable.* The implementation rubric may require evaluators to visit each school and collect observations or conduct Level of Use interviews to determine the level of implementation. There may be unanticipated costs, such as paying staff or consultants to make visits or train classroom observers for interrater reliability. If these costs have been anticipated and planned, then the question is reasonable. Alternate data-collection methods, such as a survey or sampling of classrooms, could be administered to reduce visitation costs. Another consideration about the reasonableness of this question is the rubric. Whether the rubric has been developed and field-tested or whether it needs to be developed and field-tested will affect the cost of obtaining an answer to this question. If costs and time for rubric design have been anticipated and planned for, the question is reasonable. If not, this question may be quite expensive in terms of staff costs and time to answer. The question is *appropriate* because it reflects the program's outcome. It is *answerable* if a level or stage of implementation can be assessed, especially if an implementation rubric is available, valid, and includes observable behaviors. The question *specifies the standard*—full implementation as specified by the rubric. The scoring of the implementation criteria defined within the *rubric is the measure* of implementation.

ESTABLISHING PRIORITIES IN PURSUING QUESTIONS

Stakeholders in any professional learning initiative may believe that answering multiple questions about program need, design, process, and impact is important. And, although there indeed may be value in answering numerous questions, it may not be reasonable or even appropriate to do so. Therefore, the evaluator may prioritize questions to reflect what the stakeholders believe is most important to know at this time. Narrowing or prioritizing the questions can help the evaluator design an evaluation that is more doable and useful. The evaluator might want to engage in several prioritization exercises with the stakeholders to determine which questions would be most helpful.

Weiss (1998) suggests the following considerations for selecting or prioritizing questions:

- Timeliness for program decisions
- Influence or power of stakeholders
- Contributions to address gaps in the knowledge base
- Usefulness of findings
- Alignment with the program's theory of change
- Evaluator judgment

Before moving to the next step, the evaluator culls the questions and uses the rubric in Table 5.2 to assess each question. From this process, the evaluator revises the questions and produces a narrower, clear set of questions to focus the evaluation so that it will be successful. Asking stakeholders to be involved

in this process increases their ownership and perceived value of the evaluation. If they are not engaged in the process of reviewing the evaluation questions, evaluators will want them minimally to approve them. With clear, focused, and prioritized evaluation questions, the evaluator is ready to begin building a framework for conducting the evaluation. Without good questions, the evaluator risks not only wasting precious resources, but also the integrity of the evaluation itself.

Table 5.2 Evaluation Questions Assessment Rubric

Characteristics of Effective Evaluation Questions	Not Ready to Implement or Evaluate	Revise Before Program Implementation and Evaluation Design	Ready to Evaluate
Reasonable	Answering this question requires resources or level of effort that exceeds the available evaluation resources.	Further investigation is necessary to determine the cost and level of effort needed to answer this evaluation question.	The question can be answered within the scope of the available evaluation resources, including the evaluator and staff time, skill, and the budget.
Appropriate	The question does not align with the program goal, outcome, or program design.	The question is partially aligned with the program goal, outcome, or program design.	The question aligns directly with the program's goal, outcome, and program design.
Answerable	Data to answer this question cannot be collected.	Only approximation data (something that stands as a representation of the construct) can be collected to answer the question.	Authentic data can be collected to construct answers to the question.
Success Standards	The question does not include standards of success.	The question refers to fuzzy standards of success.	The question includes or refers to established standards of success to provide criteria against which to judge success.
Measures	The question does not include a means for measuring success.	The question vaguely indicates a means of measuring success.	The question includes or clarifies the means for measuring success.
Reflects Prioritized Needs of Stakeholders	The question does not align with key stakeholders' interest and needs.	The question aligns with some stakeholders' interest and needs.	The question aligns with key stakeholders' primary interest and needs.
Usefulness	Answering this question does not add value or usefulness to the evaluation.	Answering this question adds moderate value and usefulness to the evaluation.	Answering this question adds significant value and usefulness to the evaluation.

Planning Phase

- Assess evaluability
- Formulate evaluation questions
- Construct the evaluation framework

Conducting Phase

- Collect data
- Organize, analyze, and display data
- Interpret data

Reporting Phase

- Report, disseminate, and use findings
- Evaluate the evaluation

Construct the Evaluation Framework

6

This chapter provides an overview of the tasks in constructing an evaluation framework or plan for an evaluation and describes the steps necessary to accomplish this work. The chapter also includes discussion of whether practitioners in schools, school systems, or other agencies can lead the work or if an external evaluator is necessary to support the work.

VISUALIZING THE EVALUATION FRAMEWORK

An evaluation framework is a plan that outlines how the evaluation will occur. It answers essential questions about the procedures; the types of data (qualitative and quantitative); the timeline; the data-collection methods, tools, and techniques; and the people responsible. Patton (2008) cites the opening lines from Rudyard Kipling's *The Elephant's Child* (1942) as an apt way for considering how an evaluation framework is constructed.

"I keep six honest serving men (they taught me all I knew);

Their names are What and Why and When and How and Where and Who" (p. 414)

An evaluation framework then lays out the plan and answers the questions *what*, *why*, *when*, *how*, *who*, and *where*. These questions regarding the program have already been answered in its problem identification, goals and outcomes, theory of change, and logic model.

The key questions an evaluator or evaluation team answers in constructing the evaluation framework include the following:

- What is the **unit of analysis** for the evaluation questions and the overall evaluation (individual educators, clusters of educators, individual students, clusters of students, schools, school systems, regions, etc.)?
- How will the choice of the unit of analysis influence the evaluation design and data-collection methodology?
- What changes are expected in participants and their clients? How will those changes be evident?
- Who or what are the sources of the data that can be used to answer the evaluation questions? Which people or **artifacts** are most accessible or available so as not to create an unnecessary data burden for participants? Which sources will yield more authentic data rather than approximations? Will multiple sources of data increase the rigor and credibility of this evaluation for stakeholders?
- What activities or components of the professional learning program will yield useful data for this evaluation? How are these activities determined?
- What are the best methods of collecting data from the sources? Which are feasible, cost-effective, and manageable? What are the trade-offs in selecting some methods for collecting data over others?
- Where will the data be collected?
- How can the methods for collecting data support or enhance the program's goals so that they are perceived as a part of the program rather than an intrusion in the program?
- How will the data be analyzed to answer the evaluation questions?
- Do stakeholders expect to know whether the change is *caused* by the professional learning program or *associated* with it?
- When will data be collected, findings reported, and evaluation findings be used to inform program decisions?
- Who is primarily responsible for which part of the evaluation Who else is involved?
- Why is this framework the most feasible and appropriate one to conduct the evaluation of this professional learning program?
- Have the primary stakeholders reviewed and approved the evaluation framework?
- Does the evaluator have the expertise to conduct the evaluation?

The Big Picture: Evaluation Framework Components

The evaluator answers these questions to construct the framework. The worksheet in Appendix D may help the evaluator plan.

Evaluation Framework Components

Evaluation questions

What does the program intend to accomplish (goal)?

What changes are anticipated for program participants and their clients? To what degree (outcomes)?

What are the interim benchmarks of the outcomes to measure?

Unit of analysis

What or who is being studied for this evaluation and its findings?

Information/data needed

What are the best ways to determine whether the changes have occurred? What data are needed to answer the evaluation questions?

Data sources

What/who is the best source of information about the intended change? What is already available? What might have to be created to gather the information needed? What tools, techniques, or processes will be used to collect data?

Data analysis

How will the data be analyzed and interpreted to answer the evaluation questions? Will descriptive or inferential statistics be necessary?

Timeline

When will data be collected? How frequently? Does the timeline correspond to normal cycles for student data such as benchmarks, grading period, and so on?

Location

Where will data be collected (i.e., in teams, at schools, in district meetings)?

Responsible person

Who will be the primary person responsible for each part of the evaluation?

Table 6.1 serves as a sample guide for the many decisions and possible approaches to the construction of the evaluation framework. If the questions the stakeholders and evaluator want to answer about professional learning are

Table 6.1 Sample Decisions in Constructing an Evaluation Framework

To know if the professional learning program has	The following kinds of information or data are necessary:	Information or data will be most useful if it comes from	And can be collected using the following methods:
impacted, for example, student achievement or social or behavioral success . . .	Change in students' academic performance or in their behaviors (engagement, participation, attendance, etc.)	• Students • Teachers • Principals • Artifacts (test scores, observation notes, etc.)	• Test score analysis • Performance on learning tasks • Portfolios of work samples • Records other documents such as attendance, discipline referrals, etc. • Teachers' observation notes, records, or perceptions about student achievement and behavior • Students' perceptions or reports (such as in student-led conferences) about their own achievement or behavior
impacted educator knowledge, attitudes, skills, aspirations, or behaviors	Changes in educator • knowledge (content knowledge, knowledge about students, knowledge about curriculum, assessment, school policy, procedures, etc.), • attitudes (beliefs or values such as morale, satisfaction, commitment, etc.) • skills (demonstration of competence, capacity, etc.) • aspirations (desire to act, preferences, willingness, readiness, etc.) • behaviors (evidence in authentic practice, performance, etc.)	• Students • Educators • Documents • Supervisors	• Tests • Performance tasks • Documents or records • Surveys • Observations
specific activities or components that are perceived as been most influential in impacting participant knowledge, attitudes, skills, aspirations, or behavior	Participants' perception of the relative weight or influence of various activities or components of the professional learning program; evidence of degree or scope of change occurring after each activity or component	• Program facilitators • Coaches • Participants • Supervisors • Documents • Artifacts	• Surveys • Interviews • Focus groups • Documents or records
been implemented with fidelity	Comparison between what was designed and what is occurring in practice	• Program manager • Program designer • Participants • Stakeholders	• Records and documents • Surveys • Observations • Interviews • Focus groups

about the items in the first column, the most likely kind of information needed to answer the question is listed in column 2. Column 3 contains the sources of the information that may have the highest level of authenticity and credibility, and column 4 lists some of the ways the information might be gathered from the sources. It is also a useful tool to share with stakeholders, who may be less familiar with the decisions required at this step of the process as a way of helping them understand the importance of the decisions that occur in step 3 of the evaluation process.

Making Decisions About the Framework

After delineating the professional learning program's goals and outcomes, and the purpose and questions for the evaluation, the evaluator decides whether the evaluation is worth doing and, if so, begins to construct an evaluation framework that will serve as the action plan for completing the evaluation. The evaluator may engage a team of stakeholders to provide input on what they consider feasible and credible in the framework's construction or engage the team in reviewing a draft of the framework. Investing time for thoughtful planning and engaging stakeholders are wise moves to ensure a successful evaluation. While some have questioned the engagement of stakeholders in the more technical aspects of the evaluation design, their engagement has merits in terms of the usability and perceived value of the evaluation. John Bryson and Michael Quinn Patton comment, "The vast majority of evaluators agree that it is important to identify and work with evaluation stakeholders in order to design and manage evaluation processes in such a way that evaluations serve their intended purposes for their intended users" (2015, p. 59). They continue, "The strong evidence that engaging stakeholders is effective and important for improving use should certainly give pause to the naysayers who are against all stakeholder involvement in the more technical aspects of the evaluation" (p. 60). Of particular note is their perspective on the role of stakeholders in the program or initiative being evaluated. "[E]valuation efforts focused on examining initiatives aimed at changing all or major parts of a system should probably include the mapping of changed relationships among key stakeholder groups, especially changed relationships among those stakeholders directly involved in the evaluation" (p. 59).

Choosing an Evaluation Design

In preparing the evaluation framework, the evaluator determines the overall evaluation design necessary to answer the questions posed and to satisfy stakeholder priorities. An evaluation design identifies how the evaluation will be done, what data to collect, and the ways to collect the data. The design depends primarily on the context of the evaluation, its purpose, stakeholder interest, the evaluation questions, the available resources, the validity of the evaluation, and ethical and practical issues related to data collection. No one design applies universally to all evaluations, and each has advantages and disadvantages to consider.

Practitioner-based evaluators or evaluation teams may seek the consultation of more experienced evaluators to make decisions about many parts of the evaluation framework, and especially the choice of an evaluation design. In many cases, the evaluation questions ask about the impact of the professional learning program on participants' clients. Impact evaluations require different kinds of data from planning or implementation evaluations. Gaining clarity about the questions, the data needed to answer them, and the design facilitates the construction of the evaluation framework.

The evaluator uses the evaluation purpose and questions to determine a "line of inquiry." What key constructs will be measured? How are they defined and measured? What data will be analyzed to answer the evaluation questions? To construct the evaluation design and corresponding **data plan** (the line of inquiry), the evaluator revisits this particular program's identified theory of change and logic model.

Evaluators choose from among several designs for the evaluation. Designs reflect the purpose of evaluation, need, planning, implementation, impact, and the program's outcomes. These designs then shape what and how data are collected and influence the data-collection process. Design is how the evaluation occurs. While some researchers describe multiple forms of design, such as descriptive, quasi-experimental, experimental, ethnography, or mixed method, for practitioners who are engaged in evaluation rather than research, it is easier to classify designs into three all-encompassing categories: qualitative, quantitative, and mixed method. These categories are organized primarily by the types of data that are needed to answer the evaluation questions. Each category has subcategories. Each will be described briefly. This book will concentrate on a few designs that are more common in practitioner-driven evaluation of professional learning within schools and school systems. Those who wish to gain a deeper understanding of the various designs are encouraged to study more technical texts on program evaluation. Evaluators who may be leading high-stakes evaluations for externally funded programs will find this information useful; however, it may be insufficiently rigorous for those purposes.

One decision that occurs prior to or concomitantly with design decisions is determining the unit of analysis. The unit of analysis may be individual program participants (e.g., educators who participate in the professional learning program, or the individual educators and their individual students), clusters of program participants (e.g., elementary teachers or elementary teachers and their cluster of students, such as all elementary students of the teachers who participated), individual schools, clusters of schools, individual school systems, or clusters of school systems. There are other possible units of analysis based on geography (e.g., regions of the country) and types of school systems (e.g., large versus small, rural versus urban), yet most evaluations will likely fall within the units of analysis identified. Determining the unit of analysis is applicable to both quantitative as well as qualitative designs. Patton (2015) notes, "A program evaluation could do case studies of participants to capture their holistic experiences of a program and the resulting outcomes. In such a study, the program participants are the unit of analysis. But it is also quite common to interview participants and focus the analysis on the patterns that are found question by

question: (a) patterns in how participants learned about the program, (b) patterns in what activities they found most valuable, and (c) patterns in outcomes. Responses to these specific questions become the unit of analysis" (p. 261).

Quantitative design

Quantitative evaluation designs include experimental and **quasi-experimental designs**. These designs allow the evaluator to form conclusions about whether the changes that occurred can be attributed to the program. That is, did the program cause the changes?

Experimental design. Experimental designs use **random assignment** to either a control or treatment group. Experimental designed studies meet the standard for the highest level of evidence and are used when extremely rigorous evaluations are desired. A challenge evaluators face when being asked to employ an experimental design is policy makers' desire for a proof of causality, yet these stakeholders rarely understand the complexity of the design needed to answer questions about causality.

In an experimental evaluation, the evaluator uses statistical comparisons to measure the differences among the treatment and control group before treatment on crucial factors that are likely to influence outcome attainment to ensure the groups are not significantly different. Practitioners who desire to use experimental design may use **t-tests**, for example, on years of experience, advanced degrees, area of college major, or other similar factors as well as demographic characteristics that can provide assurances that the two groups are similar prior to treatment. In some experimental designs, the evaluator may choose to conduct a pre- and posttest of the salient variables associated with the program as well. An example might be teacher knowledge about the reading strategies the professional learning program develops. The evaluator may conduct a pretest of both the control and treatment group or just the treatment group.

Following treatment, the evaluator again tests the treatment group on the salient variables associated with the program, and may test the control group as well. The evaluator analyzes the differences that occur between the pre- and posttest or between the two groups after the treatment to test for differences. Statistical analyses are again used, when appropriate conditions have been met, to measure the difference and test for its significance.

Practitioners might compare the effects of a professional learning program in a set of schools within the same district to another set of schools within the district if those schools have been randomly assigned to treatment and control groups and if they are similar on salient variables. This type of evaluation design might be best used if a district is piloting a major program of professional learning to determine its effects prior to full implementation districtwide to learn about the program's overt effect and to study issues related to implementation. Vendors may opt to use a similar design to evaluate their programs for effectiveness in naturalistic settings or in different settings such as in a rural school system or an urban school system to understand the difference in impact and operation.

Quasi-experimental design. An evaluator might choose a quasi-experimental design when random assignment to treatment and control groups is not possible. To compare the effects of the program, quasi-experimental studies construct **comparison groups** so the evaluator can determine whether the program had an effect. There are several forms of comparison groups—external, internal, and over time. For example, if a professional learning program is being implemented in one school system, another school system or set of school systems with many of the same characteristics might be selected as the external comparison group. If the program is being phased in within a district over a period of three to five years, those participating in the program may be compared to those not participating in the program. Comparison groups without some attention to the sameness of the two groups being compared or in situations where the treatment might be confounded weaken the validity of the study. Evaluators carefully select comparison groups to avoid some of the typical problems that occur in this design. In professional learning, the spread of the program to nonparticipants might occur when some teachers in a school participate in a program and others do not. In some schools, it is routine practice for teachers to collaborate with peers in learning communities and to share best practices. Those participating in the professional learning are likely to share their learning and experiences with it with nonparticipating peers. Peer effect (Jackson & Bruegmann, 2009) is a positive means for scaling an initiative, yet if these same teachers are the comparison group for professional learning, this positive attribute can have a negative impact on the overall measure of effectiveness of professional learning. For most practitioners, they would prefer the detrimental effects of positive scaling and spreading of effective practices, yet the evaluator planning a quasi-experimental design is not as likely to measure this effect.

Quasi-experimental design: Single group comparison. One form of a quasi-experimental design is the single group or internal comparison using a pretest–posttest. This allows the evaluators to measure changes following the implementation of the program. A major challenge of this design, however, is the ability to rule out other factors that might influence the effects.

Quasi-experimental design: Time-series study. Another form of comparison in quasi-experimental designs is the single group comparison over time. Both are useful for practitioner evaluations because they are less restrictive than experimental designs and permit conclusions of contribution of the program. For example, if a school improvement team was implementing visible thinking routines during a school year, it might collect data from teachers on their frequency of use of the routines with the anticipation that over time, as they became more familiar with the routines and had opportunity to practice, their use and their effects on students would increase. Measuring the frequency of use multiple times throughout the year and comparing the frequency is a **time-series design**. In this case, the results for students might be their independent application of the thinking routines in classroom tasks.

Quasi-experimental design: Multiple-interventions evaluation. A variation of the time-series approach is the multiple-interventions study. If a comparison group is not feasible and the possibility exists to repeat the intervention, the evaluator may want to compare two or more implementations of the intervention. The evaluator might compare the impact of the program in two schools, two districts, or across multiple schools or districts. The example of A Case Study: Comparisons for Professional Learning to Increase Writing Performance, on page 95 shows how an evaluator might look at a program across multiple years.

Practitioners might select a quasi-experimental design for the same reasons they would choose an experimental design, when random assignment is not feasible. They might recognize that denying the program to some participants and their clients is detrimental, particularly if the program is research or evidence based and has substantive promise of impact. They might recognize that conditions for randomization cannot be met at the most appropriate unit of analysis. Or, they may not have a suitable control group against which to measure effects.

Types of comparisons

A key word to focus on in the goal or outcome statement is the verb. If the verb suggests an increase or change, the evaluator must use some form of comparison to determine if a change occurred. Many professional learning programs ask questions about changes in student success or educator performance. Minimally, these studies require a pretest–posttest design. Another key for evaluators to tune into is a question about **attribution**—that is, "Did the changes occur because of the professional learning program?" This question requires the evaluator to use an experimental or quasi-experimental design. This means measuring effect in both a comparison or control group, a group of subjects who did not receive the treatment, as well as the group who received the intervention. For example, an evaluator might compare the performance of those students whose teachers participated in the professional learning program with the performance of students whose teachers did not have access to the professional learning intervention. Another possible comparison an evaluator might consider, if an entire school staff, for example, participated in the professional learning, is the performance of students of educators who are high-implementers with students of those who are low- or non-implementers. Using a comparison group allows the evaluator to rule out, to some degree, other factors that may influence the change and, therefore, to say with some certainty that resulting changes are associated with the professional learning program.

Impact evaluation of professional learning requires knowing whether change occurs. There are several ways to measure change. All involve comparison. Evaluators can make comparisons within the group of participants or with other groups who have not participated in the program. Choosing the basis for comparison depends on several factors that include time, financial resources, expertise of the evaluator, and availability of nonparticipants. Table 6.2 summarizes the various ways comparisons can be made in professional learning program evaluations.

Table 6.2 Options for Comparisons in Impact Evaluations

Options	Advantages	Disadvantages
Individual Comparison Matches and compares the scores for the same individuals before and after the intervention.	Looks at individual change from pretest to posttest rather than the mean or modal scores at the pretest and posttest; permits disaggregation by group such as years of experience; may provide a more accurate picture of the change.	Individual scores may not be available. Potentially may have attrition from pretest to posttest in both students and teachers so that it is not possible to form valid conclusions based on the remaining data.
Cohort Group Comparison Compares the pretest and posttest scores of the same group of participants or their clients.	Provides a view of the entire group. Provides information about the impact of the program.	Will not provide information about individual performance. May not account for differences present in the groups before the professional learning program or interventions that may have been implemented in the comparison group during the time of the professional learning program.
Panel Group Comparison Compares the posttest scores of different groups that are assumed to be the same (e.g., all new principals in one school year and all new principals in the next school year; eighth-grade students from one year with eighth-grade students from the next year).	Provides information about the impact of the program on two distinctly different groups that are assumed to be the same.	May not account for differences present in the groups before the professional learning program or interventions that may have been implemented in the comparison group during the time of the professional learning program.
Selected Comparison Group Compares pretest and posttest scores of different groups, matched because they share salient characteristics, one participating in the professional learning program and another selected for group comparison.	Provides information about the impact of the program. Provides an approach to comparison second only to random assignment. Adds strength and rigor to an evaluation if the selected or matched group shares the salient characteristics. Accounts for differences in the group *before* professional learning. May allow for conclusions about attribution.	Will not provide level of confidence in generalizations that random assignment does. Does provide a degree of rigor that some other forms of comparison do not. May be difficult to identify the salient characteristics for forming the comparison group. May be difficult to find groups with the same characteristics. May not account for differences present in the groups *before* the professional learning intervention or interventions that may have been used in the comparison group during the period of interest.

Options	Advantages	Disadvantages
Randomized Comparisons Compares participants randomly assigned to treatment or control group based on the assumption that randomization accounts for all difference between and within the groups.	Provides strong basis for drawing conclusions about causations when all salient variables that might influence the results are controlled for. Accounts for differences in the groups *before* professional learning if a pretest–posttest is done or if comparison statistics are applied. Allows for conclusions about attribution.	May be difficult to randomize at the unit of analysis of interest without some inter-group effect. Classrooms and schools are intact groups, which makes assignment of individual students, teachers, principals, or schools to a treatment group or a control group difficult. May cause denial of services to a student or educator who needs the services the program provides.
Generic Comparisons Compares the treatment group to a generic group that is presumed to have typical characteristics yet cannot be specifically matched (i.e., comparing performance of a school to the district mean for school performance or to the performance of all other high school students).	Provides a form of comparison, although this is the least strong of the options. Allows for weak conclusions of contribution.	Does not account for difference between the generic group and the treatment group that might exist before the professional learning program, potentially leading to inaccurate findings.

A case study: Comparisons for professional learning to increase writing performance

Teachers in one large urban district participated over five years in an intensive professional learning program designed to expand teachers' understanding of writing, learn how children learn to write, and improve students' performance in writing on both the district's writing sample and on related subtests of the standardized achievement test. The professional learning program involved extensive training, demonstration teaching, resource material development and dissemination, classroom coaching, and individual- and grade-level consultation. To support the change in instruction in writing, writing labs were created in the middle and high schools, lay graders were hired to assist teachers with grading writing, and student writing was published annually in a collection of student literary works. The district also instituted a pre- and posttest writing sample in each grade and required students to construct portfolios of their writing to carry with them through their educational career.

Schools were randomly assigned to participate in a three-year rotation with the unwritten assumption that all schools would participate. In the first two years of the program, schools were matched with other schools based on student achievement on standardized achievement tests and district criterion-referenced tests, and on socioeconomic status. Because of the design of the implementation of the professional learning program, the evaluator applied a

Table 6.3 Comparison Groups for Evaluating Professional Learning Program in Writing

Year 1
Year 1 schools compared with nonparticipating schools and the state
Year 2
Year 2 schools compared with Year 1 schools, nonparticipating schools, and the state
Year 1 schools compared with nonparticipating schools and the state
Year 3
Year 1 schools compared with Year 2 and Year 3 schools and the state
Year 2 schools compared with Year 3 schools and the state
Year 1, 2, and 3 schools compared with the state

multiple-intervention evaluation using the comparisons described in Table 6.3. Because of the evaluation results, the program was continued and received additional resources.

Qualitative design

Qualitative studies are another category of evaluation design and are more familiar and often more appropriate to use in practitioner-based evaluations. Qualitative designs, mostly descriptive in nature, include case and naturalistic studies. They are preferred designs when the program manager, stakeholders, or the evaluator expects the program to produce varied levels of impact on participants, and they allow the evaluator to measure the differing levels of outcomes and range of experiences of participants (Patton, 2015). Each will be described briefly.

Qualitative design: Case study. Case studies are a common form of naturalistic evaluations that examine the effects of a program on a single or multiple entities. Case studies acknowledge that units of analysis are unique and exist in unique contexts and that how one case responds to the program is likely to be different from others' responses. The cases are the unit of analysis, such as individual educators or schools. Case studies are selected when the variance of effect is expected to be substantial and is a focus of the interest of the stakeholders. Cross-case analyses examine the effects of a professional learning program across cases. Patton (2015) suggests this example of the useful application of case studies: "[A] leadership program that focuses on basic concepts of planning, budgeting, and communication skills may be able to measure outcomes with a standardized, quantitative instrument. But a leadership program that engages in helping participants think in systems terms about how to find leverage points and intervention strategies to transform their own organizations will need case studies of the actual transformation efforts undertaken by participants, for their individual endeavors are like to vary significantly. . . . Under such circumstances, qualitative case study methods and design strategies can

be particularly useful for evaluation of individual participant outcomes and organization-level impacts" (p. 185).

Qualitative design: Success case study. One form of case study, developed by Robert Brinkerhoff (2003), is the success case study in which random cases are selected from participants after classifying and assigning them to one of two groups—successful and unsuccessful—with the program. By studying the distinctions among the cases and telling the story about the success cases, evaluators can understand what influences the differences and formulate their findings, conclusions, and recommendations on the successful cases.

Qualitative design: Naturalistic study. Naturalistic evaluations allow the evaluator of a professional learning program to study its activities and the results obtained without being limited by the hypotheses associated with quantitative studies and without comparing them to something else. This approach, described as the "discovery approach" by Egon Guba (1978), seeks to study the program in its natural environment without attempting to manipulate or control for influences. Patton (2015) describes naturalistic inquiry as appropriate when programs are "subject to change or redirection." He continues, "The qualitative evaluator sets out to understand and document the day-to-day realities of participants in the program, making no attempt to manipulate, control, or eliminate situational variables or program developments but accepting the complexities of a changing program reality" (p. 49).

Mixed-method designs

Mixed-method evaluations use both qualitative and quantitative techniques to answer the questions the evaluation poses. Multiple methods may strengthen the validity of an evaluation by overcoming the weaknesses of any one design. Because they combine a quantitative design with the qualitative one they can standardize while also enriching the meaning of the study by offering an in-depth analysis of the behaviors, motivation, and attitudes of participants. For a professional learning program, using quantitative approaches to measure outcomes that can be standardized, such as student or educator performance, and supplementing that with a qualitative study of successful cases expands what stakeholders are able to learn from the study. This approach is particularly useful when standardized measures of student performance, for example, may be insufficiently sensitive to the specific professional learning outcomes for educators.

For the professional learning program focused on reading, the program outcomes suggest the need for a mixed-method evaluation design. Looking only at the intermediate outcomes and intended results (goals) and their evaluation questions, Table 6.4 and Table 6.5 delineate the evaluation design for each outcome. The predominant design is qualitative, yet the evaluator has opportunities to add quantitative elements to enrich the study, as noted in the design column.

Table 6.4 Proposed Evaluation Designs for the Professional Learning Program in Reading Intermediate Outcomes

Intermediate Outcomes	Evaluation Question	Evaluation Design
Teachers identify and solve implementation challenges within their own classrooms.	• What implementation challenges are teachers experiencing within their classrooms? • How do they solve those problems? • How well do their solutions align with the reading program's core components? • What are ways to change the design of the program to minimize the most common problems teachers are experiencing?	Qualitative: Success case study
Teachers accurately and consistently apply new reading instructional strategies in their classrooms with support from coaches.	Are all teachers accurately and consistently—as measured in three separate 40-minute observations, one by a peer, the coach, and the principal—based on the Innovation Configuration Map, implementing the new reading instructional strategies in their classrooms? What support from coaches do teachers report is most beneficial in helping them implement the reading instructional strategies?	Qualitative: Time Series (No comparison is needed.) Qualitative: Success case
Students use classroom resources for independent and guided reading.	Are students using classroom resources for independent and guided reading? Which materials are students using most often during independent reading and guided reading? How are students using classroom resources for independent and guided reading?	Qualitative: Time Series
Teachers use assessment data to adapt reading instruction based on student learning needs.	Are teachers using assessment data weekly to identify changes needed in reading instruction and integrating those changes into lesson and unit plans?	Qualitative: Artifact analysis
Teachers and coaches use student data to design reading instructional interventions for those students who need extra assistance.	What reading instructional interventions are teachers and coaches making based on student data for students who need extra assistance?	Qualitative: Artifact analysis

Intermediate Outcomes	Evaluation Question	Evaluation Design
Teachers' use of reading instructional strategies and review of student progress data increases with principal support.	What are teachers reporting about their classroom use of the new reading instructional strategies and their meetings with principals to assess the effectiveness by examining student progress data on benchmark assessments?	Qualitative: Success case study
New reading materials are used in classrooms.	How are teachers using the new reading instructional materials in the classroom?	Qualitative: Success case study
Students apply the new strategies in reading for both learning and pleasure.	How frequently do students initiate the use of the new strategies in reading both for learning and pleasure?	Qualitative: Success case study

Table 6.5   Proposed Evaluation Designs for Professional Learning Program in Reading Intended Results

Intended Results	Evaluation Question	Evaluation Design
Year 1: 60% of the students score proficient or above on the state reading test in Grades 3–8. Students read at least 30 minutes a week for pleasure.	Did 60% of all students score proficient or above on the state reading test in Grades 3–8? Are students reporting on their reading logs that they are reading for 30 minutes per week for pleasure?	Qualitative (While the scores are numerical, answering this question does not require the use of a quantitative evaluation design. No comparison is needed.) Qualitative: Success case study
Year 2: 80% of the students score proficient or above on the state reading test in Grades 3–8. Students read at least 60 minutes a week for pleasure.	Did 80% of all students score proficient or above on the state reading test in Grades 3–8? Are students reporting on their reading logs that they are reading for 60 minutes per week for pleasure?	Same as Year 1
Year 3: 100% of the students score proficient or above on the state reading test in Grades 3–8. Students read at least 60 minutes per week for pleasure. Students identify reading as a lifelong tool for learning and enjoyment.	Did 100% of all students score proficient or above on the state reading test in Grades 3–8? Are students reporting on their reading logs that they are reading for 60 minutes per week for pleasure?	Same as Years 1 and 2

Quantitative Versus qualitative designs

The age-old argument about the value of quantitative versus **qualitative data** certainly influences preferences. The desire for more scientifically based research in education blossomed with the advent of increased accountability. Institute for Educational Science (IES) guidelines for federally funded grant programs and their evaluations call for more application of experimental and quasi-experimental design in education to counteract what some perceive to be decades of soft (qualitative) research. This increasing pressure for "gold-standard designs" has only exacerbated the "quant"–"qual" divide. Fortunately, *ESSA* recognizes four levels of evidence, and IES funds some developmental studies based on promising evidence. To respond to the demand and desire for greater accountability with investments in professional learning, many evaluators and their stakeholders gravitate toward experimental or quasi-experimental evaluation designs rather than qualitative ones. In some cases, the use of the former designs is both appropriate and doable. Using experimental or quasi-experimental designs increases the generalizability of the evaluation findings. But in some cases, and frequently in public education, the necessary conditions for these designs cannot be met.

There is no perfect design—only better ones for specific evaluation questions. Evaluators are likely to be pulled in multiple directions when making the decision about design and influenced by stakeholders. Policy makers and decision makers admittedly have preferences for the kind of data and evaluation designs they find convincing. School boards, superintendents, and central office personnel may find **quantitative data** more credible. Principals and teachers are pressured by accountability demands to present quantitative data. Yet not all evaluation questions can be answered with quantitative or qualitative data alone and may require some of both to produce useful results. Rossi, Freeman, and Lipsey (2003) state

> Our position is that evaluators must review the range of design options to determine the most appropriate one for the evaluation. The choice always involves trade-offs; there is no single, always-best design that can be used universally as the "gold standard." Rather, we advocate using what we call the "good enough" rule in formulating research [evaluation] designs. Simply stated, the "good enough" rule is that the evaluator should choose the best possible design from a methodological standpoint after having taken into account the potential importance of the results, the practicality and feasibility of each design, and the probability that the design chosen will produce useful and credible results. (p. 240)

Table 6.6 summarizes the evaluation designs.

Table 6.6   Summary of Evaluation Designs

Design	Description
Experimental	Compares outcomes between a treatment and control group based on whose members have been randomly assigned; allows conclusions about the attribution of the program on results for participants.
Quasi-experimental	Compares outcomes between groups that have not been randomly assigned yet are similar in important aspects, one receiving the treatment and one serving as the control group or the comparison of a single group from a pretest to a posttest or over time; is less restrictive than pure experimental design; use when participants are not or cannot be randomly assigned to treatment and control groups; usually easier to implement in an educational setting than an experimental design; pretest–posttest and time-series studies fall into the category of quasi-experimental design.
Qualitative: Case study	Studies the effects of a program on a single or multiple entities; acknowledges that professional learning program participants and their clients are unique and exist in unique contexts and their responses to the program may vary because of the context or other factors; use when the variance of effect is expected to be substantial and is a focus of the interest of the stakeholders. The success case study is one form of case study.
Qualitative: Naturalistic	Studies the program, its activities, and outcomes obtained without being limited by the hypotheses associated with quantitative studies and without comparing them to something else in its natural environment without attempting to manipulate or control for influences.

Specialized mixed-method evaluation designs

There are multiple variations of the quantitative and qualitative designs that can be applied to evaluations. Three that might be of particular interest to professional learning leaders are **Rapid Feedback Evaluation (RTE)** (Wholey, 2015), small-sample studies, and Rapid Evaluation and Assessment Methods (REAM) (Mertens & Wilson, 2012). These designs are a form of evaluability assessment that provide quick results that allow for decision making about the viability of a larger-scale evaluation or of the potential for the program to produce its intended effects or are for exploratory programs, ones which are being examined for potential for impact. Both designs typically involve mixed methodologies, although not always. These forms of evaluation are particularly useful for teams within a school or district, or for a school improvement team.

Rapid Feedback Evaluation. RFE is a less well-known form of evaluation. It can be useful when policy makers cannot or will not wait for a full evaluation to make decisions about a professional learning program. It parallels other forms

of evaluation such as audits, but the real intention is to provide policy and decision makers confidence in continuing the program, funding it, or expanding it as a precursor to a fuller evaluation later. "RFE," according to Joseph Wholey (2015), "uses evaluation synthesis, small-sample studies, program data, site visits, and discussions with knowledgeable observers to (1) estimate program effectiveness and indicate the range of uncertainty in the estimates, (2) produce tested designs for more definitive evaluation, and (3) further clarify intended uses of the evaluation" (p. 89). RFE begins after agreement on the program's goals, applies a five-step process, described below, and produces estimated results on effectiveness in a brief amount of time. While there are challenges with RFE, it provides an option for short-term initiatives such as might occur in a team of teachers engaged in a cycle of continuous improvement or a school improvement team implementing multiple initiatives for which a full-scale evaluation might not be possible.

Steps in Rapid Feedback Evaluation include the following:

1. Collect existing data on the professional learning program.

2. Collect new data on the professional learning program.

3. Estimate the effectiveness of the professional learning program with clarity about the estimate not being a certainty.

4. Develop and/or explore options for further evaluation.

5. Determine the design and use of subsequent evaluation.

Case study: Rapid feedback evaluation of culturally responsive classrooms

The English teachers at Fenster Middle School are learning about creating culturally responsive classrooms to revamp their use of discussion techniques for the standard on using evidence to support arguments in oral and written language. They realize that cultural and language barriers prevent students from engaging fully in classrooms discussion, and they want to create conditions that foster the engagement of all students. From their reading, they have identified five promising techniques to try, and want to examine how they affect students with limited English. Each month they plan a series of lessons that integrates one technique and identify their "look-fors" to assess its effectiveness on student engagement and language development. They meet twice each month to bring their data to share with each other and clarify their use of the technique and their assessment of it. They create data displays each time they meet that summarize changes in student engagement and language use characteristics based on their look-fors. They are finding that students who had not previously engaged in large and small group discussions are engaging more readily and are using language in inventive ways when teachers consciously apply the techniques.

The teachers want to propose to the school improvement team that the techniques are appropriate for each discipline and that more teachers could

integrate some or all of them into their instructional repertoire. The English teachers use their Rapid Feedback Evaluation data to advocate for more wide-spread use of the techniques across the school. They also pull research findings on culturally responsive classrooms to support their proposal and suggest a schoolwide professional learning program and evaluation for the following school year.

Small-Scale Studies. Small-scale studies have specific purposes. One is to provide formative evaluation during implementation to adjust the program's implementation for improved results. "Because stakeholders are, at this point, in need of quickly collected information they can use to continue efficiently down the road toward mature implementation, and evaluation that is too slow-paced will not serve" states Huey Chen (2015). "A great deal of the value of formative evaluation lies in its ability to present information to stakeholders quickly" (p. 155). Small-scale formative studies focus on programmatic issues and can raise "red flags" if a program requires adjustments (Chen, 2015). In this way, small studies can point to issues needing attention that are interfering with program effectiveness and give stakeholders and program directors the needed information to make changes.

Small-scale studies are particularly useful for piloting instruments or other data collection methods to determine their effectiveness in gathering the necessary data to answer the evaluation questions. They can be useful too when sampling is difficult or the scale of the program implementation is relatively small, such as in a collaborative learning team or in a school; the study has, by its very nature, a smaller landscape to cover, yet is still necessary to provide effectiveness of the professional learning on educators and their clients. Like the case described in RTE, the smaller-scale studies may lead to larger-scale programs and evaluations over time.

Rapid Evaluation and Assessment Methods (REAM). Rapid approaches to evaluation are typically done when real-time information is essential and engagement of stakeholders and participants shapes the next series of decisions for a program. "The REAM process is an iterative one, with decisions about the need to collect more data or different data being made at each juncture of the process," according to Donna Mertens and Amy Wilson (2012). "Preliminary findings can be used to guide decisions, as the whole evaluation cycle continues to provide more refined information or information about new needs that surface" (p. 485).

Rapid evaluations can look at a slice of a program to provide formative evaluation or perspectives of the program from multiple sites in a short time. If an evaluator visits multiple schools, for example, where a professional learning program for leaders on building relationships with staff is being implemented, an evaluator can observe how the program is impacting principal interactions with staff, students, and potentially community members. "Rapid appraisal studies, also called rapid reconnaissance and rapid assessment, are aimed at

quick, low-cost data collection to answer specific, urgent questions. The purpose is to obtain a narrow, but in-depth understanding of the conditions and needs of the targeted group in a specific area to inform immediate decisions" (Patton, 2015, p. 346).

A district math coach who is the primary facilitator of a professional learning program on math practices might visit classrooms of program participants every few weeks to observe how teachers are implementing the focus math practices from the previous sessions. He uses his visits to record variations of implementation, frequency of implementation, and student responses. He shares this information with participants to clarify the practice, highlight successes, and adjust misconceptions. The specific examples from their own classrooms allow participants to reflect on their practice, ask questions, and gain greater clarity.

Creating the Data Plan

Another key part of constructing the evaluation framework is determining the data plan. The data plan has three parts: determining (1) when to collect data, both the specific activities about which to collect data to answer the evaluation questions and at what points in the program's maturation or operation; (2) the data sources; and (3) the data collection method. These decisions, along with the decision about the evaluation design, are not always perfectly linear in nature. They often occur simultaneously, with one decision requiring reconsidering and revising previous decisions.

When and about what to collect data

Using the evaluation questions, the evaluator identifies when to collect data by determining the key components of the theory of change to measure and identifies the best possible method and source for measuring the construct within the component. These are the data points for the evaluation. The evaluator confirms during this process if the design is appropriate to answer the evaluation questions. For example, in the theory of change presented in Chapter 4 on the reading professional learning program, the evaluator might consider which steps are the most significant to gather data about because they are pivotal points to the overall theory. Because each step may have its own distinct evaluation question some of which may take priority over others, the evaluator might first examine what the implications are for gathering data at each step and then streamline from there. Readers may want to review the diagram of the reading program theory of change on page 58 (Chapter 4).

The evaluator might also use the logic model to make decisions about which outcomes to measure. One option available is to measure each outcome, initial and intermediate, and the goal. While doing so might seem like an exorbitant number of data points in a program, there are only a few that do not naturally produce data as each activity is completed. In the reading professional learning program, the evaluator might measure only the intermediate outcomes rather than the initial outcomes. It is helpful to not miss opportunities for collecting

useful data that can inform decisions about the program, yet it is also important to acknowledge the cost of collecting too much data.

The evaluator wants to prevent needless data collection that infringes on program participants or taxes program staff. Expecting program participants to produce data can create a data burden that by itself will act as a barrier to the program's success. The evaluator wants to consider what types of data already exist within the system and to determine whether they might be a source of evidence before he decides that he will create and implement a new data-collection process. For example, observers naturally collect data in their observations, and student benchmark scores are available. A few steps might require a revision of data collection if the current process for data capturing does not provide the information needed or added data collection if there is not an established procedure. Or, if teachers are not naturally recording how they use student data and work samples to adapt instruction, for instance, that data collection procedure will need to be added. If coach logs are already capturing their classroom visits and reflection conversations with teachers, the log might be amended to include specific information about the use of the new reading instructional strategies. Sometimes evaluators enter the data-analysis phase awash in data, only some of which are useful to the specific evaluation questions. On the other hand, an evaluator may find when she is beginning the data analysis that she is missing data that would prove useful for future decision making about a program's implementation or impact. Time invested making thoughtful decisions related to data in the design of the evaluation framework prevents such frustrations.

Data formats

Data, like evaluation designs, come in two formats: quantitative and qualitative. Quantitative data are those that can be represented by numbers, while qualitative data are those that are represented by words or images.

Quantitative data result in scores, rankings, numbers, percent, or statistics. Sometimes those scores are from tests, surveys, or other instruments. Whenever data are represented numerically or algebraically, they are quantitative. Quantitative data are usually analyzed with descriptive or inferential statistics and presented in the form of tables, graphs, charts, or models (Weiss, 1998). Most quantitative data come from administering an instrument such as a survey, test, or other measure that results in numeric results or from transferring results into numeric values such as **counting** the number of uses of a particular instructional strategy during an observation; therefore, the evaluator rarely has personal or direct contact with participants.

Qualitative data, on the other hand, are represented in words, themes, or semantic analyses and are used in narratives, case studies, or vignettes. They result from data-collection methods such as open-ended survey questions, observations, interviews, anecdotes, or focus groups. In analyzing qualitative data, the evaluator typically searches for meaning and analyzes the data for recurring trends, patterns, or themes to make sense of the data. Collecting qualitative data usually places the evaluator into the program, and his or her presence may have an impact on the results.

Sometimes data from interviews, focus groups, or open-ended surveys are numerically coded, transforming what was qualitative data into quantitative data. For example, if an interviewer talked with students to ask about the various teaching strategies they recall their teachers using, the data might be left in the words of the students or coded using an established coding system that determined how often students spoke about particular teaching strategies.

Data sources

When the evaluator knows what data she needs to answer the evaluation questions, she decides on the best source of the information and what the best method of collecting that information is. Sometimes multiple sources of data are preferable to single sources of data. Data sources are the individuals, groups, or artifacts that provide the information needed to answer the evaluation questions in the most authentic way so that they are credible, reliable, and valid. Valid data are those that measure what is intended to be measured. Reliable data are those that are consistent across multiple situations. Credible data are those that stakeholders perceive to be useful. Data sources might be people such as educators, supervisors, peers, students, coaches, mentors, external observers, or others. They might also be documents, records, or artifacts. For example, to gather data about teachers' use of new instructional strategies, evaluators might analyze lesson plans for the presence of the strategies as an approximation of use. Actual observations provide more authentic evidence of use, yet may be prohibitive in terms of time and cost. To improve the support for their conclusions, evaluators seek to find evidence from multiple data sources and to answer their questions through multiple data-collection methods. This process, called triangulation, results in stronger, more valid conclusions. Using multiple data sources and different data-collection methods offsets some of the potential for measurement error or biases in the evaluation. Generally, the more data sources and the greater the variety of data-collection methods, the more credibility, validity, and reliability in the evaluation results.

Data-collection methods

Data-collection methods are the way in which the data are collected from the data sources. The decision about the data-collection method follows the decision about the appropriate data source for answering the evaluation questions. Evaluators do not choose a survey before they consider who the source of the data is and what data are needed from the source. Only then are they ready to determine the best method for collecting data from the source. Some common forms are survey, observation, interview, document analysis, or focus groups. The data plan leads to the appropriate data and allow the evaluator to form conclusions about how the components of the program interact to produce its intended results. In developing the data plan, the evaluator can also determine which data are more critical, which are less essential to answer the questions, and how to streamline the data-collection process so as not to collect unnecessary data or create a data burden. Both can be costly in terms of time and fiscal investment and in terms of goodwill.

Once evaluators know what data to collect they turn their attention to how to collect it. Evaluators have several options for data collection. They base decisions on increasing the validity, credibility, and reliability of their findings, and the feasibility of the evaluation plan. They strive to select data-collection methods that most authentically capture the desired data. Below are descriptions of some common forms of data-collection methodologies that can be used in the evaluation of professional learning.

Tests

Practitioners often think of tests as a means for measuring what students know, not what adults know, yet if they are valid ways of knowing if students are learning, it seems reasonable that they work for learners of all ages. Adults, however, have more test aversion than their students. Tests, however, are a means to measure change. Surveys are a form of test, for example, that can measure changes in knowledge, attitude, or aspiration.

Tests are useful for measuring student learning and come in a variety of forms. Some forms are standardized tests that are designed to measure achievement of particular criteria. Many states use this form of test to measure students' acquisition of the state-adopted standards. The typical written portion of a driver's education test is a form of standardized test, as are tests such as the PRAXIS used in many states for educator licensing. Classroom-based assessments are another form, often designed by teachers or groups of teachers to measure students' learning. When educators are engaged in professional learning, they may complete a series of specific assessments throughout a course to measure their understanding of the content and to provide guidance for the course developers on which aspects of the course might need more development or other forms of adjustment. These tests might not be standardized in a psychometric sense, but they are criteria-referenced to the course content. Tests typically are authentic measures of knowledge, and in a limited way can serve as approximate measures of attitude, skill, aspiration, and behavior. If tests are selected for measuring either participant learning or their clients' learning, the constructs measured should closely align with the content of either the professional learning or of the translation of professional learning to student learning. In other words, if teachers are learning ways to teach academic vocabulary, their tests should focus on the methods for teaching academic vocabulary, not what academic vocabulary is and why it is important, and students' tests then focus on their acquisition and/or application of academic vocabulary. The mismatch as described earlier can have negative effects on the success of the evaluation. The match of outcome and its measure is necessary so that a valid conclusion can be drawn about the link between professional learning and participant or client learning.

Surveys

Surveys are a form of test that measure opinion or preference and can measure each of the KASABs—some better than others, as in the case of attitude or

aspiration rather than behavior. Some surveys can be completed orally, such as those pesky 6:00 p.m. phone calls that interrupt family meals. Interviews are an oral survey that ask for open-ended responses. The accessibility of online survey tools makes this form of data collection increasingly practical because they provide descriptive analytics, yet a survey is not always the best method for digging deeper into respondents' reasons for choosing specific responses and may fall short in their design. Often survey developers fail to identify the constructs they wish to measure and operationalize them adequately before they design the survey items.

One of the major criticisms of surveys is that they are self-report responses that are biased by personal preference or perceptions about what respondents think is the socially acceptable or preferred response. Much of social science depends on self-reported data, and numerous studies have validated the reliability of self-reported data, especially if there are other means to triangulate to validate the findings. Even though there are threats to validity and reliability, surveys are one method for collecting data from some sources.

Interviews

As mentioned, interviews are a form of open-ended survey. Respondents are usually able to elaborate on their responses if they wish, and evaluators may probe for additional information or clarification. Structured interviews use a set of predetermined questions and probes for each interview so that the responses can be clustered and analyzed. Some interviews are less structured and more free-flowing, although there are limitations in compiling data from multiple interviews where there are no standard questions. Interviews can measure the same KASABs as surveys and have stronger ways to address behaviors than surveys. An interviewer, for instance, might ask a respondent to describe how he would enact a behavior or the specific situations in which a behavior is appropriate to use, thus providing the evaluator a better way to approximate the actual behavior, and one that is better than asking a survey question about the intent to enact a behavior. Interviews have the disadvantage of being time intensive and more complex to analyze than surveys or tests. Formulating the interview questions that resonate with respondents is another challenge.

When interviews are used as the data-collection method, the evaluator decides who the interviewer is. This decision requires consideration of the interviewer's neutrality, ability to understand and probe responses, and capacity to follow the interview protocol. The interview protocol may include open-ended questions, some form of selected choice questions, or a combination.

Focus groups

A focus group is a group interview moderated by a facilitator who uses a prepared set of questions to engage a small group of 6 to 10 participants in answering the questions. The questions are limited, as is the size of the group, to ensure that all participants can contribute and less vocal members are encouraged to share their views. Focus groups are usually recorded for later analysis. Like interviews, focus groups provide data that are more complex to

analyze, yet semantic analysis software is making some of this analysis for key words or phrases easier than coding the text.

Resources for Evaluation Instruments Related to Professional Learning

- *Online Evaluation Resource Library (OERL)*
  www.oerl.sri.com

OERL contains plans, tools, and reports from evaluation professionals. The resources are drawn from those who conducted National Science Foundation (NSF) project evaluations and include professional development modules for understanding deeper knowledge about evaluation.

- *The Evaluation Center at Western Michigan University*
  www.wmich.edu/evaluation

The center's mission is to advance the theory, practice, and use of evaluation through research, service, and leadership. It offers an array of useful checklists by preeminent evaluation scholars to facilitate evaluation practice.

- *The National Center for Research on Evaluation, Standards, and Student Testing at the University of California Los Angeles*
  http://cresst.org/

CRESST advances educational assessment and evaluation to improve policy and practice.

- *The National Science Foundation*
  www.nsf.gov

NSF offers a collection of evaluation reports on federally funded scientific programs.

Logs

Logs are forms of documentation to record occurrences of behaviors. They can be used by individuals to self-report their practice or by others to report on the practices of others. When coaches meet with teachers, for example, they often are required to log their interaction and code it by type, teacher, time, date, and follow-up required. Logs can be particularly useful for time-series studies if the content includes quantitative data that can be subjected to descriptive statistics. If coaches are logging their interactions with teacher by type, rather than the content to uphold confidentiality, it is helpful to note if some types of interactions, such as providing resources, are diminishing over time and others are increasing, such as classroom observations with reflection conversations (Killion, Harrison, Bryan, & Clifton, 2015). Logs that are anecdotal

or all qualitative in nature have similar challenges in the analysis phase that interviews and focus groups do.

Observations

Observations occur in authentic or simulated situations in which a learner is enacting the behaviors associated with professional learning. Micro-teaching simulations as a part of a weeklong workshop are a form of simulated applications that can be observed, whereas implementation in classrooms with students present is an authentic application. Observations are a useful way to measure behavior, not the other KASABs, yet it can be assumed that if the behavior is present, the other KASABs are as well. If a teacher is implementing with some accuracy a method for helping students develop academic vocabulary, the behavior of teaching academic vocabulary in an authentic or simulated situation may serve as evidence that the teacher knows about, believes in, knows how to do, and wants to develop academic vocabulary. Usually observers have a data-gathering or recording tool that focuses their attention on specific behaviors associated with the professional learning. These tools might be a tally sheet, check sheet, or list of specific behaviors with room to make notes about their observations. They may include codes aligned to the behaviors to use in recording the observation. Sometimes observers write scripts of the observation, recording what is happening and what participants are saying. These scripts are later analyzed. In other cases, observers might supplement their data gathering with anecdotes, perceptions, or judgments. This type of observation is often referred to as field notes. Sometimes video or audio recordings of the observed experience assist the evaluator in revisiting or analyzing the experience more deeply.

All observations are filtered through the observer's perception. Interrater reliability checks can minimize observer bias. Multiple observers can also mitigate observer bias. Observations are best done by trained observers to minimize some observer bias.

Rating scales

While conducting observations, observers may be asked to rate or score a set of practices. This form of data-gathering tool requires even more training for interrater reliability than other forms of observation tools because it asks raters to use a set of predetermined criteria and to score or judge observed experience. A panel of judges at a gymnastics event or a forensics event who use established, known criteria that are consistently applied are examples of the application of **rating scales**. Raters, those who use the criteria to form a rating, can be internal or external to the professional learning program and may be content area experts, process experts, program administrators, participants, or supervisors of the participants.

Rating scales may result in a single score or multiple scores in several different categories. Many forms of educator performance appraisals use rating scales in addition to observation notes. Innovation configuration (IC) maps are useful forms of a rating scale for assessing implementation of professional

learning because they delineate a range—from ideal to unacceptable—of behaviors associated with implementation of the professional learning outcomes for educators. Developers of IC maps, Gene Hall and Shirley Hord, stress that they are used primarily for educative and assessment purposes rather than evaluative purposes; however, many evaluators find them useful to use as guides to developing evaluation tools such as a rating scale. Rubrics are another form of rating scales that can be useful for measuring the quality of a product or a practice. Both IC maps and rubrics provide a continuum of strong practices to weak practices to help the rater form a judgment.

Extant data sources: Documents and artifacts

Documents and artifacts are data sources found in the educational system that can be collected for analysis. If a school is implementing a socio-emotional learning program, they have as a goal to reduce discipline referrals. One evaluation question might be about the impact of the program on student behavior. To answer this question, they might gather three years of discipline referrals and analyze them for total number, frequency, and type of behavior problem by student group to answer the evaluation question. Documents and artifacts provide information about the knowledge, skills, and practices of program participants and students. Most artifacts or documents exist naturally within the environment in which the program operates. Some examples are attendance records, lesson or unit plans, educator or student work samples, meeting agendas and minutes, and anecdotes or correspondence. For example, students' products that serve as demonstrations of their knowledge or skills can be collected and assembled in portfolios and are available to others for review. Artifacts can serve as evidence of growth over time or the outputs from program activities. The challenge with artifacts is analyzing them, so evaluators will often create rubrics, checklists, or rating scales to use for this purpose.

Selecting Instruments

When selecting a data-collection method, the evaluator first considers if it will produce credible, valid, and reliable data. Next the evaluator considers if some form of the data already exists before deciding a new source is needed. The evaluator then determines if an existing data-collection method or instrument can be used, or adapted, or if it is necessary to construct a new one. Constructing instruments requires extra time for development and field-testing. While there are advantages to using previously developed instruments, there are also disadvantages. Existing instruments may be field-tested and determined to be valid and reliable. In some cases, they will be normed and standardized, yet they may not align precisely with the constructs of the evaluation or be appropriate for the context or the population who use them.

When the evaluator chooses to develop new instruments, he must be certain they are valid and reliable so that the data collected are accurate. Valid instruments are ones that can measure the constructs intended. When the

instruments measure abstract concepts such as persistence or engagement, the concept of validity is more complex and depends on a clear operational definition of the construct. Reliable instruments are ones that yield consistent results—if the same person completed the instrument without any intervention, she would have a consistent score, one without much variance. Evaluators ask the following questions about the instruments they decide to use:

Do they measure the constructs identified as important?

Do they represent the constructs as defined in the program?

Are they appropriate for the age and language of the population completing them?

Are they free from bias?

Are they clear and can they be completed in a reasonable amount of time?

Are they reliable?

Choosing an Appropriate Data-Collection Method. The choice of the data-collection strategy depends on what information is needed. While some data-collection strategies are more time-consuming and costlier than others to implement, decisions are made based on their potential for collecting valid and reliable data. For example, an interview is more time-consuming and can be costlier than administering a survey. Yet, if the evaluator believes the quality and depth of the information from interviews may be better, she should use interviews to collect data, if possible, rather than compromise the integrity of the evaluation. Some data-collection methods require more resources than others. Making decisions about data collection based on what is preferred rather than what is affordable will ensure the integrity of the evaluation. If resource limitations require choosing a less appropriate data-collection method, the evaluator engages stakeholders in understanding the trade-offs and considers a sampling process as a potential way to reduce costs. Any decision about the data-collection method is based on the purpose of the evaluation, program outcomes, data sources, and intended uses of the evaluation.

Case Study: Mannsfield Middle School

Mannsfield Middle School wanted to improve students' literacy performance, particularly how students score on the state reading assessment. To do this, both the principal and teachers wanted more strategies for teaching literacy and reinforcing literacy in all content areas. First, teachers needed to know more about the reading process. As middle school teachers, most had taken only one course in reading in the content areas. Consequently, they did not understand how children learned to read or how to teach adolescents the basic reading processes they lacked.

The school staff engaged in more than 30 hours of professional learning that included a workshop, coaching, observations with feedback, and

study groups. The administrative team conducted weekly walk-throughs of classrooms to examine teachers' practices and provide information to the entire staff about how the various strategies were being implemented. The principal met with each staff member to help him or her develop a personal professional growth plan to identify specific goals for improvement and strategies for achieving those goals. Coaches worked one-on-one with teachers in their classrooms and with grade-level and department teams, devoting most of their time to assisting new staff members. The evaluator worked with the leadership team in the school to establish various ways to collect data about changes in teacher knowledge and practices and student learning without disrupting classrooms or burdening teachers or students with additional testing.

Table 6.7 summarizes the data the evaluator used in the evaluation. The evaluator chose to use multiple types of data sources and data-collection methods to look at the impact of teachers' increased knowledge and practices on student achievement from different perspectives. The program leaders and evaluator wanted to know whether (1) student achievement increased as measured on the state test when teachers implemented the new strategies; (2) students' attitudes about reading were more positive; (3) teachers regularly used the strategies (their behaviors); and (4) students could describe their reading behaviors. With this information, the evaluator determined whether teachers' acquisition of knowledge and additional practices in literacy positively influence students' literacy achievement.

Table 6.7   Data-Collection Plan for the Mannsfield Middle School Evaluation Framework

Data	Data-Collection Methods	Timeline
Student achievement	Pretest (previous year's middle grade students) and posttest (current year's middle grade students) reading scores on state reading assessment	May and May
Teacher behavior	Walk-through logs	Weekly
Student behavior	Student interviews	Quarterly with representative sample of students
Students' attitudes about reading	Pretest and posttest student surveys	Twice a year, in the fall and spring

Selecting sources for data and the method for collecting the data are pivotal decisions in the construction of the evaluation framework. The evaluator may have determined the most appropriate data to collect and the best method for collecting but, if the source is not accurate, the entire data set and

evaluation can be compromised. It may seem appropriate to ask teachers to recall information about their lessons, yet checking their classroom lesson plans or student work may be more accurate. When selecting the data sources to use, the evaluator considers whether the data from each source are likely to be accurate, which sources might be more expedient to tap, and whether the actual data collection will pose any excessive burden, potential harm, or threat to the source.

Data Analysis and Interpretation

Evaluators consider the format of the data they are collecting and identify the best data-analysis process to use with the data collected. In constructing the evaluation framework, evaluators plan for how they will analyze data, yet their plan might change once the data are actually collected. This chapter and Chapter 7 have details about data analysis and interpretation. Data analysis is the procedures used to calculate or synthesize the data. For example, if students complete interviews about how they are applying the new reading strategies in their independent reading, the evaluator might choose to identify which strategies students use and how often students mention each strategy. This is a numerical or quantitative way to summarize qualitative data. They may supplement their numerical analysis with statements or responses from some students that characterize common responses and perhaps add outlier examples. Evaluators may also determine if students are describing a strategy accurately, if their interview questions yield sufficient information to make this determination, and report the number of times students report using a strategy accurately or inaccurately.

Evaluators make decisions about analysis based on the evaluation questions, the type of data collected, the purpose of the evaluation, and the validity and reliability of the data. Data analyses might be descriptive in nature, such as calculating difference scores, means, modes, ranges, percentage, or using themes, trends, or common responses. Sometimes evaluation questions call for more than descriptive forms of analysis, so evaluators apply inferential statistics such as standard deviation, correlation coefficients, t-tests, or others. The power of the data analysis increases the rigor of the evaluation, yet the evaluation design and conditions must be appropriate for the application of the inferential statistics used.

Interpretation is the process of making sense of the analyzed data. When the evaluator has completed the analysis and displayed the results in a variety of formats such as tables, graphs, and charts, she invites stakeholders to engage in a discussion about the meaning of the analyzed data. The purpose of engaging stakeholders is to seek multiple perspectives, particularly from those who have been closest to the work and to use those perspectives to understand what the data say and what implications they have for the professional learning program, its participants, their clients, and the program director or manager. More details about data interpretation are included in Chapter 7.

Timelines and Responsibilities

Another component of the evaluation framework is setting timelines and assigning responsibilities. Before an evaluation framework can be approved and enacted, the evaluator determines the timeline for collecting the necessary data, who will be responsible for collecting and managing them, who will analyze them, and who will be invited to participate in the interpretation of the analyzed data. Creating the timeline and assigning responsibilities is one way to keep the work on track, provide notification to both informants and data collectors so they can plan accordingly, and establish milestones to assess if the evaluation is on track.

Reviewing and Approving the Evaluation Framework

Evaluators, once the evaluation framework is completed, ask primary stakeholders to review and approve it. Whether the evaluator is an external one, an internal practitioner, or member of a team of practitioners, she uses this opportunity to explain what the evaluation design is to others and seeks approval for it. Some stakeholders may not have the depth of understanding of the technical aspects of evaluation to know with confidence that decisions regarding the evaluation framework are accurate and appropriate, yet they can weigh in on some aspects such as the timeline, responsible persons, when staff will be completing some aspects of the evaluation, the proposed cost of the evaluation, and the anticipated usefulness of the results. The review and approval process may be a formality that seeks support for the evaluator's work and the evaluation itself. When stakeholders have an opportunity to review and approve the evaluation framework, their commitment to the evaluation is likely to increase and the evaluator's work will potentially be more valued.

The most significant criteria for reviewing an evaluation framework are its feasibility, appropriateness to the evaluation questions and intended purpose, and the evaluator's expertise. Feasibility is a determination of whether the evaluation can be accomplished within the resources available, the time available, and the expertise or capabilities of the evaluator or evaluation team. Appropriateness is a determination of whether the evaluation framework will yield the answers to the evaluation questions. Evaluator expertise is a determination about the skillfulness of those who will conduct the evaluation.

If there are disagreements about any aspect of the evaluation framework, the evaluator seeks to make modifications without compromising the integrity of the evaluation. The evaluator also explains honestly and clearly the rationale for various decisions and implications for any changes that may have some detrimental effect on the evaluation's integrity or usefulness. Often, especially in the case of an external evaluator, stakeholders respect the expertise of the evaluator. Internal evaluators are often working as a part of a team of practitioners who are collaborating on the decisions within the design of

the evaluation framework and they can continually examine the impact of each of their decisions on the evaluation.

CAUTIONS FOR EVALUATORS AND STAKEHOLDERS

Attribution and Contribution

The design of an evaluation influences the conclusions an evaluator can draw from it. Some evaluations allow the evaluator to draw conclusions that changes that occur are the result of the program and nothing else. *Attribution* is a term used in experimental studies, or under certain circumstances in quasi-experimental ones, to imply that the program or some aspect of it is solely responsible for the changes that occur. Making claims of attribution is possible only if a comparison can be made with a nonparticipating group when subjects are randomly assigned to participating and nonparticipating groups. Such claims are strengthened if both a pre- and a posttest comparison is made between the two groups. Attribution claims are possible if the changes that occur always occur with the intervention and not with any other intervention and if removing the intervention returns the observed change back to its previous condition.

In complex systems such as schools, it is likely that professional learning contributes to changes such as improvements in student achievement. In other words, the conclusions are about how educator learning is a contributing factor to the changes rather than the changes being attributed to professional learning. Most evaluation studies are not designed to provide evidence that the program is completely responsible for the changes. Claims of *contribution* acknowledge there are other factors that might have an impact on any changes occurring, such as new curriculum, new instructional materials, improved student test-taking skills, a different cohort of students, other professional learning, different educators, or a new principal at the school. When the conditions for conclusions of attribution are not met (i.e., random assignments of participants to treatment and control groups), an evaluator may identify the changes associated with the professional learning program (contribution), yet cannot state that the program is solely responsible for the changes (attribution).

Seeking Permission

Evaluators, both internal and external, must follow policies or procedures that exist regarding human subjects and their engagement in evaluation or research studies. Some school systems have their own policies regarding the use of district data. Evaluators have a responsibility to understand these policies and to follow them precisely.

Evaluators respect the security, dignity, and self-worth of the respondents, program participants, clients, and other stakeholders with whom they interact. Evaluators must abide by professional ethics and standards regarding risks,

harms, and burdens that might be engendered to those participating in the evaluation; informed consent for participation in evaluation; and informing participants about the scope and limits of confidentiality. Examples of such standards include federal regulations about protection of human subjects, including the ethical principles of such associations as the American Anthropological Association, the American Educational Research Association, the American Evaluation Association, or the American Psychological Association. (See *Program Evaluation Standards Statements* in Appendix B.)

Sometimes schools and districts ask parents to sign blanket permission forms granting permission to use student records or routine classroom practices or work for research and evaluation. If this is not the practice, districts can inform parents that their children's records will be a part of an evaluation study and give them an opportunity to exempt their child from involvement.

Similar procedures are required for staff members who are asked to participate. They minimally must be given an overview of the evaluation and its purpose, be told how data from them will be used and if the data will be confidential and anonymous, and be given an opportunity to not participate without sanction. Some district contracts and state policies include specific guidelines about the involvement of staff and students in research and evaluation. Evaluators must adhere to these guidelines in all circumstances unless specific exemptions are granted.

Cost of Evaluation

Evaluations are an investment. There are costs associated with either paying for direct services of an evaluator or in staff time invested in the evaluation or a combination of both. Decisions about the evaluation framework must consider the resources available for the evaluation without compromising the integrity of the evaluation or the data. The cost of evaluations is one reason that educators do not conduct more of them. Yet valuable information can result from low-cost evaluations. When designing an evaluation framework, evaluators consider what is achievable with various levels of fiscal support for an evaluation. Some program directors realize that cutting corners too closely may not provide the data they, decision makers, and policy makers want from a program. If corners are cut too closely, the evaluation may be less useful to them and may be less valid. When program directors have options about what is possible at different levels of funding, they may opt to budget more for the evaluation to produce the results that will be valid, reliable, and useful.

The cost of conducting evaluations varies widely and depends on the evaluation questions, the requirements of the evaluation, the cost of the program, and the rigor required. While a range of 10 percent to 20 percent of total program budget is usually recommended by granting agencies for evaluations, there is no universally accepted standard for funding evaluations. Table 6.8 provides some options for evaluation designs based on cost.

Table 6.8 General Guidelines for Evaluation at Different Cost Levels

Range of Cost	Typical Characteristics
Low Cost	• Allows for some collection of data, usually extant, about a program's implementation, such as numbers of participants, participant satisfaction with the program, and minimal data about initial and intermediate outcomes. • Permits description of program implementation. • Provides little, if any, information about program's impact on which to base decisions. • Can be used for some compliance requirements. • Provides little, if any, information about changes in participants or their clients that occur during in the program. • Provides a single report format.
Moderate Cost	• Allows for adequate data collection about a program's implementation and impact to answer the evaluation questions. • Permits adequate data analysis to form possible conclusions about changes in participants or their clients that occur during in the program to answer the evaluation questions. • May permit conclusions about whether the program is responsible for the changes. • Focuses on short-term rather than long-term changes. • Provides one to two report formats.
High Cost	• Allows comprehensive data collection from multiple sources and with multiple methodologies to provide reliable, valid, and credible conclusions about the program's merit, worth, impact, and significance. • Provides sufficient evidence to determine whether changes are sustained over time. • Provides support from the evaluator or evaluation team to facilitate dissemination and use of evaluation results. • Provides recommendations regarding program design, implementation, management, and effects. • Provides multiple report formats.

Adapted from Administration of Children, Youth, and Families (n.d.). *A program manager's guide to evaluation.* Retrieved December 21, 2006, from www.acf.hhs.gov/programs/opre/other_resrch/pm_guide_eval/index.html

INTERNAL OR EXTERNAL EVALUATOR

Because impact evaluation requires specialized knowledge, program designers decide early on whether to use an internal or external evaluator. Reading through the next section may provide some guidance, although some may want to read the remainder of the chapter and return to the next section before making this decision about and internal or external evaluator.

Before planning an evaluation framework can begin, the program director and stakeholders collaboratively and carefully consider whether to have an

external or **internal evaluator**. The information in the following section summarizes the pros and cons of both approaches and suggests ways for program leaders and the evaluator to share responsibilities.

Conducting an evaluation requires competency in the field of evaluation. Some of the decisions about the evaluation framework and conducting the evaluation can be technical, and so it is important early in the process for the person responsible for the evaluation to acknowledge his or her strengths and limitations and to identify the support system available to assist at this stage.

Several options are available for conducting evaluations with either an internal or an external evaluator. Each has its advantages and disadvantages. When making decisions about who conducts the evaluation, the following questions and guidelines adapted from *The Program Manager's Guide to Evaluation* (Administration of Children, Youth, and Families, n.d.) might be helpful (see Table 6.9). Table 6.10 will also assist with this decision. If there is a preponderance of *no* answers checked in response to the questions in Table 6.11, it may be best to wait until there are adequate funds to hire an outside evaluator. If there is a balance of *yes* and *no* responses and the answer to Question 1 is *yes*, an in-house staff member can serve as the evaluator. Weighing the response to each of these questions and considering the advantages and disadvantages of each type of evaluator will help program directors make the decision about who should conduct the evaluation.

Some programs have a greater cost or perceived significance than others (because of the nature of the program or the source of funding) and may require the objectivity of an external evaluator even though there may be might in-house expertise for conducting the evaluation. When programs have large price tags, are controversial, have divided support, or are viewed as the "silver bullet" for solving problems, it may be best to have an outside evaluator lead the evaluation.

If the stakeholders decide to hire an external evaluator, program directors will want to work closely with the evaluator to establish the parameters and expectations for the work to be done. Often a written contract between the external evaluator and the program director specifies important agreements, such as the purpose of the evaluation, timeline, payment, involvement of participants, and deliverables. One expectation should be for strong collaboration between the evaluator and the program stakeholders. When evaluators work closely with program directors and engage them in the decisions about the evaluation, the evaluation will be more valuable and useful. In addition, evaluators will be building the capacity of the program staff to conduct their own evaluations and appreciate the value of evaluations.

Responsibilities of both the program directors and the evaluator are listed on pages 121–123. If program directors act as evaluators, with or without support of colleagues, they will assume the responsibilities of the evaluator in addition to the responsibilities of the program director.

Table 6.9 External Versus Internal Evaluation

Independent or external evaluation is best when	• funders, sponsors, or governing agencies require it; • concerns about credibility of the evaluation process may arise; • concerns arise that the decision making during the evaluation may be influenced by the self-interest of the stakeholders; • using an external agent can increase the objectivity or the perceived validity of the decisions about the evaluation; and • decisions cannot be made internally for some reason.
Internal practitioner evaluation is best when	• participants want to ensure that the evaluation is useful for them; • a sense of ownership among the stakeholders is important; • there is an intent to engage in continual improvement throughout the program; and • building the capacity of others to conduct evaluations or use evaluation processes is a priority.

Table 6.10 Internal Versus External Evaluator

Options for Evaluators	*Advantages*	*Disadvantages*
Outside evaluator without support from the program staff	• Expertise available • Objectivity • Credibility of results • Efficient process • May offer new perspective • May save time	• May disenfranchise program stakeholders. • May not be as useful as possible to program stakeholders. • Incurs a cost to hire evaluator. May not have access to essential data or sources. • Evaluator may not have investment in the program or its evaluation.
Outside evaluator with support from the program staff	• Expertise available • Objectivity • Credibility of results • Useful results • Efficient process • May offer new perspective	• May take time away from program services. • Staff may feel burdened. • Incurs a cost to hire evaluator and may incur costs from involving staff.
In-house evaluator with support from the program staff, in-house experts, and other technical experts	• Technical assistance available • Useful results • May not require extra costs • Builds capacity	• Greater time commitment of program staff. • Coordination of services from different people. • Objectivity may be compromised. • Cost of staff time and reassignment of current responsibilities.

Options for Evaluators	Advantages	Disadvantages
Program director with support from an outside evaluator or consultant	• Useful results • May not require extra costs • Builds capacity	• May detract focus from program implementation. • May take time from program management. • Staff may feel burdened by extra responsibility. • Evaluator may be less committed to evaluation. • Objectivity may be compromised.
Program director without support	• Less expensive • Useful results • Builds capacity	• Time commitment may detract from implementation. • Objectivity may be compromised. • Credibility of results may be questioned. • Experience may limit evaluation options and quality.

Table 6.11 Questions for Determining the Need for an Internal or External Evaluator

Program Resource Questions	Yes	No
1. Does the program being evaluated have significant cost or a perceived importance?		
2. Will an internal evaluation have the necessary credibility?		
3. Are additional funds available, or can existing resources be redirected for the evaluation of this program?		
4. Are evaluation data collected as a regular part of the program's operation?		
5. Are there staff in-house, such as an assessment coordinator or a research and evaluation expert, who can lend expertise to the evaluation?		
6. Have the staff conducted similar evaluations previously with success?		
7. Do staff members have the appropriate expertise for this evaluation?		
8. Is the program design aligned with the evaluation's purpose?		

Responsibilities of Program Directors in Evaluation

- Work closely with the evaluator to ensure that he or she understands the program, the context, the purpose of the evaluation, the stakeholders and audience(s) for the evaluation report, and how the evaluation will be used.

- Provide input and assistance to the evaluator about the evaluation questions and the evaluation framework.
- Keep program staff and other stakeholders informed about the progress of the evaluation.
- Keep the evaluator informed about modifications in the program.
- Meet regularly with the evaluator to stay informed about the evaluation process, solve problems related to it, discuss its progress, and contribute to the data interpretation.
- Coordinate any in-house evaluation responsibilities.
- Review the draft report for clarity and usefulness and help the evaluator write for the intended audience.

Evaluator Responsibilities

- Work collaboratively with the program director, staff, and key stakeholders.
- Design the evaluation questions and framework and present a written agreement about the evaluation framework to the program director.
- Meet regularly with the program director to review the progress of the evaluation, solve problems related to the evaluation, and provide updates on the evaluation.
- Protect confidentiality and anonymity of data sources as appropriate.
- Adhere to evaluation standards and guidelines (see Appendix B).
- Complete all aspects of the evaluation framework according to the written plan.
- Conduct a valid, unbiased, thorough evaluation with integrity.
- Present the evaluation findings to stakeholders.

A SUMMARY: MAKING DECISIONS ABOUT THE FRAMEWORK

An evaluator has multiple choices about possible designs for an evaluation study, but the options are often limited by several factors. Some of the most significant determining factors are resources, including time, personnel, and funding; intended use of the evaluation findings; and the stage at which the evaluator became involved. One major challenge a program director and evaluator have is knowing the degree to which the evaluation study itself is worth the investment. If resources are limited, the evaluator's choice of design may be limited. To ensure the integrity of professional learning programs, meet standards of excellence, and make data-informed improvements, evaluation, even low-cost, practitioner-driven ones, is essential. Rossi, Freeman, and Lipsey (2003) state

> Our position is that evaluators must review the range of design options to determine the most appropriate one for the particular evaluation. The choice always involves trade-offs; there is no single, always-best design that can be used universally as the "gold standard." Rather, we advocate using what we call the "good enough" rule in formulating research [evaluation] designs. Simply stated, the "good enough" rule is that the evaluator should choose the best possible design from a

methodological standpoint after having taken into account the potential importance of the results, the practicality and feasibility of each design, and the probability that the design chosen will produce useful and credible results. (p. 240)

If the evaluation is integral to making significant decisions related to program continuation or resources, the professional learning leader and evaluator will want to lobby for the resources they believe are essential to conducting a credible evaluation. If they are obligated to cut too much, the credibility of the entire evaluation and ultimately any decisions based on it are compromised.

A Case Study: Writing Case

Hubbard Middle School staff could no longer ignore their students' deficiency in writing after the last state assessment. Their scores were substantially below the state mean on the two writing assessments. The state's holistic scoring system gave them little information about why student scores were so low. Some teachers voluntarily analyzed the writing samples using the district's writing rubric to determine their students' strengths and gaps. They determined that all students, and especially those considered at risk, lacked the ability to organize ideas and employ language conventions correctly (grammar, punctuation, capitalization, spelling, etc.).

To address these problems, teachers committed to work together as a staff to improve students' writing performance through the application of a schoolwide writing process. They created a plan that included the following components:

- Conduct a writing sample in the fall and spring.
- Establish three, multidisciplinary study groups on adolescent writing to examine research and strategies for addressing the areas of greatest need.
- Meet weekly to study together and design lessons to apply the research on the writing process in the core subjects.
- Bring in an external consultant four times throughout the year to work with teachers in teams and individually as a coach to support implementing the writing process across disciplines.
- Keep writing portfolios for all students throughout the year and engage students in reviewing their portfolios using the district writing rubric.
- Observe teachers in other schools using the writing process to refine teacher skills.
- Design interdisciplinary writing tasks to use throughout the year.
- Engage in peer observation within their school as they were learning to apply new writing instruction strategies.
- Assess the effectiveness of their implementation of the strategies by examining student writing at least once a month.

The assistant superintendent commends them on their extensive plan to improve student writing. She asks several hard questions that they need to answer to gain her support to hire the external consultant.

The assistant superintendent wants answers to these questions at the end of the year:

1. How do you know that your efforts are making a difference in student performance in writing and especially in organization and language conventions?

2. Which of the many interventions you are implementing had the greatest impact on classroom instruction?

To support the principal and school improvement team with the evaluation, she assigns a district staff person to serve as the external support for some data collection and analysis. Table 6.12 depicts the evaluation framework for the evaluation of writing professional learning program.

Table 6.12 Evaluation Framework for Hubbard Middle School Writing Professional Learning Evaluation

Types of Changes	Question	Data Source	Data-Collection Method	Data Analysis Method	Timeline	Responsible Party
Improved student writing in areas of organization of ideas and language conventions	Did student writing scores in the areas of organizing ideas and language conventions improve on the state writing assessment by 10% from the spring to spring testing?	State writing assessment in Grades 7 and 8	State test	Difference in scores in panel groups	Spring 2018 through Spring 2019	Principal and school improvement team, with support from district testing coordinator
Language arts teachers' teaching practices in language conventions and organization of ideas	Are all language arts teachers implementing explicit instruction in organizing ideas and language conventions into their classrooms at least once a week?	Teacher lesson plans	Document/ artifact collection	Percentage of teachers by counting occurrences in a 20% sample of lesson plans during three separate weeks of the school year	Designated weeks, one in early October, one in early February, and one in early May	District staff assigned serve as the external support for the evaluation and analyze lesson plans based on a rubric

Types of Changes	Question	Data Source	Data-Collection Method	Data Analysis Method	Timeline	Responsible Party
All teachers integrating practice opportunities in organizing ideas	Are all teachers providing authentic opportunities for students to practice organizing ideas within the context of writing assignments or tasks?	Student assignments and work samples	Document/ artifact collection	Percentage of teachers by counting occurrences in a 20% sample of student assignments and work samples during three separate weeks of the school year	Designated weeks, one in early October, one in early February, and one in early May	District staff assigned serve as the external support for the evaluation and score student assignments and work samples based on rubric
Teachers' efficacy in writing instruction	To what degree do teachers feel competent to teach writing? What is contributing to their increase in efficacy and competence?	Teachers	Pre- and posttest survey	Pre- and posttest difference scores with descriptive statistics	Fall (pretest) and May (posttest)	District staff assigned serve as the external support for the evaluation and analyze survey results
Teacher attitude about professional learning program in writing	What aspects of the school's efforts to improve student writing do teachers believe had the greatest impact on their practice in teaching writing?	Teachers	Focus groups with 20% of teachers selected randomly by school improvement team	Semantic analysis of responses in three categories: factors that influenced instruction, perceived weight of factors, and desire to continue implementing new practices	Late May	District staff assigned serve as the external support for the evaluation and conduct focus groups and analyze responses

Evaluators might use the rubric in Table 6.13 to review their evaluation frameworks for completeness, feasibility, and appropriateness.

Table 6.13   Evaluation Framework Rubric

Evaluation Framework	Not Ready to Begin Evaluation	Revise Before Evaluation Begins	Ready to Begin Evaluation
Data sources	The evaluation framework fails to specify the data sources needed to answer the evaluation questions.	The evaluation framework specifies the data sources needed to answer the evaluation questions.	The evaluation framework specifies multiple data sources for each type of data needed to answer the evaluation questions and for triangulation purposes.
Data-collection methods	The evaluation framework fails to specify what data-collection methods will be used to collect data from various data sources to answer the evaluation questions.	The evaluation framework names data-collection methods, yet does not specify which will be used for each data source.	The evaluation framework specifies multiple data-collection methods to collect data from each data source to answer the evaluation questions and for triangulation purposes.
Data analysis methods	The evaluation framework fails to specify how the data collected will be analyzed and interpreted to answer the evaluation questions.	The evaluation framework specifies how some of the data will be analyzed and interpreted to answer the evaluation questions.	The evaluation framework specifies how all the data collected will be analyzed and interpreted to answer the evaluation questions.
Timeline	The evaluation framework fails to specify timelines for completing the various tasks within it.	The evaluation framework specifies timelines for completing some, but not all, tasks within it.	The evaluation framework specifies timelines for completing all tasks within it including when data are collected at various data points, when data are analyzed and interpreted, when the report is finished, and when the findings are reported.
Person(s) responsible	The evaluation framework fails to specify who is responsible for the various tasks within it.	The evaluation framework names people responsible for some, but not all, of the tasks within it.	The evaluation framework states clearly who is responsible for which tasks within it including who collects, manages, analyzes, interprets, and reports data.
Feasibility/ appropriateness	The program director and primary stakeholders have not reviewed and approved the evaluation framework for feasibility and appropriateness for the resources, purpose of the evaluation, and usefulness.	The program director and primary stakeholders have reviewed the evaluation framework for feasibility and appropriateness for the resources, purpose of the evaluation, and usefulness.	The program director and primary stakeholders have reviewed and approved the evaluation framework for feasibility and appropriateness for the resources, purpose of the evaluation, and usefulness. The evaluator confirms that the evaluation framework is within his or her level of expertise.

Planning Phase

- Assess evaluability
- Formulate evaluation questions
- Construct the evaluation framework

Conducting Phase

- Collect data
- Organize, analyze, and display data
- Interpret data

Reporting Phase

- Report, disseminate, and use findings
- Evaluate the evaluation

Collect Data

7

In this stage, the evaluator is gathering data as planned and being thoughtful about altering the data plan to ensure that the data needed to answer the evaluation questions are collected. Alterations might include collecting less or more data, changing the data-collection method, or changing the time when data are collected. If the evaluation framework was thoughtfully planned, alterations will be limited, yet even with the best plans, evaluators may find reasons to make changes. If a plan to interview program participants proves too challenging to schedule or an insufficient number of participants agree to be interviewed, the evaluator may opt to use focus groups or a survey to supplement data collected from the completed interviews or to replace interviews completely. In another situation, while collecting data during focus groups, an evaluator hears that principal support has been an influential factor in teachers' application of new learning, the evaluator might decide to interview principals to learn more about how they are supporting teacher application.

Evaluators also consider the implications of creating a data burden that negatively influences the program. A data burden might result from collecting too much data or a data-collection method that requires significant investment or effort from data sources, such as asking them to do extra work. Data burden might disrupt the program because it distracts participants or causes them to lose interest in the program.

Questions the evaluator asks at this stage include the following:

1. Are the data sources and data-collection methods yielding the intended data and considered credible by key stakeholders?

2. What problems are occurring in the data-collection process, and how are they being resolved?

3. What other data might be useful to collect to expand usefulness of the evaluation and enrich responses to the evaluation questions?

4. What data are redundant and might be reduced or eliminated?

5. How do I manage the data collected?

6. How can I ensure accuracy and precision in the data-collection process?

In their extensive discussion of the pitfalls of evaluations, Harry Hatry and Kathryn Newcomer (2015) identify several problems related to data collection. Many problems they identify will be overcome by carefully completing steps 1–3 of the evaluation process. Several problems involving the collection of data are discussed in this chapter.

SELECTING DATA COLLECTORS

The data collector has the potential to influence the data collected. If an interviewer behaves in a way that is not culturally sensitive to a respondent, the respondent may not respond naturally or truthfully. If a focus group facilitator tends to listen to those in the group with greater authority than those who have less, the responses of the group will be skewed. If a professional learning program director administers surveys and observes respondents completing them, respondents may feel intimidated and respond as they think the director prefers. If a principal asks staff members to share artifacts or documents, staff members may select their best examples rather than a range of examples, thus skewing the pool of artifacts.

Evaluators consider the effect of data collectors on their sources and seek to mitigate overly negative or positive effects. A neutral person is preferable, for example, than a supervisor as an interviewer. A person without direct responsibility for the program's success is preferable to someone involved in the program. Each data collector has an ethical responsibility to practice unbiased data collection and acknowledges perceived biases that might influence his or her neutrality or ability to collect the data honestly, accurately, and with integrity.

PILOTING INSTRUMENTS, DIRECTIONS, AND PROTOCOLS

To ensure that the data-collection process runs as smoothly as possible and yields valid, reliable, and credible results, it is mandatory to pilot all instruments, directions, and protocols prior to full implementation of the data collection and make any adjustments needed. Sometimes the smallest issues may create major problems for participants. If evaluators know these problems in advance of the full-scale data-collection process, they can be corrected. If, for example, a focus group protocol involves a question that is stated in terms that will be unfamiliar to those in the focus group, the validity of the responses will be diminished.

The pilot test helps the evaluator determine whether the instrument's directions, or protocols, are effective in collecting the needed data, the directions are clear, the time allocated is appropriate, and whether respondents encounter any unanticipated problems. The evaluator analyzes instruments and protocols used in the pilot test to assess whether the responses parallel what he or she expected and whether there are any items or questions that were consistently skipped or caused confusion. Asking participants to comment on their experience during the pilot data collection is another way to learn about the effectiveness and efficiency of the data-collection process. Evaluators might use a process called cognitive laboratory in which a representative set of respondents complete the instrument or engage in the protocol and simultaneously state what they think as they are responding. This type of process alerts the evaluator to language, vocabulary, or syntax that present some form of bias.

TRAINING DATA COLLECTORS

Sometimes evaluators engage others to collect data in the field. The field might be a classroom, school, team meeting, or a professional learning session. Those who gather data for the same evaluation must accurately and consistently collect data to ensure that the data are valid and reliable. Hatry and Newcomer (2015) recommend that "consultation among data collectors should continue throughout the data collection phase or the evaluation. Initial training may not adequately anticipate all the context-specific challenges for data collectors" (p. 708). Intentionally preparing data collectors increases data collectors' accuracy and the consistency.

Training for data collectors includes

- program overview;
- review of all data-collection instructions and guidelines;
- discussion of problems that may occur during data collection;
- practice session, where data collectors complete some or all the data-collection processes or instruments themselves;
- discussion about respondent confidentiality;
- strategies for managing and keeping data in a safe place;
- procedures for submitting data; and
- sources of help when problems occur.

If the data-collection process is complex, a written manual as a reference with the information above is helpful for data collectors.

MANAGING DATA COLLECTION

The ease of managing data collection depends on the specificity of the data plan. If the plan clearly delineates who will collect the data, where the data will be

collected, when the data will be collected, and how the data will be collected, data collection is likely to run smoothly. A master schedule of the data-collection process can help track the activities and provide a checklist to ensure that steps are not missed. It is advisable to have one person or a team, depending on the scope of the data-collection process, responsible for monitoring all data-collection activities. For example, one person might be responsible for collecting student data, another might collect teacher data, and a third might collect school documents and artifacts.

Because data may be cumbersome, evaluators compensate by establishing a specific place and specific format for all collected data. Data systems available in many education agencies and school systems may reduce the cost and burden of data collection, yet they may require new queries or even programming to yield the necessary data. Evaluators work closely with the data system managers to develop or specify the parameters for templates or input systems for collecting data and determine who will be responsible for inputting data—the evaluator, data collectors, or someone else. The evaluator also ensures that those responsible for inputting data are doing so accurately and periodically cross-check data input for that purpose. If others will work with data to organize it, for example, the evaluator specifies the parameters for such organization.

Another consideration for data systems is ensuring that any data are safeguarded and kept confidential, especially if they involve any information about human subjects. To manage this, an evaluator carefully determines who has access to or uses the data collected.

Yet another consideration in managing the data collection process is monitoring for inappropriate involvement in the data-collection process of program directors, managers, or providers to avoid any contamination of the data or subjective biases.

The evaluator monitors the data-collection process by

1. creating a firm timeline for collecting and submitting data;

2. making random observations of the data-collection process;

3. checking with respondents to determine whether the data have been collected;

4. ensuring the safekeeping of all data; and

5. viewing the data-collection process as a part of the program itself.

Administration of Children, Youth, and Families, U.S. Department of Health and Human Services. (n.d.). *A program manager's guide to evaluation.* Retrieved December 21, 2006, from www.acf.hhs.gov/programs/opre/other_resrch/ pm_guide_eval/index.html

SCHEDULING DATA COLLECTION

A data plan is developed during the design of the evaluation framework, yet sometimes in the program's implementation, the timing for data collection is off. The evaluator may find that it is too early to collect data. Perhaps the program started later than anticipated or the participants were not ready to implement as scheduled. Sometimes unexpected situations interrupt the program, such as a change in priorities or an unexpected task that requires completion. In other cases, the preconditions may be at an unusually low, crisis, or non-normal point so a program's true effect is not fully known. For example, if student behavior in a school following a community incident involving gangs reached a low point, a school's program to address the situation through professional learning may demonstrate higher-than-normal positive effect because the starting point had been exacerbated by the incident. In these situations, the evaluator is faced with a decision regarding adjusting the data-collection schedule or in the case of the student behavior to change the pretest date to another time, such as a mean of the previous three years, to reflect a more accurate picture of the current state.

ADDING OR ELIMINATING PLANNED DATA COLLECTION

The success of the evaluation depends on the quality of the data. Occasionally during the data-collection process, evaluators may realize that important data are not being collected. This is not unusual. The evaluator may find some unanticipated information in a series of interviews with students that leads her to wonder whether teachers' views about the same question parallel those of their students. If this seems important, the evaluator may add a question to teacher interviews to triangulate the information she is collecting from students. The evaluator may also find redundancies in the data and may consider eliminating one data source, although this decision should be made with great care so as not to compromise the ability to triangulate data.

ACCOUNTING FOR DROP-OFFS

One challenge evaluators face is drop-off in program participants and evaluation informants. Changes in key stakeholders, such as program administrators or providers, participant engagement, or pre- and posttest respondents, are some types of drop-offs that evaluators can expect. Some of the changes are natural attrition, yet other forms might be investigated for their impact on the professional learning program's impact. If, for instance, teachers in one school opt out of a professional learning program after it begins and they are a part of the treatment group, the effect on the evaluation will be significant if the sample size does not account for the drop-off or if the drop-off decreases the representative nature of the treatment group. Holding interviews or focus groups

with teachers who opted-out can provide the evaluator with insights about the reasons for their decision. The evaluator can probe to determine if program burden, management, or support contributed to their decision, as this information will be particularly useful to the evaluation.

SCORING INSTRUMENTS

The data-collection process might include scoring instruments, tests, or artifacts. If, for example, professional learning program participants complete an interview, the interviewer may be asked to code the interview and enter the codes, key words, phrases, or terms in an electronic recordkeeping tool. If data collectors gather artifacts as evidence, they might be asked to identify features of the artifact and record those. To ensure that the scoring process is accurate and consistent if there is more than one scorer, data collectors receive training to ensure interrater reliability. If computerized scoring is used, periodic checks on the data can prevent any major problems.

Knowing the kind of scores needed for the analysis and producing those will eliminate having to repeat scoring. Table 7.1 describes the most common types of scores that can be produced from quantitative data and how those data are used.

Table 7.1 Types of Scores and Their Uses

Score	Definition	Compared With
Raw score	The number of items answered correctly (assuming there are correct and incorrect responses).	Nothing
Percentile	Scores range from 1 to 99 and indicate the percentage of students scoring at or lower than the test score in question; percentiles cannot be averaged, summed, or combined because the differences between percentile points are not equal.	Norm group
Mastery scores	Notation that indicates a level of performance typically based on a range of raw scores.	Test group or defined criterion performance
Standard scores	A recalculation of the raw score that provides equal-interval scales for comparison across students and tests and for mathematical calculations; includes NCEs and scaled scores.	Norm group
Stanines	Rough approximations of an individual's performance relative to the performance of others in the group; scores are divided into nine equal groups ranging from 1 to 9, with 1 being the lowest.	Norm group
Rubrics	Descriptors representing a range from excellent to poor performance to guide scoring of tasks or products.	Criteria-based performance
Gain scores	Score indicating how much a student has improved or progressed; typically a problematic score because the reliability and validity of the pre- and posttest may doubly impact the gain score; gain scores may have different meanings at different points on the scale.	Self; cohort group

Data collection requires methodical and systematic processes that include substantial detail and frequent cross-checks. At all phases of the data-collection process, steps must be precise and accurate. Erring at this point jeopardizes the evaluator's ability to analyze data accurately and form valid conclusions. While timing can influence the results, those involved in gathering data allocate enough time to the data-collection step to ensure that the work can be done with care.

Table 7.2 delineates the salient components of the fourth step of the evaluation process. It can guide the evaluator in assessing the preparation for and the completeness and accuracy of the data-collection process.

Table 7.2 Data Collection Rubric

Data Collection	Not Ready to Collect Data	Revise Before Collecting Data	Ready to Collect Data
Selecting data collectors	Data collectors have a vested interest in the program's success or failure.	Data collectors understand the impact of their biases on the evaluation, yet have not been screened for neutrality.	All data collectors are neutral, unbiased, and trained in maintaining objectivity toward the program, its participants, and the results of the evaluation.
Piloting instruments, directions, and protocols	The evaluator does not pilot instruments, directions, or protocols.	The evaluator pilots instruments, directions, or protocols.	The evaluator pilots instruments, directions, or protocols with multiple respondents and revises them based on the pilot results.
Training data collectors	Data collectors receive no training in the use of the instruments, directions, and protocols.	Data collectors receive training in the use of the instruments, directions, and protocols.	Data collectors receive training in the use of the instruments, directions, and protocols and practice using them before collecting data.
Managing data collection	The evaluator develops an inadequate system for managing data collection.	The evaluator develops a structured, orderly system for managing data collection and storage; for safeguarding and maintaining confidentiality of the data collected; and for ensuring that no inappropriate involvement of those responsible for the program occurs.	The evaluator develops a structured, orderly system with redundancies to monitor for accuracy and consistency for managing data collection and storage; for safeguarding and maintaining confidentiality of the data collected; and for ensuring that no inappropriate involvement of those responsible for the program occurs. Data collectors receive training on using the system for data management.

(Continued)

Table 7.2 (Continued)

Data Collection	Not Ready to Collect Data	Revise Before Collecting Data	Ready to Collect Data
Scheduling data collection	The evaluator schedules data collection in the construction of the evaluation framework and does not revisit the planned schedule.	The evaluator schedules data collection in the construction of the evaluation framework and reviews and adapts the schedule to accommodate changes in program implementation.	The evaluator schedules data collection in the construction of the evaluation framework and reviews and adapts the schedule to accommodate changes in program implementation and to eliminate undue low points in preconditions if a pretest is used. The evaluator considers and responds to the impact of the timing of data collection on data sources.
Adding or eliminating planned data collection	The evaluator makes no accommodations in the data-collection procedure for adding or eliminating data collection.	The evaluator acknowledges needed additional data or redundancies in data collected, yet does not alter the data-collection procedure.	The evaluator is sensitive to the need for additional data or for redundancies in data. The evaluator adjusts the data-collection procedure to collect additional needed data and eliminate redundant data.
Accounting for drop-offs	The evaluator makes no accommodations for accounting for drop-offs in respondents.	The evaluator addresses drop-offs in respondents and analyzes the remaining sample or pool of respondents to ensure that it represents all participants.	The evaluator addresses drop-offs in respondents and analyzes the remaining sample or pool of respondents to ensure that it represents all participants. The evaluator investigates reasons for program attrition, particularly those related to the program's design or implementation, and plans to report those reasons as a part of the evaluation.
Scoring instruments	Data collectors receive no training in scoring or coding data collected and inputting data into the data management system.	Data collectors receive training in scoring or coding data collected and inputting it into the data management system.	Data collectors receive training in scoring or coding data collected and inputting it into the data management system. Redundancies are in place to cross-check for accuracy and interrater reliability in scoring procedures.

Organize, Analyze, and Display Data

8

Organizing, analyzing, and displaying collected data are the initial processes in transforming words and numbers into meaning. The other parts include interpreting analyzed data and reporting the results. According to Michael Quinn Patton (2008), data analysis involves "organizing raw data into an understandable form that reveals basic patterns and constitutes the evaluation's empirical findings" (p. 478). The goal of data organization, analysis, and display is to create a set of manageable information by sorting, arranging, and processing the data collected (Weiss, 1998). The consistent use of thorough and methodical processes is the hallmark of a successful data analyst. John Creswell (2002) describes analyzing data in quantitative research as both statistical analysis and "describing trends, comparing group differences, or relating variables" (p. 55). In qualitative data, he continues, data analysis includes text analysis and "describing the information and developing themes" (p. 55). Since each analysis is a unique, dynamic, evolving process, the process is time-consuming, yet filled with discoveries. Throughout the data analysis process, the evaluator is constantly looking at new ways to combine, unpack, rearrange, and connect data to understand the program being evaluated. In their chapter on qualitative data analysis, Delwyn Goodrick and Patricia Rogers (2015, p. 593) cite this statement by Janice Morse (1994) as a description of the qualitative data analysis process:

> Data analysis is a process that requires astute questioning, a relentless search for answers, active observation, and accurate recall. It is a process of piecing together data, of making the invisible obvious or recognizing the significance from the insignificant, of linking seemingly unrelated facts logically, of fitting categories one with another, and of attributing consequences to antecedents. It is a process of conjecture and verification, of correction and modification, of suggestion and

defense. It is a creative process of organizing data so that the analytic scheme will appear obvious. (Morse, 1994, p. 25)

Data analysis is a process that typically causes some anxiety in educators because they remember their graduate school statistics courses. Yet, data analysis does not always require statistics. It might involve descriptive processes such as counting, **clustering**, sorting, finding patterns, and calculating differences rather than inferential statistics.

Practitioner evaluators bring into this work their years of experience in analyzing student data. Since the inception of the *No Child Left Behind Act* of 2001 and even prior to it, educators in schools have been deeply immersed in analyzing a wide variety of student learning data for accountability purposes and improvement efforts. The practices of examining data, disaggregating it by student group, and making sense of it apply to data analysis in the evaluation of professional learning. Perhaps unlike some steps of the evaluation process, this step should be familiar to practitioners. The key difference is that in addition to student learning data, evaluations of professional learning frequently require the addition of data about educator learning.

The evaluator answers several questions while engaged in quantitative or qualitative data analysis in this step of the evaluation process:

1. How will I organize, sort, and arrange the data collected to prepare it for analysis?

2. What types of data analysis will I use to examine the data?

3. How can I display the analyzed data to facilitate data interpretation?

4. How can I formulate descriptions of the analyzed data to facilitate data interpretation?

5. How will I involve stakeholders in all aspects of the analysis process?

Evaluators make decisions about data analysis during the construction of the evaluation framework. Readers may want to review Table 6.6 to refresh their understanding of qualitative and quantitative analysis. The procedures for data analysis are presented here because they occur at this point in the process. Evaluators base their decisions on the evaluation's purpose, planned uses, questions, data sources, and data-collection methods. Sometimes, depending on the success of the data-collection process, the evaluator adjusts the planned analyses of the data-collection plan, especially if data have been eliminated or others added.

Two products emerge from data analysis. The first is the analyzed data displayed in multiple formats. The second is a set of findings that are statements describing or summarizing the analyzed data. Depending on the evaluation questions, the data displays might provide a depiction of the overall program results, deeper analyses of some aspects of the program, or a combination of both. For example, the evaluator, in answering the overall program evaluation question regarding the effect of a professional learning program on educator and student learning, might decide to take a closer look at data from two schools, one where the results were high and one where the results were low, to

uncover factors that might have influenced the difference. So, in addition to looking at the overall program effects on the aggregated group of educators, schools, and students, the evaluator takes this opportunity to engage in further analysis to enrich the meaning of the data and the usefulness of the evaluation.

ORGANIZING DATA

Evaluators can drown in data. The more streamlined and condensed the data processes are, the easier the analysis will be. If, for example, the evaluator is reviewing data from **extant data** sources, it may make more sense to extract the informative sections, sort them, and work solely with the extracted sections than to work with an entire artifact. Advances in technology make the work of managing databases much easier than just a few years ago. While reducing the data set can make them more manageable, evaluators should be careful not to eliminate any useful data or alter the data in ways that might skew their meaning. The evaluator may lose the ability to triangulate or conduct an in-depth analysis if any data are lost or eliminated. Triangulation is the examination of data from multiple data sources or multiple data collection formats to find alignment. Triangulation might occur if multiple observers, a coach, peer, and principal, were observing classroom practice or if a survey, interview, and work product were examined for information about teacher practice. For example, the evaluator may decide to take a closer look at one school's data to understand better what occurred in the program in this school since it was the highest performing one in the district's pool of schools participating in the professional learning program. The evaluator should always have such options at any point in the data analysis and interpretation processes. Sometimes the extraneous data may provide opportunities to understand what factors influence success or failure in specific contexts.

Organizing data requires several steps. Developing coding systems for organizing data, sorting data into categories, and formulating and testing the viability of the categories with some of the data to ensure the categories accurately reflect the full range of data collected are processes in which the evaluator needs proficiency. Proficiency in organizing data includes accuracy, clarity, and consistency. Being flexible early in the data-organizing process and testing coding systems and categories ensures that the final categories are the most logical for further analysis.

Another task in data organization is handling missing data. If half the sample of third-grade teachers did not respond to a survey on how often they used a new instructional strategy, the evaluator must decide what to do about the missing survey responses. He might ponder whether he sent sufficient notifications to teachers about responding, the communication system broke down, or the lack of response was caused by some unanticipated situation. In these cases, the evaluator might choose to extend the deadline, engage principals in understanding the lack of responses or seeking their assistance in collecting the surveys, and, if possible, talk with some teachers to understand the lack of response. Sometimes, despite a well-planned and executed data collection, data

are missing. The rate of attrition and its effect on the representativeness of the pool of respondents are issues to examine fully. Missing data issues occur frequently in pretest–posttest designs where there may be a pretest and no posttest or vice versa. Sometimes this problem occurs in coding the data collection to maintain anonymity. Careful coding systems can help eliminate some missing data problems.

The evaluator may engage stakeholders in exploring options related to missing data. Ultimately, the evaluator decides whether to fill in the data gaps and how to do so, seek the missing data, devise a method to indicate that the data are missing, or perhaps opt for some combination of these tactics. The evaluator reports decisions about handling missing data in the evaluation report.

The last part of the data-organization process is to examine any abnormalities in data that may influence or affect the analysis process. The evaluator is particularly looking for any illegitimate or irrelevant data. Some of these abnormalities are incorrect codes, typographical or data entry errors, or extraneous data outside the scope of the evaluation. The evaluator especially reviews the outliers in the data to check for their accuracy. Occasionally the information that falls beyond the scope of the evaluation may be useful to the program directors, even if it is not useful to the evaluator. For example, if a series of interviews were used, the evaluator would list all the responses to one question together and carefully review the list to determine whether any response is not related to the topic of the question. The response might be related to another question in the interview or deemed unrelated to any question and set aside for later review and consideration. Or, in looking at a set of numerical scores, the evaluator might notice that one response is a 6 from a range of *five* possible responses. The evaluator returns to the original data set to find the correct response and replaces the incorrect response with the correct one. Careful organization of the data ensures that the data analysis is based on the most complete and accurate data rather than spurious information.

DATA-ANALYSIS METHODS

While the data-analysis process can be complex, it need not be. The evaluation questions are the primary factors in choosing an analysis method. All analyses involve the examination of one or more variables. In evaluations of the professional learning programs the common variables are changes in educator practice and their effects on participants' clients. When a single variable is analyzed in an evaluation, the evaluation is a **univariate analysis**. For example, measuring changes in educator performance before and after the professional learning program is a univariate analysis. When two variables are analyzed, the analysis is bivariate. An example is examining differences in the implementation of new instructional practices with differences in student scores on benchmark assessments. When three or more variables are examined, the analysis is considered multivariate. An example of a **multivariate analysis** might be examining the teacher perception of level of support, level of implementation, and student results.

Analyses also use two types of data that yield different kinds of results. Like the evaluation designs, they are quantitative (numbers) and qualitative (words, documents, artifacts) and are based on the types of data collected.

Quantitative analyses. Quantitative analyses are required in experimental and quasi-experimental evaluations. Quantitative analyses can be either complex or simple. Descriptive statistics, such as numbers, counts, percentages, means, or ranges, are simpler forms of quantitative data analysis. A common data-analysis method is calculating the mean or mean differences. Means are best when reported with both the range of scores and the standard deviation. Standard deviation is a measure of the variation among scores. Software programs make the calculation of descriptive and inferential statistics easy. Most practitioner evaluations depend on descriptive statistics to measure change. Sometimes descriptive statistics are coupled with inferential statistics for deeper analysis.

More sophisticated forms of quantitative analyses are inferential statistics for use in experimental and quasi-experimental evaluations. Inferential statistics require that certain conditions be met, such as the size of the treatment and control groups. The use of inferential statistics as tests for significance or measures of association allows the evaluator to determine whether the difference that occurs between two variables such as the pretest and posttest scores of a single sample or between the scores of the treatment and control group is statistically significant. A test for significance allows the evaluator to determine whether something more than chance produced the differences that occurred, namely the professional learning program. Statistical operations never fully eliminate error in estimating that a relationship exists; they merely specify the probability that an error does exist because there are multiple factors—sampling, evaluator bias, simple mistakes, or data validity or reliability—that may can cause errors in estimating a relationship.

Qualitative analyses. Qualitative analyses are used when the data are not numerical. Qualitative analyses seek patterns or themes within words across the various data sources using induction. In some evaluations, however, an evaluator may code or categorize the responses into numerical values to use in quantitative analyses. In open-ended survey responses, for instance, the evaluator seeks to find patterns or commonalities among the responses. Each one becomes a category. To conduct a qualitative analysis, the evaluator usually identifies the categories of responses, labels each category, and tests the categories against the open-ended responses. Once the evaluator is comfortable with the categories, he assigns each response to a category. The evaluator may count the number of times respondents' responses fit into each category, thereby turning the qualitative data into quantitative data. In these cases, evaluators will want to be sure they can associate the responses with the respondent to examine patterns that may exist among them. The evaluator will want to know if the differences in the category of responses in an interview are associated with other factors such as the years of experience. In this case, the evaluator may want to examine if other factors are associated with novice teachers, those

who have taught less than three years, or higher levels of implementation when compared to teachers who have taught for more than 10 years. This form of analysis then requires the evaluator to disaggregate responses by various types or attributes of respondents, much in the same way educators examine how students in different populations perform.

Evaluators who have collected demographic data, either about the participants, the participants' work environments, or the participants' clients, in their data-collection process may want to use the demographics as one variable and compare it to a program variable for a bivariate analysis. An example might be comparing the impact of a professional learning program on novice principals to its effect on more experienced principals. Another way of using demographic data is to compare the effects of a professional learning program on teachers in schools with large populations of students with limited English with schools with smaller populations of students with limited English.

In bivariate and multivariate analyses, the evaluator seeks to find relationships among variables. These analyses are applied to quantitative data using inferential statistics such as correlations, *t*-tests, **chi-square**, or analysis of variance. Inferential statistics, when the conditions are met for their use and when evaluators have proficiency in applying them, can increase the reliability and credibility of results.

Evaluators may find that descriptive statistics such as simple differences in means are more useful and meaningful to some stakeholders who will use the evaluation reports. If evaluators anticipate that stakeholders may benefit from an explanation of the analysis procedure, they should include it in the report or presentation of results to eliminate confusion, misinterpretation, or misuse of the results. Practitioner evaluators are more likely to use descriptive statistics because they are comfortable with them, and they are sufficiently powerful to answer many evaluation questions practitioners have.

Theodore Poister (2015) notes that employing a systematic process to analyze the data and gain a holistic picture of what a program's performance looks like first—by examining changes over time in individual key outcome indicators; comparing actual performance against targets; comparing the data against data for other similar programs; breaking the data down by organizational units, geographical areas, or grantees, if service delivery is decentralized; and breaking the data down by other relevant factors such as client characteristics. "Then they can examine trends in multiple outcomes indicators collectively to see whether a composite portrait of a program's performance emerges. In addition, they can assess the meaning of the outcome data in conjunction with other types of performance indicators, such as indicators for outputs, service quality efficiency, or client satisfaction, to get a fuller picture of program operations and performance" (p. 127). There are multiple analysis techniques, and those particularly useful in the evaluation of professional learning are described in Table 8.1. Some evaluations, because of the nature of the evaluation questions, may require two or more different analysis methods.

Table 8.1 Types of Data Analysis

Types of Data Analysis	Definition	Uses	Example
Describing	Narrative portrayal of the program's activities, implementation, and/or effects; frequently accompanied by descriptive statistics, such as mean, median, mode, and range; does not attempt to compare, but rather uses numbers or words to explain, portray, or represent data	Useful in qualitative studies to describe or explain the program, factors influencing effects, or effects; requires descriptive statistics	Written description of the program's purpose, goals, activities, and so on that might include the number of times principals participated in coaching, average frequency of teachers' use of a particular instructional methodology, or the pre- and posttest scores of students when teachers use the instructional strategies; summary of barriers to implementation
Counting	Numerical description of the program, its activities, its participants, and so on; frequently includes descriptive statistics such as mean, median, mode, and range	Useful in qualitative, quantitative, and mixed-method evaluations; requires descriptive statistics	Mean hours of coaching within a professional learning program; percentage of time coaches interact one-on-one with teachers during instruction; percentage of students who achieve proficiency on a particular test; number of times barriers to implementation are mentioned by teachers and principals
Factoring	Algebraic calculation that breaks down and examines the weight of the variables or factors in results achieved	Used in quantitative evaluations; requires inferential statistics	Factors and their weights contributing to student academic success, such as attendance, previous academic work, parents' involvement in school activities, or teacher behaviors; teacher motivation, performance level, principal support, and availability of resources in teachers' implementation of professional learning
Clustering	Formulation of classes, categories, or groups based on common features, characteristics, or attributes	Qualitative or quantitative evaluations to form groups to describe program activities, implementation, participant perceptions of effect and for further analysis of differences; sometimes is a precursor to descriptive or inferential statistics to comparison	Teacher-identified influences in high implementation of new instructional practices; student report on teacher practices that strengthen their reading level; common, reported benefits of the professional learning program for students
Comparing	Examination of the similarities and differences in the features of the participants before, during, and after the program; may be either narrative or numerical using descriptive or inferential statistics	Qualitative and quantitative evaluations; often used with descriptive and inferential statistics	Difference between students' level of success on a classroom performance task in geography before their teachers began examining student work with their peers measured against students' level of success on a classroom performance task in geography after their teachers regularly examined student work with their peers

(Continued)

Table 8.1 (Continued)

Types of Data Analysis	Definition	Uses	Example
Finding trends and patterns	Identification of recurring patterns, trends, or commonalities, most often in qualitative data	Useful for qualitative evaluations to make sense of text-based data; requires qualitative data	Students' use of scientific language when describing their lab activities; novice principals' biggest challenges
Examining outliers	Identification and study of data at the extreme ends of a data set to determine what, if anything, is different from data tending more toward the mean	Useful in qualitative and quantitative evaluations	Looking at attributes of teachers with low implementation scores, yet whose students perform at the high end of student scores
Finding covariation	Examination of concurrent attributes where changes in one feature occur in tandem with changes in another attribute or vice versa	Useful in quantitative evaluations, although can be used in qualitative evaluations; requires quantitative data for numerical **covariations**, yet may be narrative	Increase in teachers' use of writing to learn in social studies and math and the increase in students' proficiency on the schoolwide writing sample in language arts
Eliminating rival explanations	Use of data to rule out other plausible explanations for the changes observed	Useful in both quantitative and qualitative evaluation; examines anomalies, trends, or patterns; appropriate for either qualitative or quantitative data	Improvement in students' performance in history is better explained by teacher implementation of new instructional strategies than by students' increased attendance
Modeling	Depiction of how a program works with a graphic display that shows relationships, sequence, and significance of program activities	Useful in quantitative and qualitative evaluations, and strengthened with inferential statistics that calculate the power of the relationship	Diagrams of how the coaching influences teacher and student learning; timing of principal intervention in the teacher professional learning program

Table 8.2 provides some evaluation questions with examples of appropriate descriptive and inferential statistical analysis techniques.

Evaluators use both qualitative and quantitative analyses in their evaluations, yet to measure impact or effect of a professional learning program on educator practice and their clients' practice or learning, evaluators need a form of comparisons, calculated with either descriptive or inferential statistics. When evaluators seek to answer questions such as did the professional learning program contribute to or cause changes in educator practice or in student learning, the evaluator must be able to compare minimally two sets of data. The comparison might be between pre- and posttest results of program participants, posttest scores of participants in the professional learning and nonparticipants, or possibly between high and low implementers.

Table 8.2   Sample Questions and Appropriate Analyses

Evaluation Question	Analysis With Descriptive Statistics	Analysis With Inferential Statistics
Did professional learning increase teacher content knowledge?	Comparing pre- and post-knowledge	Examining the weight of factors related to teachers with pre- and post-professional learning content knowledge, such as years of teaching, previous experience with the professional learning content, grade or subject taught
Did principals who more frequently and accurately implemented instructional leadership strategies acquired in professional learning feel more supported than principals with low implementation?	Comparing high- and low-implementation	Finding covariation
Do teachers' use of social-emotional learning strategies influence students' sense of belonging in the school and classroom?	Describing	Factoring; finding covariance; comparing
Does the type of coaching interactions influence teachers' use of new instructional strategies?	Describing; comparing; clustering	Factoring; finding covariance

Evaluations of professional learning programs might include comparisons of

- teachers' frequency of use of the instructional methodologies with student performance;
- teachers' performance levels compared to those defined in the goal (univariate analysis);
- performance, work products such as assignments or lesson/unit plans, and student performance of teachers who participated in the professional learning program to those of teachers who have not participated in the professional learning program (multivariate analysis);
- the content knowledge of teachers who participated in the professional learning program and their students' performance on benchmark assessments to the content knowledge of teachers who did not participate in the professional learning program and their students' performance (bivariate analysis); and
- performance of the same group of students before their teachers participated in the professional learning program and after their teachers' participation (univariate analysis).

A useful way to examine the impact of a professional learning program using a bivariate analysis is comparing educators' level of proficiency or implementation (as determined through classroom observations or self-report) with

Table 8.3   Sample Bivariate Analysis for the Evaluation of Professional Learning

Educator Level of Proficiency/ Implementation	Client Performance Scores
High	X
Medium	X
Low	X

a variable related to their clients, such as student performance on an assessment. A display of this analysis technique appears in Table 8.3.

One caution associated with bivariate or multivariate analysis is the tendency to infer a causal (attribution) relationship among data sets when the data and analysis permit only inferences about a relationship (contribution), its strength, and direction. Maintaining clarity about attribution and contribution even in the analysis step serves evaluators well moving forward.

Practitioner evaluators who feel uncertain about their own capability in using descriptive or inferential statistics can seek support from someone more knowledgeable in the area. Applying the most appropriate analysis procedures is an ethical responsibility of an evaluator and one that has serious consequences in the credibility and ultimately the usability of an evaluation if done inaccurately.

INVOLVING OTHERS IN ANALYSIS

Engaging the program directors and/or stakeholders in the data-analysis process has several benefits. It may increase their understanding of the data used in the analysis, their perceived value of the evaluation, and the usefulness of the evaluation. It may also identify areas to illuminate, emphasize, or dig deeper into the evaluation report. Ultimately, as Patton (2008) notes, they are the ones who will use the analyzed data to make subsequent decisions about the program. Involvement of others in data analysis depends on their level of comfort and competence with data analysis. Evaluators may decide that it is more appropriate to involve others in the interpretation phase rather than in the data-analysis phase.

Patton (2008) recommends increasing stakeholders' comfort with and ability to analyze data. He suggests two approaches, a simulated analysis that "involves fabricating possible results and interpreting the action implications from the made-up data" (pp. 472–473). He continues, "The simulated analysis is a check on the design to make sure that all the relevant data for interpretation and use are going to be collected. (remember this session occurs before actually gathering data). All too often, at the analysis stage, and after data collection, evaluators and stakeholders realize that they forgot to ask an important question" (p. 473). He adds that the simulated use session, in which the

analyzed data are used to make decisions, "prepares stakeholders for the real analysis later" (p. 473). The simulated use exercise helps set realistic expectations for the results, including strengths and limitations of the evaluation design. The simulated use exercise helps stakeholders explore their expectations about the professional learning program, prepares them to engage productively in the analysis of authentic data, builds interest in the data-analysis process and their commitment to use the data, and helps the evaluator refine the data-collection process. It gives the evaluator a concrete basis for knowing whether the results are like those expected by stakeholders. Evaluators use this information about similarity or discrepancy in writing their evaluation report. When the discrepancy is substantial, evaluators may add more detail and evidence to support their conclusions. Comparing stakeholder expected results with the actual results often provides them with new insights and an appreciation for the evaluation process.

Questions to Guide Data Analysis

If an evaluator chooses to engage others in the analysis process, he may facilitate the process with a protocol or series of questions to guide the analysis. The questions below provide sample questions that can initiate the process. This list of questions is not exhaustive, and it may be used in a variety of sequences. Sometimes answering one question leads the evaluator to ask and answer other questions. The key purpose of the analysis is to take the data apart, to find relationships, and to identify patterns, trends, or describe the information. It is not to explain or find meaning. That is the purpose of the next step of the evaluation process, interpreting data.

- What percentage of the total population is represented?
- Were groups (year of experience, type of preparation, gender, advanced degrees, age, etc.) within the population adequately and fairly represented?
- What patterns or trends exist in the data?
- What anomalies occur in the data?
- What are the results for the overall group or various groups of participants and their clients?
- How does the performance of various groups differ (e.g., gender, socio-economic status)?
- How consistent are the patterns within a group, such as grade levels, schools, departments, and across groups such as in different departments?
- How do the data compare with other similar data sets (such as last year's or the last several years') or with other schools with similar students?
- What outliers—those responses that fall far from the modal response—exist? How do they differ from the mean, median, or modal responses?

- What strengths and weaknesses are evident in the data?
- What changes occurred in the KASABs (knowledge, attitudes, skills, aspirations, or behaviors) of participants and/or their clients?

Creating a Safe Place for Data Analysis

If the evaluator chooses to include stakeholders and/or participants in the data-analysis process, he or she begins with creating a safe environment for data analysis. When they feel safe in taking risks and being objective, honest, and vulnerable during the data-analysis process, there is greater likelihood that their engagement initiates further change in their practice, more collaboration, and ongoing engagement in data analysis for continuous improvement. If stakeholders and participants feel judged, they will be less objective and open to examining the data. To create a blame-free environment that allows them to participate without fear, the evaluator sets clear norms or agreements for the data-analysis process, such as maintaining confidentiality, focusing on issues not people, and clarifying and addressing the problem rather than finding blame. The evaluator can increase safety by removing names or other identifying indicators or having stakeholders and participants analyze group rather than individual data. By creating a safe environment for the data-analysis process, the sense of safety may transfer to the interpretation process if the same stakeholders and participants are involved.

Encouraging a Collaborative Analysis Process

Organizing and analyzing data require methodical, detail-oriented work, understanding of and ability to conduct various data analyses, and ability to display data analyses visually to facilitate understanding. During this step of the evaluation process, the evaluator is advised to collaborate with stakeholders frequently to ensure that the data analyses and displays are useful and easily understood. The more stakeholders understand and participate in the organization and analysis of data, the less suspicious they will be of the data and how they are used to draw conclusions.

DISPLAYING DATA

How the evaluator displays data often influences how the data are interpreted. The data displays created by the evaluator help others to make sense of the data to contribute to the overall conclusions and recommendations included within the evaluation report. It is helpful if the evaluator displays the same data in multiple formats rather than a single one. In this way, during the interpretation step, stakeholders can identify which display best conveys the data for the intended audience so that the data are most useful. As Theodore Poister notes when discussing performance data (2015), "Presenting data in useful formats can also facilitate what they mean. Thus evaluators . . . are encouraged to use

a variety of display formats (dashboards, spreadsheets, graphs, pictures, and maps) to present performance data clearly. They are also urged to keep presentations simple and straightforward and to focus on conveying meaningful information effectively rather than presenting glitzy visuals" (p. 127).

Data displays typically include charts, graphs, and tables. They might also include models, diagrams, relationship charts, contingency tables, matrices, organization charts, communication pattern diagrams, checklists, theories of change, flowcharts, logic models, decision trees, timelines, **scatterplots**, and process maps. A danger in data analysis and display, as Patton notes (2008), is oversimplification. "In striving for simplicity, one must avoid simplemindedness. This happens most often in evaluation when results are boiled down, in the name of simplicity, to some single number—a single percentage, a single cost-benefit ration, or a single proportion of the variance explained. Striving for simplicity means making the data understandable, but balance and fairness need not be sacrificed in the name of simplicity. Achieving balance may mean that multiple findings have to be represented through several different numbers, all of them presented in an understandable fashion" (p. 481).

The goal of these data displays is twofold: (1) to create a way to display the data to facilitate the interpretation process and (2) to use them to support conclusions formed about the professional learning program.

Several forms of data displays for the same data set follow to show comparisons. Each provides a different view of the data from two elementary schools, both with the same student demographics and levels of student performance in writing on the district writing sample. The writing samples are completed at the end of the school year in Grades 2–6. One school, School A, participated in a professional learning program on the writing process throughout the current school year. The other school, School B, is scheduled to participate in the program in the second year of its districtwide implementation. The district professional learning and curriculum team responsible for the implementation of the program within the district uses a multiple interventions evaluation design to answer the summative evaluation question: Did teacher participation in the professional learning and implementation of the professional learning on the writing process contribute to student writing performance?

The following tables and figures provide examples of the data display techniques. Table 8.4 is a set of raw data, organized by grade level, from the writing professional learning program. It includes teacher and student pretest and posttest scores from two schools, School A and School B.

Table 8.5 extracts the raw data for School B from Table 8.4 and adds the change in teacher and student pretest–posttest scores.

Table 8.6 summarizes the pretest–posttest changes in teacher and student performance for both School A and School B and includes the standard deviation for each.

Table 8.7 summarizes the mean changes in teacher and student pretest–posttest scores by grade level.

Figure 8.1 is a bar chart of the pretest–posttest differences in teacher implementation between School A and School B by grade level.

Table 8.4   School A (N = 32) Raw Scores and Mean Changes Pretest–Posttest

Grades	Ts (listed randomly by grade; coded for anonymity) N = 32	School A: Pretest T implementation scores (Range 1 [low] to 6 [high])	School A: Pretest student scores by teacher (Range 1 [low] to 4 [high])	School A: Posttest T implementation scores (Range 1 [low] to 6 [high])	School A: Posttest student scores by teacher (Range 1 [low] to 4 [high])	School A: Pretest-posttest change in T implementation (Range 0 [no change] to 5 [high degree of change])	School A: Pretest–posttest change in student scores by teacher (Range 0 [no change] to 3 [high degree of change])
Grade 2	1	1	1	3	1	2	0
	2	1	1	5	4	4	3
	3	2	2	6	3	4	1
	4	1	1	2	1	1	0
	5	1	2	5	4	4	2
	6	1	1	1	1	0	0
	7	2	1	3	1	1	0
Grade 3	8	2	1	2	1	0	0
	9	1	2	5	4	4	2
	10	2	1	6	4	4	3
	11	2	3	6	3	4	0
	12	2	1	4	4	2	3
	13	1	1	5	3	4	2
Grade 4	14	1	2	3	3	2	1
	15	2	1	2	1	0	0
	16	2	2	5	4	3	2
	17	1	1	6	4	5	3
	18	1	2	3	2	2	0
	19	2	1	1	1	-1	0
	20	2	2	3	2	1	0

Grades	Ts (listed randomly by grade; coded for anonymity) N = 32	School A: Pretest T implementation scores (Range 1 [low] to 6 [high])	School A: Pretest student scores by teacher (Range 1 [low] to 4 [high])	School A: Posttest T implementation scores (Range 1 [low] to 6 [high])	School A: Posttest student scores by teacher (Range 1 [low] to 4 [high])	School A: Pretest–posttest change in T implementation (Range 0 [no change] to 5 [high degree of change])	School A: Pretest–posttest change in student scores by teacher (Range 0 [no change] to 3 [high degree of change])
Grade 5	21	2	2	2	2	0	0
	22	1	1	4	4	3	3
	23	2	2	5	4	3	2
	24	2	1	5	2	3	1
	25	2	2	6	3	4	1
	26	1	1	4	3	3	2
Grade 6	27	2	2	3	2	1	0
	28	1	1	2	1	1	0
	29	1	1	4	2	3	1
	30	2	2	2	3	0	1
	31	2	2	5	4	3	2
	32	1	2	4	2	3	0
	Grand Mean	1.53	1.50	3.81	2.59	2.28	1.09
	Standard Deviation	0.53		1.50		1.51	

Figure 8.2 is a bar chart of the pretest–posttest differences in student performance between School A and School B by grade level.

Table 8.8 presents the correlation, using **Pearson's** *r*, between student performance and teacher implementation.

Pearson's *r* is an inferential statistic that measures the relationship among two variables to determine the degree of relationship that exists between the variables. The value of a Pearson's *r* ranges from −1 to +1, and the closer the value is to either −1 or +1 the stronger the relationship. A value of +1 indicates that as one variable increases, so does the value of the other one. A value of −1 means that as one variable increases the other decreases.

Figure 8.3 is a bar chart that summarizes the mean pretest–posttest score changes between School A and School B.

Table 8.5 School B (N = 36) Raw Scores and Mean Changes Pretest–Posttest

Grades	Ts (listed randomly by grade; coded for anonymity) N = 36	School B: Pretest T implementation scores (Range 1 [low] to 6 [high])	School B: Pretest student scores by teacher (Range 1 [low] to 4 [high])	School B: Posttest T implementation scores (Range 1 [low] to 6 [high])	School B: Posttest student scores by teacher (Range 1 [low] to 4 [high])	School B: Pretest-posttest change in T implementation (Range 0 [no change] to 5 [high degree of change])	School B: Pretest-posttest change in student scores by teacher (Range 0 [no change] to 3 [high degree of change])
Grade 2	1	1	1	2	1	1	0
	2	1	1	1	1	0	0
	3	2	2	1	2	−1	0
	4	1	2	2	4	1	2
	5	2	2	3	2	1	0
	6	1	2	1	1	0	−1
	7	2	2	1	2	−1	0
	8	1	2	1	2	0	0
Grade 3	9	1	1	2	2	1	1
	10	1	1	1	1	0	0
	11	1	1	1	2	0	1
	12	1	2	1	2	0	0
	13	2	1	2	1	0	0
	14	2	2	2	2	0	0
	15	2	1	3	1	1	0
	16	1	1	1	1	0	0
Grade 4	17	1	2	2	2	1	0
	18	2	3	2	3	0	0
	19	1	2	1	2	0	0
	20	3	2	2	2	−1	0
	21	3	3	5	2	2	−1
	22	2	1	2	1	0	0
	23	2	2	2	2	0	0

Grades	Ts (listed randomly by grade; coded for anonymity) N = 36	School B: Pretest T implementation scores (Range 1 [low] to 6 [high])	School B: Pretest student scores by teacher (Range 1 [low] to 4 [high])	School B: Posttest T implementation scores (Range 1 [low] to 6 [high])	School B: Posttest student scores by teacher (Range 1 [low] to 4 [high])	School B: Pretest–posttest change in T implementation (Range 0 [no change] to 5 [high degree of change])	School B: Pretest–posttest change in student scores by teacher (Range 0 [no change] to 3 [high degree of change])
Grade 5	24	2	2	4	2	2	0
	25	2	2	4	3	2	1
	26	1	1	1	1	0	0
	27	1	2	1	2	0	0
	28	2	1	2	1	0	0
	29	2	1	2	1	0	0
	30	3	3	5	3	2	0
Grade 6	31	1	1	1	2	0	1
	32	2	1	3	1	1	0
	33	2	1	2	1	0	0
	34	1	1	1	1	0	0
	35	2	1	2	1	0	0
	36	1	1	2	1	1	0
	Grand Mean	**1.58**	**1.97**	**1.69**	**2.28**	**0.36**	**0.11**
	Standard Deviation	**0.64**		**0.95**		**0.68**	

Table 8.6 School A Versus School B Change in Means

School	Mean Change in Pretest–Posttest Teacher Implementation	Mean Change in Student Performance Scores on Benchmark
School A mean	2.28	1.09
School A standard deviation	1.51	
School B mean	0.36	0.11
School B standard deviation	0.68	

Table 8.7 School A Versus School B Change in Means by Grade Level

	Grade	School A	School B	Mean Change School A to School B
Mean change in pretest–posttest teacher implementation	2	2.29	0.13	2.16
	3	3.00	0.25	2.75
	4	1.71	0.29	1.42
	5	2.67	0.86	1.81
	6	1.83	0.33	1.50
Mean change in student performance scores on benchmark	2	0.86	0.13	0.73
	3	1.67	0.25	1.42
	4	0.86	−0.14	1.00
	5	1.50	0.14	1.36
	6	0.67	0.17	0.50

Figure 8.1 Mean Change Pretest-Posttest in Teacher Implementation

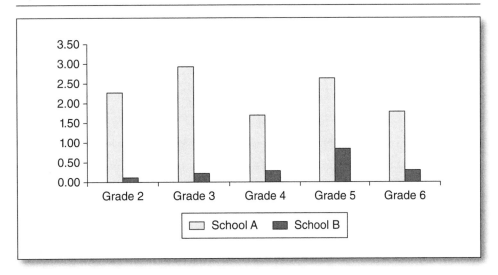

Figure 8.2 Mean Change Pretest–Posttest in Student Scores by Grade

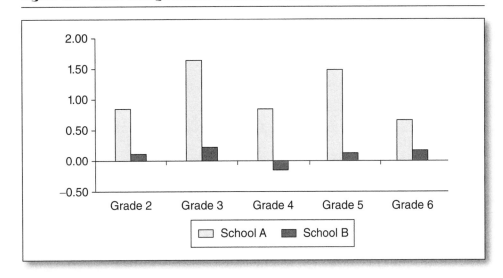

Table 8.8 A School A Versus School B Pearson's *r*

School	Pretest Teacher Implementation by Student Scores	Posttest Teacher Implementation by Student Scores
School A	0.28	0.76
School B	0.64	0.95

Figure 8.3 Pretest–Posttest Change in Means in School A and School B

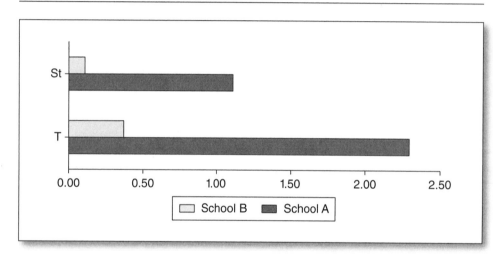

Summarizing Analyzed Data

Statements of finding describe the analyzed data or observations about the data in summary statements. One way to think about this process is grouping independent, isolated bits of information (data) into a more meaningful, yet broader, finding. The diagram below shows the process of moving from analyzed data to a finding.

Figure 8.4 Simple Example of Stating a Finding

Analyzed data
Student scores on district benchmark writing sample from May to May.

Data-analysis method
Comparing student benchmark scores from May prior to implementation of professional learning to May of last year of implementation

Finding
Mean scores for student performance in writing improved by 8 percent.

Table 8.9 is a useful format for constructing findings based on data. The table demonstrates how the evaluator uses data to arrive at a finding.

Table 8.10 displays other findings about the professional learning program in School A and School B.

Findings summarize, describe, or make observations about the analyzed data. They are drawn directly from the data without interpretation or explanation. They are stated succinctly with strong, clear, unbiased language. Findings are rarely disputed. Their meaning and explanations, however, will have different meaning to stakeholders and participants, who bring their different perspectives to make sense of the findings.

The amount of support for a finding matters. If there is one or two points of evidence to support a finding, the finding may not be as strong. When more

Table 8.9 Sample Findings From Data on School A and School B

Data Source and Data-Collection Method	Data/Evidence	Data Analysis	Finding
Teacher observation and self-report using Innovation Configuration Map for implementation of writer's workshop	136 teacher (pretest and posttest) implementation scores (64 in School A and 72 in School B) from combined pretest and posttest observations and self-report scores	Comparing mean change in teacher implementation from pretest to posttest scores for School A and School B	There was a greater change in teacher pretest and posttest scores in School A (2.28) than in School B (0.36).
Student scores on district benchmark writing samples in two years, prior to implementation of professional learning program and year of implementation of professional learning program	1,632 student performance scores (pretest and posttest) (781 from School A and 851 from School B) on two district benchmark writing samples (May of year prior to implementation of the professional learning program and May of the year the professional learning program was implemented)	Comparing change in student performance scores on district benchmark writing sample from pretest (May of year prior to the implementation of the professional learning program) to posttest (May of year in which professional learning program was implemented)	There was a greater change in student pretest–posttest scores in School A (1.09) than in School B (0.11).

Table 8.10 Other Findings About Professional Learning in Writer's Workshop

1.	Teachers who participated in the professional learning on writer's workshop implemented those practices at a higher level than teachers who did not participate in the professional learning.
2.	There is evidence that some teachers who did not participate in the professional learning on writer's workshop did implement some practices associated with writer's workshop.
3.	Students of teachers who participated in the professional learning on writer's workshop performed better on the district benchmark assessment in writing than students of teachers who did not participate.
4.	The professional learning program on writer's workshop positively influences teacher practice and student achievement in the schools where writer's workshop was applied at high levels.

data are used to support a finding, the finding is stronger. Robust findings are those that have multiple types of support and therefore deserve confidence. Triangulation—having data from more than one source to support the finding—is one way to ensure that the findings are robust. If a teacher survey, student achievement data, and an expert all report that teacher practice is changing and student performance is improving when those practices are visible, the finding is stronger. Using quantitative data to support qualitative data or vice versa is another way to triangulate data sources and strengthen the interpretation process. Figure 8.4 is an example of a robust finding with strong support. It describes findings drawn from data about the comparison between 22 high-implementation writer's workshop classrooms, as measured by teacher self-report and principal, coach, and expert observations with 24 low-implementation classrooms. If some data points were missing, the support would be weaker for this finding. A finding that is weaker will be considered differently by the stakeholders, participants, and evaluator when they engage in data interpretation.

Figure 8.5 provides an example of a finding about the writer's workshop professional learning program drawn from the School A and School B data previously presented with its corresponding support from the analyzed data.

Data organization, analysis, display, and summary facilitates the next step of the evaluation process: interpreting the data. When the evaluator chooses to engage others in the process of data analysis, she ensures that they have the capacity to contribute productively to the data-analysis processes being applied, feel safe engaging in the work, and committed to being objective, methodical, and fair. Evaluators can use the rubric in Table 8.11 to check the completeness of the data organization, analysis, and display and summarizing findings step.

Figure 8.5 Sample Finding With Strong Support

> **Finding:** Teachers implementing writer's workshop at high levels have more students performing at higher levels on the district's spring writing benchmark.
>
> <u>Support 1</u>: Teachers report that students enjoy writer's workshop.
>
> <u>Support 2</u>: Students of teachers who implement writer's workshop at high levels perform twice as well as students of teachers who implement writer's workshop at low levels.
>
> <u>Support 3</u>: Seventy-three percent of fifth-grade students in high-implementation classrooms score proficient or above on the state writing assessment compared to 43 percent in low-implementation classrooms.
>
> <u>Support 4</u>: Eighty-four percent of students in high-implementation classrooms in interviews described the writing process accurately compared to 38 percent in low-implementation classrooms.
>
> <u>Support 5</u>: Students in the 22 high-implementation classrooms published 546 books during the school year compared to 187 books in the 24 low-implementation classrooms.
>
> <u>Support 6</u>: School librarians indicate that students in high-implementation classrooms checked out 2.5 times the nonfiction books than students in low-implementation classrooms.
>
> <u>Support 7</u>: Principal walk-through records report observing writer's workshop core components in 83 percent of classrooms visited at least twice compared to 28 percent of low-implementation classrooms.
>
> <u>Support 8</u>: Teachers in high-implementation classrooms report greater satisfaction and enjoyment in teaching writing than teachers in low-implementation classrooms.

Table 8.11 Data Organization, Analysis, and Display and Summarizing Findings Rubric

Data Organization, Analysis, and Display, and Stating Findings	Inaccurate and Incomplete Data Organization, Analysis, and Display	Partially Accurate and Complete Data Organization, Analysis, and Display	Accurate and Complete Data Organization, Analysis, and Display
Considering engagement of stakeholders	The evaluator or evaluation team fails to consider the appropriateness of engaging stakeholders.	The evaluator or evaluation team decides whether to engage stakeholders in the data-analysis process, and if they decide to involve them, invites them.	The evaluator or evaluation team determines the advantages and disadvantages of engaging stakeholders in the data-analysis process, decides based on their consideration, and, if they plan to involve stakeholders, select and prepare them for the data-analysis work. If they decide not to engage stakeholders, they prepare a brief rationale explaining their decision.

Data Organization, Analysis, and Display, and Stating Findings	Inaccurate and Incomplete Data Organization, Analysis, and Display	Partially Accurate and Complete Data Organization, Analysis, and Display	Accurate and Complete Data Organization, Analysis, and Display
Organizing data	The evaluator or evaluation team neglects to organize data by establishing and reviewing categories, codes, or other systems for data organization and checking for and correcting inaccuracies in data entry.	The evaluator or evaluation team organizes data by establishing categories, codes, or other systems for data organization and checking for inaccuracies in data entry.	The evaluator or evaluation team, with the engagement of stakeholders if appropriate, organizes data by establishing and reviewing categories, codes, or other systems for data organization, and checking for and correcting inaccuracies in data entry.
Handling missing data	The evaluator or evaluation team neglects to establish a method for handling missing data or checking the impact of attrition on the data analysis.	The evaluator or evaluation team has a logical and consistent method for handling missing data or checks for the impact of attrition on the data analysis.	The evaluator or evaluation team, with the engagement of stakeholders if appropriate, has a logical and consistent method for handling missing data and checks for the impact of attrition on the data analysis.
Addressing anomalies in the data	The evaluator or evaluation team neglects to review the data for anomalies or to address anomalies in the data.	The evaluator or evaluation team reviews the data for anomalies and yet fails to address them.	The evaluator or evaluation team, with the engagement of stakeholders if appropriate, reviews the data for anomalies and addresses them.
Analyzing data	The evaluator and/or evaluation team apply methods of data analysis that are insufficient, inappropriate, or will not answer the evaluation questions accurately.	The evaluator or evaluation team accurately applies the appropriate data analysis to some data and to answer the evaluation questions.	The evaluator or evaluation team, with the engagement of stakeholders if appropriate, accurately applies the appropriate data analysis to all available data and to answer the evaluation questions.
Displaying data	The evaluator and/or evaluation team do not provide displays of analyzed data.	The evaluator or evaluation team, with the engagement of stakeholders if appropriate, presents the analyzed data in only one format.	The evaluator or the evaluation team, with the engagement of stakeholders if appropriate, displays analyzed data in multiple, useful formats to facilitate interpretation.
Summarizing analyzed data in findings	The evaluator and/or evaluation team states fuzzy findings with inadequate support.	The evaluator or evaluation team, with the engagement of stakeholders if appropriate, makes statements of findings that summarize the analyzed data and are supported by one form of analyzed data.	The evaluator or evaluation team, with the engagement of stakeholders if appropriate, makes clear, logical statements of findings that summarize, make observations about, or describe the analyzed data, and are supported by multiple forms of analyzed data.

Planning Phase

- Assess evaluability
- Formulate evaluation questions
- Construct the evaluation framework

Conducting Phase

- Collect data
- Organize, analyze, and display data
- Interpret data

Reporting Phase

- Report, disseminate, and use findings
- Evaluate the evaluation

Closely linked with data analysis is data interpretation. Many, in fact, view analysis and interpretation as a single step, yet they are treated separately in this process because the distinction is significant. Interpretation is the meaning-making process that comes after the data have been organized, counted, sorted, analyzed, and displayed and requires the engagement of stakeholders and preferably program participants. At this step of the process the evaluator seeks to answer the following questions:

1. Who will be involved in the data interpretation process?

2. What do these analyzed data mean?

3. How do stakeholders and participants interpret these analyzed data?

4. What do these analyzed data mean in terms of the program's future?

5. What recommendations can we (the evaluator, stakeholders, and participants) make about the program and its effects?

Michael Quinn Patton (2015) offers a detailed description of this step of the evaluation process:

Interpretation, by definition, involved going beyond the descriptive data. Interpretation means attaching significance to what was found, making sense of findings, offering explanations, drawing conclusions, extrapolating lessons, making inferences, considering meanings, and otherwise imposing order on an unruly but surely patterned world. The rigors of interpretation and bringing data to bear on explanations include dealing with **rival explanations**, accounting or disconfirming

cases, and accounting for data irregularities as part of testing the viability of an interpretation. All of this is expected—and appropriate—as long as the researchers own the interpretation and make clear the differences between description and interpretation. (p. 570)

Patton (2008) describes how analysis and interpretation differ. Analysis is the first of a four-part process, he says, and "involves organizing raw data into an understandable form that reveals patterns and constitutes the evaluation's empirical findings" (p. 478). Patton states, "*Interpretation involves deciding what the findings mean. How significant are the findings? What explains the results? Even when those receiving evaluation findings agree on the acts and findings, they can disagree vociferously about what the findings mean*" (p. 486; italics in original). Patton (2008) acknowledges that while evaluators and researchers understand the distinction between analysis and interpretation, the stakeholders and participants engaged in the interpretation process often do not. This lack of clarity requires the evaluator to build the capacity of stakeholders and participants to understand the distinction so they can engage fully in the interpretation process.

Patton (2008) also recommends that evaluators emphasize the following four points to distinguish analysis and interpretation and to reinforce the significance of the interpretation process.

1. "Numbers and qualitative data must be interpreted to have meaning. . . . No magic formulas, not even those for statistical significance can infuse meaning into data. Only thinking humans can do that" (Patton, 2008, p. 486).

2. "Data are imperfect indicators or representations of what the world is like" (Patton, 2008, p. 487).

3. "Statistics and qualitative data contain errors" (Patton, 2008, p. 487). Hatry and Newcomer (2015) warn about overreliance on statistical significance and underreliance on practice significance of the program's effect. Most evaluations, they suggest, that use a 95 percent confidence interval may be overkill unless the program involves safety or health elements. Further, they warn that relying solely on "statistical significance as the only criterion for detecting differences can be misleading to officials using the information" (pp. 717–718).

4. "Look for interocular significance" (Patton, 2008, p. 487), the significance that comes from using what lies between one's eyes to examine, question, and explain findings drawn from analyzed data.

Interpretation turns data into meaning. It involves three parts: interpretation, judgment, and recommendations. Patton (2008) delineates the three steps included in the interpretation process: (1) "Interpretation, which involved determining the significance of and explanations for the findings" (p. 478); (2) "judgment, which brings values to bear to determine merit or worth and decide whether the results are positive or negative" (p. 478); and (3) "recommendations, which involve determining the action implications of the findings" (p. 478).

In data interpretation, the evaluator or evaluation team serves as facilitators during meaning-making meetings of stakeholders and participants. Patton (2008) suggests four steps for interpreting data. The first is building agreement among stakeholders and participants on the findings that emerged from the data analysis and organization phase. This happens by reviewing the findings from the analyzed data and drawing conclusions from them. The next step is elaborating possibilities and options to explain the findings. In this step, those engaged in interpretation use data to support their possibilities and options. Because perspectives may differ based on role, experience with the professional learning, or level of engagement with it, there is likely to be a variety of possibilities or options proposed and some may be contradictory.

Once consensus is reached, the stakeholders and participants, facilitated by the evaluator and evaluation team, make their judgments about the program and prepare recommendations about the program. Judgments are grounded in the interpretation of the findings and lead to the evaluator, evaluation team, stakeholders, and participants determining merit and worth of the program, its impact on participants and their clients, and the social justice of a program. These judgments serve as the basis for recommendations related to the program's continuance, discontinuance, upgrades, modifications, or revisions and to extract learnings to inform future professional learning. The recommendations then become the impetus to spur actions on the part of stakeholders. Donna Mertens and Amy Wilson (2012) advise that moving beyond data to recommendations and ultimately actions requires "additional knowledge beyond the evaluative data . . . (e.g., contextual variables, organizational culture, political considerations)" (p. 38).

UNDERSTANDING FINDINGS

The process of interpreting data to explain the findings, make judgments, and formulate recommendations requires inductive thinking. It calls for the evaluator to facilitate conversations of stakeholders and participants to generate explanations for the findings that are useful, logical, significant, and relevant. To facilitate the interpretation process, the evaluator invites stakeholders and participants to answer questions, such as the ones below, to consider multiple possibilities, and to ultimately reach some agreement. The process might begin with a dialogue about how stakeholders and participants understand and feel about the findings and then move to more discussion with the questions below guiding their interaction. To simulate this process, readers may want to gather a small group of colleagues, reviewing the findings in Figure 8.4 on page 153, and facilitating the group's discussion as they answer the questions.

The questions evaluators, joined by stakeholders and participants, answer in the interpretation process include the following:

1. What do these findings mean for this professional learning program?

2. What else might be influencing the results we identified? What other factors were at play during the same time as this program that might have influenced the results? If we had to estimate whether these other factors or the professional learning was more influential, how would we answer and what evidence supports this estimate?

3. What worked, what didn't, and why? How do we know?

4. How do we feel about the set of findings? What prompts those feelings?

5. Which aspects or components of the professional learning program seemed to contribute the most or the least to the outcomes produced?

6. What might have interfered with the program's success?

7. What might have accelerated the changes we noticed?

8. What are the implications of these findings for this professional learning program and others?

9. Does this program have merit and worth? How significant are the merit and worth of this program?

10. Did this program produce the intended outcomes for participants and their clients?

11. Did this program serve those with the greatest need fairly and equitably?

12. What surprised us that we didn't anticipate?

13. What recommendations can we make about the professional learning program based on these findings?

14. What did we learn about professional learning as a result of this evaluation that will help us improve future professional learning?

15. What conclusions can we draw from the evaluation of this professional learning program?

Because alternative interpretations are possible, the evaluator might ask those involved in interpreting data to combine the data and findings in different clusters, perhaps by role group, to explore other possibilities. Interpretations seek to explain why the findings might have occurred, how the findings are perceived by stakeholders and participants, and with other combinations of data or information items. The evaluator can make greatest sense of the findings by trying out several possible interpretations, engaging program stakeholders in dialogue about which interpretations might be most feasible from their perspective, and examining the analyzed data to determine which interpretations are most supportable.

More support makes the finding more credible and harder to ignore and gives the program stakeholders more information to examine possible implications and potential actions as a result of the evaluation. Patton (2008) suggests the use of a claims matrix (Table 9.1) to categorize claims or findings from an evaluation as either major or minor, strong or weak. The claims matrix is a useful tool to help the evaluator determine which findings are more important to present to stakeholders. Patton recommends that evaluators seek to make major claims with strong support.

The most powerful, useful, and credible claims are those that are of major importance and have strong empirical support (Patton, 2008).

Table 9.1 Patton's Claims Matrix

Rigor of Claims	Importance of Claims	
	Major	Minor
Strong	*	
Weak		

Michael Quinn Patton, *Utilization-focused evaluation: A new century text* (4th ed.). Claims Matrix from pp. 498–499. ©2008 by SAGE. Reprinted with permission.

*GOAL: Strong claims of major importance.

The most powerful, useful, and credible claims are those that are of major importance and have strong empirical support.

Characteristics of a Claim of MAJOR IMPORTANCE

- Involves making a difference, having an impact, or achieving desirable outcomes
- Deals with a problem of great societal concern
- Affects large numbers of people
- Provides a sustainable solution (claim deals with something that lasts over time)
- Saves money
- Saves time, that is, accomplishes something in less time than is usually the case (an efficiency claim)
- Enhances quality
- Claims to be "new" or innovative
- Shows that something can actually be done about the problem; that is, claims the problem is malleable
- Involves a model or approach that could be used by others (meaning the model or approach is clearly specified and adaptable to other situations)

Characteristics of a STRONG CLAIM

- Valid, believable evidence to support the claim
- Follow-up data over time (longer periods of follow-up provide stronger evidence than shorter periods, and any follow-up is stronger than just end-of-program results)
- The claim is about a clearly specified outcomes intervention (model or approach) with solid implementation documentation
- The claim is about clearly specified outcomes and impacts: Behavioral outcomes are stronger than opinions, feelings, and knowledge.
- The evidence for claims includes comparisons:
  - To program goals
  - Over time (pre-, post-, follow-up)
  - With other groups
  - With general trends or norms
- The evidence for claims includes replications:
  - Done at more than one site
  - More than one staff person attained outcomes

(Continued)

(Continued)

- o Different cohort groups of participants attained comparable outcomes over time
- o Different programs attained comparable results using comparable approaches
- Claims are based on more than one kind of evidence or data (i.e., triangulation of data):
  - o Quantitative and qualitative data
  - o Multiple sources (e.g., kids, parents, teachers, and staff corroborate results)
- There are clear logical and/or empirical linkages between the intervention and the claimed outcomes
- The evaluators are independent of the staff (or where internal evaluation data are used, an independent, credible person reviews the results and certifies the results)
- Claims are based on systematic data collection over time

CAVEAT

Importance and rigor are not absolute criteria. Different stakeholders, decision makers, and claims makers will have different definitions of what is important and rigorous. What staff deem to be of major importance may not be so to outside observers. What is deemed important and rigorous changes over time and across contexts. Making public claims is a political action. Importance and rigor are, to some extent, politically defined and dependent on the values of specific stakeholders.

Related Distinctions

1. Program *premises* are different from but related to and dependent on program *claims*.

   Premises are the basic assumptions on which a program is based, for example, that effective, attentive parenting is desirable and more likely to produce well-functioning children who become well-functioning adults. This premise is based on *research*. The program cannot "prove" the premise (though supporting research can and should be provided). The program's claims are about the program's actual implementation and concrete outcomes; for example, a program might claim that the program yielded more effective parents who are more attentive to their children. The program does not have to follow the children to adulthood before claims can be made.

2. Evidence is different from claims—but claims *depend on* evidence.

   Claim: This program trains welfare recipients for jobs, places them in jobs; as a result, they become self-sufficient and leave the welfare rolls.

   Evidence: Numbers and types of job placements over time; pre-, post-, and follow-up data on welfare status; participant interview data about program effects; employer interview data about placements.

Michael Quinn Patton, *Utilization-focused evaluation: A new century* (4th ed.). Claims Matrix from pp. 498–499. ©2008 by SAGE. Reprinted with permission.

FORMING JUDGMENTS ABOUT THE PROGRAM'S SUCCESS

At this stage, the evaluator, working alone or preferably with the engagement of both stakeholders and participants, makes a claim about the program's success based on the interpretation step. *Success* traditionally means that the program met its goals and outcomes as defined by the standards for success. While this is a preferred definition of success, evaluators, stakeholders, and participants may find that success has multiple meanings for them, one of which is meeting the standards of success. For example, if a school leadership team implemented a professional learning program to increase teacher practice and student achievement in problem solving, their goal might be to increase student performance in problem solving on both quarterly benchmark assessments and the state annual math test. Their standard of success for all students might include both an overall increase in performance year over year of 10 percent; however, the team may also want to set goals for student groups who have been underperforming and underserved. They may establish a separate, maybe higher standard of success of 15–20 percent for students with limited English, disabilities, and past low performance so that they are able to close gaps in learning. The leadership team might deem the program successful if high-poverty students achieved a 22 percent gain, yet the school mean increase was only 8 percent.

Standards of success, established in the program planning phase and reviewed in the first step of the evaluation process (evaluability assessment), serve as the criteria against which the program's results are measured. If student achievement is the intended goal, and the evidence collected and analyzed demonstrates that student achievement has increased and the increase meets or exceeds the standards established for acceptable performance, the evaluator can conclude that the program is successful.

Standards for success prevent the evaluator from making judgments that are arbitrary and subjective. A standard is a statement of desired impact of the program and seeks to answer the questions, "How good is good enough?" and "How do we define success?" With specific standards of desirable results in place, the judgment process is less capricious and less subjective. The standards will reflect expectations for the program's results and, therefore, the actual results will be more meaningful and useful to program stakeholders. If the program's objective was to raise student achievement by 10 percent on a program-specific test of mathematics and the data indicate only an 8 percent gain, the evaluator may claim that the program did not achieve its intended results, yet is on its way to doing so. Sometimes a program does not meet its standards for success, yet there is evidence of improving results. The program may be approaching the level of desired success, and the planners miscalculated the time for the effects to be evident. The evaluator and interpretation team may examine factors that prevented the program from reaching the desired success. Perhaps the original timeline was too brief. Perhaps program staff lacked the skills to deliver the program. Perhaps program participants were reluctant to get involved in the early stages. Whatever the reasons, evaluators who have data about how the program

worked and information about the program's operation and implementation will be better able to offer explanations for the program's results and to recommend ways to improve it. Success might also be present if the program has not met all its intended outcomes at the level desired, yet has improved other related or unanticipated conditions. In the case of the school leadership team mentioned above, they may also consider the program successful even if it falls short of achieving its intended standard of success because it is both close to the desired level and because other indicators support their decision.

The value of glass-box evaluations (see Chapter 3) is particularly evident at this stage of evaluation. Programs may or may not achieve their intended results, yet the glass-box evaluation provides the evidence to examine various program activities to determine if they produce the initial or intermediate outcomes. Ending programs that have some evidence of improvement bypasses the opportunity for strengthening the program's design or implementation or to learn what worked and what didn't. Ending programs that have some evidence of success may ultimately be a huge loss to students, educators, and the field of professional learning. Program managers must juggle their priorities with deliberation when deciding to continue a program that is not yet producing visible evidence of success with renewed effort so that it will in the near future. To end an evaluation with a finding that the program has not met its anticipated results, without seeking to identify, understand, and examine possible reasons why, leaves program stakeholders and participants empty-handed. Every evaluation has the potential to generate useful conclusions to inform future professional learning planning, implementation, and evaluation.

Making Claims of Attribution or Contribution

When forming judgments, it is important to revisit concepts of attribution and contribution discussed in Chapter 6. There is an intense desire and demand to show that there is a cause–effect relationship among professional learning, changes in educator practice, and increases in student achievement. Perhaps because the argument is so intuitively strong, the desire to assume or suggest causality is stronger than a fear of misrepresenting evaluation findings. Policy makers and other decision makers often ask advocates for professional learning to show that there is such a cause–effect relationship and that investments in professional learning are more valuable than other means for improvement. Evaluators strive to ensure that stakeholders and participants who engage in the interpretation phase understand the distinction between attribution and contribution and whether the evaluation design permits a legitimate claim of attribution, that is, the professional learning program solely is *responsible for* the changes that occurred, either in educators or their clients. *Attribution*, on the other hand, suggests that *nothing other than* the professional learning program was responsible for the change in student achievement. Claims of attribution assert that a cause-and-effect relationship exists and that measurable and identifiable changes can be attributed solely to the professional learning program. But claims of attribution are possible only in strictly controlled experimental studies, something rarely done in the real-life context of education.

For example, many school systems have hired coaches to support improving teaching and learning in core content areas. In School P, in the two years following the introduction of coaching in math and literacy, student achievement improved substantially. School S also implemented coaching the same year as School P; however, its student achievement scores did not improve over the same period. Since neither school nor teachers were randomly assigned to the treatment of coaching, an attribution claim that coaching in School P is responsible for the changes in student achievement is neither valid nor credible. While coaching may have been a factor that influenced change, to make a claim of attribution requires statistical confirmation that the schools are somewhat similar in salient characteristics and random assignment to the treatment or control group. In addition, a sample of just two schools further seriously limits the credibility of this claim.

Contribution means that the professional learning program was *a contributing, influencing, or supportive factor*, yet it was *not solely responsible* for the changes observed. It acknowledges that other factors that have not been studied are present and likely also contributed or influenced the observed changes. Professional learning frequently occurs in tandem with new standards, curricula, instructional resources, equipment, technology, or other innovations. These variables and others such as attributes of program participants and their clients influence the change. To determine which of the many variables influence the observed changes from professional learning, evaluators would need to conduct randomized control studies that allowed them to control for each of the variables in isolation of others. In complex systems such as education, these types of studies have significant ramifications and implications.

To explore the example of coaching in School P and School S further, the evaluator uses the theory of change and the data collected at significant points within the chain of activities designed to produce the changes to determine if coaching is an influential factor. In all likelihood, the evaluator collects data to know (1) if, how often, and how long teachers met with coaches; (2) if the content of and types of interactions coaches and teachers had related to content teaching and learning; (3) what changes teachers made in instruction that coaching prompted or supported; (4) if teachers feel supported by coaching; and (5) if student achievement is improving on some valid and reliable measure of learning. If the evaluator can, using data, provide evidence to show that teachers met with coaches to discuss teaching and student learning in the content areas and were supported by coaches to change their instructional practice in ways that advanced student learning, the evaluator can make a claim that, in this school, given all the conditions present and the evidence available, it is likely that coaching in the core content areas contributed to improvement in student achievement. In addition, the evaluator would seek to explain other possible factors that also might be contributing to the increase in student achievement.

The distinction between attribution and contribution is critical for evaluators. In education, most evaluations are not designed to result in conclusions about cause and effect. Most professional learning evaluations, and especially

those done by practitioners, focus on merit, worth, and impact in the form of contribution rather than attribution. When policy makers or other publics want evaluations that can claim attribution, an evaluator has a rich opportunity to teach them about the difference and to clarify the evaluation's purpose so evaluation is deemed to be credible, useful, and valuable. Involving policy and decision makers in the planning phase of the evaluation and again in the interpreting phase and seeking their approval of the evaluation framework are proactive approaches to minimize confusion about attribution and contribution claims.

Determining Merit and Worth

The evaluator, preferably with the support of stakeholders and participants who engage in interpretation, form summative judgments about the professional learning program. A critical part of evaluation is to form judgments about the merit, value, worth, and significance of a professional learning program. The intent is to make a judgment about the program to inform decisions about its continuation, expansion, redesign, replication, or discontinuation for example. Michael Scriven (1991) delineates the intent of summative judgments about a program that declare the overall effectiveness of a program. "Summative evaluation of a program (or other **evaluand**) is conducted after completion of the program (for ongoing programs that means after stabilization and for the benefit of some external audience or decision maker (for example, finding agency, oversight office historian, or future possible users). . . . The decisions it services are most often decisions between these options: export (generalize), increase site support, continue site support, continue with conditions (probationary status), continue with modifications, discontinue. The aim is to report *on* it [the program], not report *to* it" (p. 340).

A value judgment, according to Sarah Mathison (2005), is "judgment about the merit, worth, or value of something" (p. 443). They are not "subjective, individualistic, arbitrary" (p. 443), but rather result from "weighing and synthesizing criteria or evidence" (p. 443). Ultimately, the evaluator is determining whether the program is valuable to those who participated (worth) and if it produces the intended results (merit). Merit, summarize Donna Mertens and Amy Wilson, "is the absolute or relative quality of something, either intrinsically or in regard to a particular criterion" (2012, p. 6). They add, "Worth is an outcome of an evaluation and refers to the evaluand's value in a particular context. Worth and merit are not dependent on each other, and an evaluand may have intrinsic merit but may not have worth" (p. 6).

Patton (2008) explains the difference between merit and worth: "Merit refers to the intrinsic value of a program, for example, how effective it is in meeting the needs of those it is intended to help. Worth refers to extrinsic value to those outside the program, for example, to the larger community or society a welfare program that gets jobs for recipients has merit for those who move out of poverty and worth to society by reducing welfare costs" (p. 113). Programs may have perceived worth and little merit or vice versa. A coaching program

may not produce the intended results of increasing student achievement (merit), yet may be perceived by principals as worthwhile because they have an extra set of hands to help with administrative tasks (worth), even though that is not the purpose of coaching. On the other hand, coaching may be perceived as time-consuming and intrusive by teachers (without worth), yet it contributes to more job satisfaction, sense of collaboration and support, and improved student learning (merit).

Mertens and Wilson highlight Ernie House's (1990) comments about the political nature of judgments of merit based on criteria established. He notes that what might be considered good for one group may not be appropriate for another. When the criteria are established, and the program meets those criteria, the evaluator makes a claim of merit. This situation emphasizes that the process of making claims of merit or worth must include the perspectives of stakeholders and participants so that their explanations and insights can illuminate the judgments made about the program. To extend House's caution, Patton (2008) stresses that making judgments solely on the data without considering "the politics, values, competing priorities, the state of knowledge about a problem, the scope of the problem, the history of the program, the availability of resources, public support, and managerial competence" (p. 115) may be shortsighted.

When the judgments made seem contradictory to the data, it is even more important to acknowledge the engagement of stakeholders and participants and to engage them in sharing the findings and their interpretations, the next step of the evaluation report. It is not unusual for participants particularly to perceive a program as less than worthwhile, especially when they are so closely involved in a professional learning program, burdened by new expectations, confronted with their attitudes and aspirations, and overwhelmed with the challenge of changing years of habits and practice while juggling new knowledge and skills.

It is reasonable for participants to experience dissonance and disequilibrium, and it is crucial that program directors and stakeholders understand the full impact of the changes the professional learning program is expecting. Learning is not a light-switch activity, especially when the learning, as Katz and Dack (2013) suggest, "is a permanent change in thinking and behavior" (p. 13). Learning at this level requires dissonance. This is a strong reason to recognize that judging the success of professional learning based on participants' enjoyment of an event is a weak and insufficient measure of a professional learning program. Sharing the evaluation findings may offer encouragement and evidence of the impact of the hard work participants are engaged in to increase student achievement and serve as motivation to continue their commitment to faithful implementation. Demonstrating in an evaluation that their efforts are providing evidence of change, even though it might not yet be at the level expected or desired, can affect participants' aspiration to continue growing and learning as professionals.

Evaluating professional learning provides program directors, stakeholders, and participants with crucial information to make decisions about the

program. Not all programs will be successful immediately, yet without understanding the merit and worth of a program using evaluation data as well as perceptions of those engaged in it, it is difficult to know what to adjust to strengthen the program's impact and overall value. Formative evaluation coupled with summative evaluation offer insights and evidence for improving those programs that may be long-term change initiatives or have had a rocky launch. The evaluator's responsibility in the interpretation stage is to help program directors, stakeholders, and participants understand the evaluation findings, interpret the data-supported findings, draw conclusions from the findings, understand their implications, make judgments from their more direct experience with the program, and to make recommendations about the program.

Making Recommendations

The last part of the data-interpretation step in the evaluation process is formulating recommendations about the program's design or operation to increase its merit, worth, and impact. Recommendations suggest changes that identify the next steps for the program. George Grob (2015a) notes that evaluators might consider whether to call these recommendations, which he contends sound "authoritative, compulsory, and imposing" (p. 727) or to use terms such as *suggestions for improvement* or *options to consider*, which may be perceived as less dictatorial. Recommendations depend on deductive and inductive thinking; use the data, findings, and interpretations; and identify where opportunities exist for making revisions in the program. The revisions are hypotheses about what actions are needed regarding the program. Until further evaluation is conducted, there is no certainty that the recommendations, if enacted, will produce positive results. Recommendations can focus on changes in the program's operation, policies, resources, personnel, or activities. "Well-written, carefully derived recommendations and conclusions can be the magnet that pulls all the other elements of an evaluation together into a meaningful whole," notes Patton (2008). "Done poorly, recommendations can become a lightning rod for attack, discrediting what was otherwise a professional job because of hurried and sloppy work on last-minute recommendations" (pp. 501–502). Evaluators will return to the evaluation questions and the evaluation's purpose as guides for formulating recommendations. As such, there he may include more short-term, immediate recommendations related to formative evaluation questions and longer-term ones related to summative evaluation questions.

Evaluators may make recommendations without consultation with program stakeholders or participants, or may consult with them in developing recommendations. When evaluators engage others in this process, they have the advantage of multiple perspectives to expand and enrich the potential recommendations, yet they are limited by the potential biases each brings to the process. Those who participate in formulating recommendations often bring personal interests and needs into the conversations. As Ingrid Guerra-Lopez notes, "[T]he likelihood that solutions that stakeholders come up with will be

implemented is significantly higher than the likelihood that solutions you [evaluator] come up with will be implemented. Although people sometimes have a difficult time articulating what ends they are really after, there is usually no shortage of ideas about how to get there, primarily because most people's work is focused on those ends" (2008, p. 222). Guerra-Lopez suggests a framework for generating, prioritizing, and selecting recommendations to include in the evaluation report. To generate recommendations, she suggests that the evaluator, stakeholders, and others

1. define the problem the recommendation seeks to address or solve;

2. identify the requirements or criteria for the problem solution;

3. generate potential recommendations or alternatives;

4. identify the advantages and disadvantages of each recommendation;

5. rank the alternatives using the defined criteria; and

6. decide which recommendations to advance.

Steps to determine which recommendation to implement would include understanding the level of effort and cost to implement each recommendation, the potential or expected impact, and the feasibility of each recommendation. Following this analysis, program directors and stakeholders would rank the alternatives based on the level of effort, potential for impact, and feasibility and decide which to implement. This process may or may not include the evaluator.

Patton (2008) recommends guidelines for developing useful, practical recommendations. The list below is adapted from his recommendations and focuses on the process and product.

1. Determine in collaboration with stakeholders and evaluation funders whether to include recommendations in the evaluation, the specific focus area for recommendations, and if they prefer options or alternatives in the recommendations (i.e., different ways to approach adjustments).

2. Generate multiple recommendations before narrowing the list.

3. Develop recommendations that follow clearly and logically from evaluation findings.

4. Include recommendations both about leveraging positive findings for more impact and for strengthening the program by addressing gaps, problems, or challenges encountered.

5. State recommendations in clear, specific, precise language.

6. Focus recommendations on what is within the sphere of control of stakeholders. Include, when possible, the potential level of effort, cost, benefits, and challenges with implementing recommendations.

7. Exercise political and cultural sensitivity in writing recommendations.

8. Consider how to engage stakeholders in using the recommendations.

Evaluators might use a criteria matrix to facilitate the discussion and decisions about proposed recommendations. Figure 9.1 is an example of a criteria matrix. Adding a weighted value to each criterion is another way to assess the proposed recommendations.

Not all evaluations include recommendations. Evaluators, preferably working in collaboration with stakeholders and participants, determine whether recommendations are appropriate in an evaluation. Not all experts on evaluation agree that evaluation reports include recommendations. Some suggest that the work of an evaluator is finished when the evaluator has finished her primary work, rendering judgement (Scriven, 1993). Michael Scriven notes that the evaluator is responsible for making a judgment about a program, and that alone is the end of his responsibility. He adds that there is a considerable distance from the judgment to a recommendation that requires a significant understanding of the local context. Others, however, argue that the evaluator is in a unique position to offer recommendations because he has a comprehensive and nuanced understanding about a program that is unlike any one stakeholder's. The data collection, analysis, and interpretation process gives him a broader, deeper, and multidimensional view of the program's design, operation, and effects. This understanding may be visible to others in the data itself or it may be more opaque, emerging from the convergence of data and perspectives.

The challenge for evaluators in collaborating with stakeholders and participants to develop recommendations is to maintain objectivity and neutrality. One way external evaluators or internal evaluators who work in a different department can avoid the challenges of insufficient understanding of the local context and build on his unique perspective about the program is to engage primary stakeholders minimally and preferably representative stakeholders and participants into the entire interpretation step. Practitioner evaluators, those who are closest to the program and responsible for its evaluation, will almost always have recommendations about the program's operation and design to increase its effectiveness.

Figure 9.1   Criteria Matrix

Recommendations	Criterion 1	Criterion 2	Criterion 3	Criterion 4	Criterion 5	# Criteria Met
Recommendation 1						
Recommendation 2						
Recommendation 3						
Recommendation 4						
Recommendation 5						

Sometimes evaluators may not have the expertise or there is insufficient data available to make recommendation about the program. In these cases, they can turn to research and best practices, experts in the field, other similar programs, and other evaluation of similar programs to develop helpful and useful recommendations (Grob, 2015a; Weiss, 1998). Practitioner evaluators may not have sufficient information or understanding of the options available to them for improving professional learning programs, so they reach out to the research or others for more information before formulating recommendations.

Decisions about a program's continuation or discontinuation are not the responsibility of the evaluator, nor are they included as part of the recommendations. Program directors and policy and decision makers make those decisions based on the evaluation.

The following questions may assist evaluators in the interpretation process:

1. What do these findings mean to various program stakeholders and participants?

2. Have we sought diverse perspectives on the findings from a representative set of stakeholders and participants whose views may vary?

3. Does this program have worth, that is, is it seen as a valuable part of the school's or district's mission, or is it perceived as valuable to the program participants?

4. Does this program have merit, that is, can it produce the intended outcomes for the educators and their clients?

5. Is this program significant, that is, does it address a significant problem or need in a feasible, practical, reasonable way?

6. What implications do the judgments have for the program, the stakeholders, participants, sponsoring school, school system, or education agency?

7. What recommended actions can either improve the program or its results?

The interpretation step of evaluation is a significant opportunity to understand the program, what makes it successful, and what contributes challenges. When the evaluator, particularly those who are practitioners within schools and school systems, purposefully engages stakeholders and participants in this step, the meaningfulness and usefulness of the evaluation is exponentially increased. Evaluators serve as facilitators, guiding the work with processes, information, teaching, dialogue, and discussion to support engagement, reasonableness, and fairness in the process. Thoroughness in this step makes the transition to writing the evaluation report, disseminating it, and using the results of the evaluation substantially easier.

The rubric in Table 9.2 may guide evaluators in assessing the data-interpretation step of the evaluation process.

Table 9.2 Data-Interpretation Rubric

Data Interpretation	Incomplete Data Interpretation	Partially Completed Data Interpretation	Completed Data Interpretation
Engaging others	The evaluator engages only a few stakeholders in the data-interpretation process.	The evaluator engages some stakeholders and participants in the data-interpretation process.	The evaluator engages representative stakeholders and participants with diverse perspectives in the data-interpretation process.
Seeking meaning	The evaluator facilitates discussion among a few stakeholders to establish their understanding of the findings.	The evaluator facilitates dialogue and discussion among some stakeholders and participants to seek consensus about the meaning of the findings.	The evaluator facilitates dialogue and discussion among representative stakeholders and participants to seek consensus about the meaning of the findings and the explanations for their occurrence.
Judging merit	The evaluator, alone or with the support of a few stakeholders and participants, uses the data, findings, and interpretations to judge the program's merit.	The evaluator, with the support of some stakeholders and participants, uses the data, findings, and interpretations to judge the program's merit.	The evaluator, with the support of a representation of stakeholders and participants, uses the data, findings, and interpretations to judge the program's merit.
Judging worth	The evaluator, alone or with the support of a few stakeholders, uses the data, findings, and interpretations to judge the program's worth.	The evaluator, with the support of some stakeholders and participants, uses the data, findings, and interpretations to judge the program's worth.	The evaluator, with the support of a representation of stakeholders and participants, uses the data, findings, and interpretations to judge the program's worth from the perspective of diverse stakeholders and participants.
Judging impact	The evaluator, alone or with the support of a few stakeholders, uses the data, findings, and interpretations to judge the program's impact.	The evaluator, with the support of some stakeholders and participants, uses the data, findings, and interpretations to judge the program's impact on participants and/or their clients.	The evaluator, with the support of a representation of stakeholders and participants, uses the data, findings, and interpretations to judge the program's impact on participants and their clients.
Judging significance	The evaluator, alone or with the support of a few stakeholders, uses the data, findings, and interpretations to judge the program's significance in terms of the intended outcomes and the capacity of planned actions to solve identified problems in culturally appropriate, reasonable, feasible, and practical ways.	The evaluator, with the support of some stakeholders and participants, uses the data, findings, and interpretations to judge the program's significance in terms of the intended outcomes and the capacity of planned actions to solve identified problems in culturally appropriate, reasonable, feasible, and practical ways.	The evaluator, with the support of a representation of stakeholders and participants, uses the data, findings, and interpretations to judge the program's significance in terms of the intended outcomes and the capacity of planned actions to solve identified problems in culturally appropriate, reasonable, feasible, and practical ways.

Data Interpretation	Incomplete Data Interpretation	Partially Completed Data Interpretation	Completed Data Interpretation
Making claims	The evaluator, with a few stakeholders, summarizes the judgments about the program.	The evaluator, with the support of some stakeholders and participants, formulates claims about the program's merit, worth, impact, and/or significance that are drawn from the data and findings.	The evaluator, with the support of a representation of stakeholders and participants, states major and minor claims about the program's merit, worth, impact, and significance that are drawn logically from the data and findings.
Making recommendations	The evaluator, with a few stakeholders, makes recommendations about the program.	The evaluator, with the support of some stakeholders and participants, offers multiple, clear, practical, categorized, and actionable recommendations.	The evaluator, with the support of a representation of stakeholders and participants, offers multiple, clear, practical, categorized, and actionable recommendations with their benefits, costs, level of effort, and limitations that are within the sphere of the stakeholders' control.

Report, Disseminate, and Use Findings

10

Disseminating and using the findings of the evaluation requires the evaluator to prepare and share interim and final reports about the evaluation study and to facilitate the use of the evaluation. While many evaluators understand the need to produce a report that summarizes the evaluation, explain the methodology used, provide data, findings, interpretations, and recommendations, they often fail to understand the role their report plays in motivating and engaging stakeholders in making decisions for improvement. As Patton (2008) notes, "Use is a process, not a report" (p. 518). The report is a tool that summarizes the evaluation and promotes its use. How it is structured can leverage interest, engagement, and support for the use process.

Reports can be offered in a variety of written and oral formats. There is no "best" format for an evaluation report, according to Patton (2008). As he states, "[T]he best format is the one that fulfills the purposes of the evaluation and meets the needs of the specific intended users in a specific situation. In many cases, multiple reporting strategies can be pursued to reach different intended users and dissemination audiences" (p. 509). In this step, the evaluator considers answers to several questions:

1. Will there be interim, formative reports or only a final, summative report?

2. Who constitutes the various audiences that will receive and use the evaluation report?

3. Who is the primary audience for and users of the evaluation report?

4. What are the most crucial elements that the primary audience wants included in the evaluation report to meet their utilization needs? For example, how much does it want to know about methodology, data sources and collection tools, and other technical aspects?

5. Will there be one, or multiple, evaluation reports tailored to various audiences?

6. What are the best formats of the final report for various audiences to facilitate its use?

7. What is the best way for sharing the report with the various audience (i.e., a face-to-face presentation, an online meeting, a discussion group)?

8. How will various audiences interact with the report (i.e., a meeting in which they discuss the meeting, an opportunity to ask the evaluation team questions)?

9. What voice or tone is best for the written report (i.e., conversational, authoritative, informal, traditional)?

10. Will the report be disseminated to and used widely or by a limited audience? Primarily to internal stakeholders? Made available to the general public? Available to members of the community and media?

11. Who will be the disseminators of the report? Who will be speaking about the evaluation? What information or materials will they need to speak both accurately and effectively about the evaluation?

12. What layout or design issues must be considered in preparing the final report? For formal publication, will the evaluator need to adhere to certain specifications in word processing? Or if the report will be translated to PDF or html files for Web-based distribution, what is the best way to format the document?

13. Will there be a press release or press briefing?

14. What is the role of the evaluator in disseminating the report and facilitating its use? Will the evaluator have any ongoing relationship with the program, program staff, or organizations?

INTERIM VERSUS FINAL REPORTS

Sometimes evaluators prepare interim reports about the progress of the program and final reports that include judgments and recommendations about the program as a whole. The two differ in that the interim report does not attempt to report on the program's impact, but rather focuses on the process, implementation, outputs, initial outcomes, or operation of the program. The interim reports are about formative evaluations that present status reports on what is occurring. Interim reports may include recommendations for fine-tuning, modifying, or changing some aspect of the program to improve implementation. Program directors and stakeholders may agree not to share them as widely as summative evaluation reports.

One or more interim evaluation reports may be required by the program manager or funder. Typically, programs funded by federal, state, or local agencies or public or private foundations require at least one interim report that

describes the program's progress, frequently includes a budget expenditure report, and indicates any variations in what was proposed and approved and their rationale. Interim reports may include documentation about the number of clients served, the occurrence of program activities, unexpected challenges and how they were addressed, progress on program outcomes, and practical suggestions for adjustments in the program operation or design. Tools such as tables, charts, or heat maps might indicate progress on goals. Table 10.1 is a framework an interim report's progress on program goals.

Interim reports are often briefer than summative reports, yet length is never a criterion for quality of evaluation reports. Interim reports are practical, direct, and useful for those managing the program, and they encourage immediate consideration about adjustments in the program. They provide the program director, stakeholders, and potentially participants with a status report that includes a summary of successes to date, ways to leverage successes to advance the work, challenges or issues identified, and considerations for handling them.

Final reports, on the other hand, focus on the professional learning program's merit, worth, impact, and significance. They focus on summarizing the evaluation, forecasting next possible actions, and encouraging stakeholders to act. The summative evaluation report is not intended to be a historical or biographical account of the program's development, description, or operation. Rather, it is intended to provide the value judgments about the program with supporting data. While the evaluation report might include a brief synopsis

Table 10.1   Framework for Progress on Program Outcomes

Program Outcomes	Not Started	Early Implementation	Refined Implementation	Completed
Principals refocus their time and responsibilities to increase the frequency and effectiveness of in-depth conversations using classroom data with selected teachers weekly about teaching practices and related student learning.			X	
Teacher strengthen data-driven instruction by collecting, using, and discussing data to address learning gaps in student performance.		X		
Teachers refine their use of collaborative learning teams to identify and solve instructional challenges using classroom data, opportunities to learn with and from each other, and examine the effects of their changed instruction.		X		
Student performance on benchmark assessments increases.		X		
Teachers understand how to access and use data from the data warehouse for classroom instruction purposes.				X

about the program and its activities, it is mostly focused on the judgments about the program and recommends how those judgments can be used.

Although final reports most often focus on the impact of a professional learning program, some evaluations are conducted for different purposes. Some evaluations are designed to identify specific problems or needs to address. Some are done to assess a program's theory of change. Some are done to improve implementation. In these cases, the final reports naturally focus on the evaluation's purpose.

FORMATS FOR AND ATTRIBUTES OF THE SUMMATIVE EVALUATION REPORT

Most evaluators submit a written report of the evaluation study, although this is not always in the traditional, scholarly format. The formats vary extensively and are facilitated with opportunities available through technology. What was once a traditional hundred-page report may now be presented in infographics, slides, press releases, press briefings, summary documents, policy papers, briefs, technical reports, conference presentations, small group presentations, newspaper or newsletter articles, social media postings, videos, face-to-face or online presentations, journal or magazine articles, brochures, flyers, or all of the above. The options continue to grow as communication vehicles continue to grow. George Grob (2015b) describes six formats for an evaluation report: (1) **Mom test**, a succinct two-sentence statement of the essence of the report, often used in an oral presentation; (2) the killer paragraph, a written version that includes the Mom test statement and enough explanation to deliver down a hallway; (3) the outline, an essential tools to help a writer organize and synthesize information; (4) the two-page executive summary, which provides the high-level information with sufficient detail; (5) the 10-page report, as Grob describes it, "the best investment in reaching our goal to make a difference in the world. . . . It will reach more thought leaders than anything else" (p. 750); and (6) the technical report, designed primarily for researchers, policy analysts, other evaluators, program staff, and others who want detailed information about the program's and the evaluation's design, operations, and methodology. Increasingly, evaluators provide multiple forms of their reports to meet the various needs of stakeholders and to improve access to and use of the evaluation for programmatic decisions. For example, an evaluator might provide an executive summary, a one- to five-page summary report with bullets and highlights for wider distribution or posting on a school or district's website, and a technical and comprehensive report. Sometimes the evaluator prepares presentation materials for an oral presentation. Other times, a more formal, scholarly, academic evaluation report is necessary. The evaluator, in collaboration with key stakeholders and other primary users of the evaluation, makes decisions about the format, style, and structure of any reports to ensure that they are in the most useful formats.

Simplicity and clarity are the goals of both oral and written reports. The evaluator strives to ensure that the language and tone of the evaluation are

neutral, unbiased, and informative. Reports should be easy to understand and free of jargon or technical terms not widely known to likely audiences. Preparing the report is not the time for the evaluator to impress an audience with his or her technical knowledge about evaluation, but rather to become the teacher. Evaluators are trained to clarify and simplify a complex process so that others can understand it and use the results effectively in making decisions for improving both the program and its results. George Grob (2015b) describes this, as mentioned above, as the "*Mom* test." He stresses that this is not about "dumbing down" the report, but rather finding its essence. "Failure to pass the Mom test is the most common and significant weakness in evaluation reports that fail to inspire action. The main reason for failing the test is not the difficulty of finding words to succinctly express the report's message. It is because there is no message. The author may have provided lots of findings and good recommendations, but no kernel, no unforgettable nub that attracts attention and compels the reader's interest" (pp. 740–741).

Patton (2008) begs for simplicity in evaluation reports and presentations so that the information will be accessible and understandable to those who intend to use its results:

> Simplicity as a virtue means that we are rewarded not for how much we complicate the analysis or impress with our expertise but for how much we enlighten. It means that we make users feel they can master what is before them, rather than intimidate them with our own knowledge and sophistication. It means distinguishing the complexity of analysis from the clarity of presentation and using the former to inform and guide the latter. Simplicity as a virtue is not simple. It often involves more work and creativity to simplify than to rest content with a presentation of complicated statistics as they originally emerged from analysis. (p. 479)

Clarity is another attribute of evaluation reports that evaluators want to address. What is said will have a long-term impact on the program stakeholders. The way it is said will also influence the degree to which people will be able and willing to understand and use the message.

Mary Jean Taylor, a program evaluator and colleague, shared the story below with the author via e-mail:

> I was coming back from meetings in Washington, D.C., and happened to be seated next to a scientist from Ball Aerospace. We got into a fairly lengthy conversation about the organizational behaviors that led to the *Challenger* disaster, writing, and rocket design. . . . I made some comment about the importance of writing clearly so you could be understood, and he noted that they used a different criterion for clear writing—*to write so that you could not be misunderstood.* I immediately liked the idea and try to use it as my standard. (personal e-mail, September 9, 2001)

The standard used at Ball Aerospace for writing is a high bar for written work. Preparing the evaluation report sometimes seems anticlimactic; but the

report stands long after the work is completed as evidence of the thought, effort, and energy that went into the entire evaluation, and it is the primary vehicle to promote use of the evaluation for program decisions. The evaluators and all those who help to write the report should be aware of the need to remain concise, unbiased, and accurate. According to the Accuracy Standards section in *Program Evaluation Standards*, "A8 Communication and Reporting Evaluation communications should have adequate scope and guard against misconceptions, biases, distortions, and errors." (Yarbrough, Shulha, Hopson, & Caruthers, 2011). These standards appear in Appendix B. In addition to accurate reporting and concise writing, when reporting on sources of information used in a program evaluation, evaluators need to provide enough detail to make the accuracy of the information evident, yet not to breach promises of confidentiality or anonymity.

The evaluator keeps the purpose of the evaluation in the forefront when preparing either an interim or a final report. A secondary goal of evaluations of professional learning—to contribute to the conceptual knowledge about the field of professional learning—may be addressed as well if stakeholders are comfortable with this addition. Evaluation, then, becomes a mechanism to help stakeholders understand (1) how the professional learning program achieved its outcomes, (2) what factors enhance and inhibit the changes intended, and (3) how these changes influenced participants, their clients, the school or school system, and potentially other professional learning.

Evaluations help stakeholders develop new insights and perspectives about their work. Sometimes program staff are too close to see how even simple changes dramatically increase the impact of the program. For example, teachers in one program appreciated it when the coach left a short note after a classroom observation and conference listing key points from the conference. Teachers referred to these notes, they said, as reminders about implementing new practices and a way to assess their own progress. They also viewed them as motivation to move ahead. Teachers said they were sometimes flustered or anxious in the conference later with their coach and didn't remember all the details. The coaches were previously unaware of the impact of their notes and had been leaving them inconsistently because they had believed the practice was not helpful. When coaches learned the perceived value of their notes, writing them became a part of every classroom visit.

TYPICAL COMPONENTS OF A
TRADITIONAL FINAL EVALUATION REPORT

While the formats for evaluation reports are changing rapidly, the more traditional final report continues to include some common components. The list that follows includes more common components and can be used to guide discussion with the primary audience about what components they want in their evaluation report. It is not intended to be a list of required components. Sometimes, before a final draft of a report is completed, evaluators meet with those who will use the report to talk about the findings and

the "look and feel" of the report. Discussing the findings and recommendations with key program stakeholders, the director, and others in advance of preparing the final draft of the report will increase their understanding and acceptance of it. Mertens and Wilson (2012) list the common elements of a scholarly evaluation report, often one intended to be published in a professional journal.

> "Introduction (this established the broader context of the report and situates the study in extant literature)
>
> Evaluand (this describes the intervention or program)
>
> Methodology (this includes a description of stakeholders, data collection strategies and instruments, participants, and data analysis)
>
> Results (this presents the findings of quantitative, qualitative, and mixed-methods data analysis)
>
> Conclusions (this presents and explanation of the findings and their implications, usually with recommendations for next steps)" (p. 476)

In describing the structure of a collaborative outcomes report, a form of reporting that is a participatory approach to an impact evaluation, Patton (2015) offers a similar list.

1. "A narrative section explaining the program context and rationale

2. A 'results chart' summarizing the achievements of the program against a program logic model

3. A narrative section describing the implication of the results, for example, the achievements (expected and unexpected), the issues, and the recommendations

4. A section that provides a number of 'vignettes' providing instances of significant change, usually first-person narratives

5. An index providing more detail on the sources of evidence" (p. 624)

While an evaluation serves as a vital and formal part of the information base upon which future decisions about the program's design, status, and resources can be made, it is typically not the *sole* source of information. Evaluation serves as one part of a much broader knowledge base about the program that policy and decision makers have accumulated over time. Nearly all written reports and even oral ones will have several common elements: the program's outcomes, the questions the evaluation seeks to answer, the answers, the findings about the analyzed data, and recommendations. Even brief articles, brochures, or executive summaries include these same elements. Refer to Table 10.2 for a list of possible components.

Table 10.2 Possible Components of Evaluation Reports

1. EXECUTIVE SUMMARY/ABSTRACT	4. EVALUATION DESIGN
Program outcomes	Data collection
Evaluation questions	Data sources
Summary of findings	Data analysis
Implications	5. EVALUATION FINDINGS
Recommendations	Findings
2. INTRODUCTION	Interpretations
Purpose of the evaluation	Limitations
Outcomes of the professional learning program	Implications
Evaluation questions	6. RECOMMENDATIONS
3. OVERVIEW OF THE PROGRAM	Future actions
Program description and context	Possible resources
Program outcomes and activities	Potential uses
Resources	7. APPENDICES
Stakeholders	Acknowledgment or list of participants in the evaluation
Participants	Supplemental data displays
Theory of change and/or logic model	Instruments used
	Supporting documents

For evaluation reports that are not in a traditional, scholarly, or academic format, they typically include basic information. Dean Spaulding (2008) describes these as the cover page, executive summary, methods, and body of the report. Even a two-page summary of the evaluation report can incorporate these elements.

The guidelines below offer suggestions about the summative evaluation report (Grob, 2015b; Mertens and Wilson, 2012; Patton, 2008, 2015; Spaulding, 2008).

1. Meet with primary stakeholders to determine the best formats for and expectations for the evaluation reports, the intended audiences and appropriate formats to reach them, and the primary users and the best formats for their use.

2. Write clearly, succinctly, and with precision so that what is written cannot be misunderstood. Construct crisp sentences and paragraphs in active voice.

3. Write for the intended audience.

4. Include a crisp, brief (one to two pages) executive summary that can stand alone, minimizes explanation about methodology, and emphasizes findings, explanations, recommendations, and reasons for confidence in the evaluation.

5. Use well-constructed, labeled figures, tables, graphics, or images only as appropriate to summarize data, display data, and promote understanding of the support for findings, yet limit overuse of them or the use of images or graphics merely for design purposes if they are not directly connected to the report content.

6. Connect figures, tables, or graphics with the text.

7. Share drafts for response and suggestions and to check expectations with primary stakeholders and intended users.

8. Answer each evaluation question with sufficient supporting evidence.

9. Use neutral, unbiased language.

10. Protect the human and legal rights of participants and stakeholders; be sensitive to and respectful of cultural differences, and uphold promises of anonymity or confidentiality.

Evaluators want to be cautious about the use of graphics in their evaluation reports. While the use of graphics (charts, tables, figures, photos, images, etc.) can enhance understanding, they can also distract from it or contribute to misunderstanding. Evaluators should use them as appropriate, yet limit overuse of them or the use of images or graphics merely for design purposes if they are not directly connected to the report content. Grob (2015b) notes that evaluators like to use graphics because they add interest and visual appeal as well as provide tools for explaining or demonstrating ideas. He adds that these reasons are the same ones for avoiding their use: "Use graphics to highlight and clarify your message. Don't use them for anything else. Is the graphic you noticed while skimming the report about the main message? Is it about the major findings? Is it about the most important recommendation? If so, it should be there. If not, it should not be used" (p. 756). He adds a tip that the labels for graphics can be stated in brief sentences so the graphic can be easily understood. The evaluator ensures that any graphic used has sufficient clarity to have meaning when it stands alone and is described in the text of longer written reports.

Evaluators too want to acknowledge those who contributed to the evaluation. If anonymity is desired, the evaluator makes a general statement about the roles of participants, yet including specific names heightens the credibility of an evaluation. Before including names, though, the evaluator will want to seek permission to include them. Contributors can be included in an appendix or listed separately on a website, for example. Evaluators also consider authorship of the evaluation reports with the team of evaluators who contributed to the evaluation and with primary stakeholders. Authorship naturally includes

all contributors to the report. Evaluators should not shy away from identifying themselves as the author of an evaluation report, regardless of whether they are internal or external evaluators.

Disseminating the Results

Evaluators are not solely responsible for disseminating the evaluation report unless they have been contracted to do so or they are practitioners doing their own evaluations. In the latter case, the evaluator or evaluation team does disseminate the results of their work. Evaluators respect that the education agency that commissioned the evaluation is the owner of it and ultimately has the authority to determine the breadth of dissemination. The evaluator might facilitate discussion with the program director or stakeholders to determine who will receive a copy of the report or some form of it and what essential aspects of the evaluation results are important to share with which audiences. While the standards for program evaluation recommend that evaluation reports are widely available to program participants and stakeholders, the ultimate decision rests with the school, district, or agency.

Evaluators can be instrumental in cultivating how stakeholders share evaluation reports. Many stakeholders, such as a school or district improvement team, may not immediately see the value of sharing their evaluation report beyond the typical narrow audience made up perhaps of district senior management. Yet, the results of nearly all evaluations have value for others engaged in the program or similar programs or those designing, leading, or evaluating other professional learning programs. The communities that fund and support professional learning programs also share an interest in the results of evaluations to learn how investments are leveraged for improvement. Sharing results, for example, in a local newspaper of a district's investment in early release time for teacher collaboration can help the community understand and realize the value of providing non-contact time for this purpose and help them understand that the investment is considered significant enough to evaluate and refine its value.

When program evaluation is a part of the routine work of schools and school system staff and the results of evaluations are broadly disseminated, the opportunities to use existing work to inform other future or existing work exponentially increase. A program manager of a districtwide professional learning program may discover from engaging in discussions about the professional learning on mathematical practices that sufficient attention to principal engagement and specific responsibilities was a missing element and he can use that information to review his program's design to determine if it addresses this critical component. The evaluator of a professional learning program for office managers might realize that there is a need to engage supervisors of the managers in some way. The evaluation results, therefore, can strengthen professional learning in many diverse areas within an education setting.

When considering the formats for an evaluation report, the evaluator and key stakeholders consider all the possible audiences they want to receive the report, the best format in which to present the results, and how to engage the audience in interacting with the results.

Some options for distributing the results of an evaluation, including the report and other forms of disseminating the results, are listed in Table 10.3. The list is not intended to be comprehensive. With the availability of technology-enabled media, the options continue to grow.

Table 10.3   Potential Ways to Distribute Evaluation Results

- Published on a website in multiple formats for multiple audiences, such as the executive summary, technical report, presentation materials, blogs, and so on
- Published reports in newspapers, newsletters, magazines, professional journals, and others
- Face-to-face presentations, discussion groups, and the like with
  - School board or district accountability teams
  - School leadership teams;
  - Faculties or parent organization
  - Participant groups
  - Community groups
  - Parent groups
  - Student leadership groups
- Local media
  - Television
  - District's cable program
  - Student news program
  - Community or local government program
- Inclusion in other reports
  - Quarterly reports
  - Annual reports
  - Strategic updates
  - Social media postings

Table 10.4 summarizes formats of the evaluation report by audience.

Table 10.4   Typical Evaluation Report Formats for Various Audiences

Audience	Formats of the Report
Primary stakeholder Program director and program's supervisor, such as the superintendent, assistant superintendent, board of education, funder or funding agency, program staff	Full report Technical report Presentation with accompanying materials Executive summary Abbreviated report

(Continued)

Table 10.4   (Continued)

Audience	Formats of the Report
Secondary stakeholder Program participants	Executive summary
	Full report
	Abbreviated report
	Presentation with accompanying materials
	Blog
	Case studies
	Webpage articles
	Newsletter, newspaper articles
	First-person narratives
	Infographic
	Video case studies with participants demonstrating changes in their work environment
Public Community members, parents, various committees not directly involved in the project	Executive summary
	Abbreviated report
	Brochure
	Flyer
	Blog
	Local news media print article or film story
	Summary in other reports
Other agencies, districts, schools	Full report
	Technical report
	Executive summary
	Abbreviated report
Education policy makers, evaluators, program directors	Full report
	Technical report
	Policy paper

Evaluators may encourage stakeholders to gather responses from those who access and review the evaluation results by embedding brief surveys in the reports and other results. This information helps them monitor dissemination and assess if they are reaching their intended audiences. It might also provide information about who is interested in evaluation of professional learning. Stakeholders might invite those who read about the results to respond to a few questions such as those below:

In what form did you learn about the evaluation results?

_____ District newsletter article

_____ From a friend or colleague who is a district employee

_____ From a neighbor, friend, or community member who is not a district employee

_____ Blog post

_____ Report in local newspaper

_____ Technical report

_____ Community meeting presentation

___ School meeting presentation

___ Other _____ (please specify)

To what degree was the presentation of the evaluation results clear?

___ Very clear

___ Moderately clear

___ Unclear

How useful were the evaluation results to you?

___ Very useful

___ Somewhat useful

___ Not useful

Are you interested in learning more about the evaluation results?

___ Yes

___ No

Facilitating Dissemination

Primary stakeholders, with the support of the evaluator if desired, can facilitate the usefulness of the evaluation to the program staff by leading study or discussion groups focused on the report. Primary stakeholders might invite strategically selected, representative individuals to participate in study groups or open them to any interested individuals. These study groups differ from a presentation about the findings that an evaluator might make to the primary stakeholders in conjunction with the presentation of the final results or to others at the request of the primary stakeholders. The purpose of the study or discussion groups is to engage stakeholders or interested individuals in understanding the evaluation results and their implications. Participants prepare in advance for the meeting by reading the report and consider the questions they have. A facilitator skillful in managing discussion organizes an agenda or selects a protocol to guide the discussion. Several examples of processes for structuring study groups are provided in Tables 10.5 and 10.6. A variety of different text-based response protocols might be considered to guide discussion of the report, although facilitators of discussion groups will want to be sure that the protocol's purpose is appropriate for discussing text of the nature of evaluation reports and that she is skilled in using the protocol.

Table 10.5   Study Group Process

Step 1: Identify and invite potential members

Identify and invite members to participate in the study group. Potential members may be strategically selected members who represent various program stakeholders, participants, or others who are interested in participating because they hold an interest in the results of the evaluation.

(Continued)

(Continued)

Step 2: Prepare and share pre-reading guide

Prepare and share with those who plan to attend the study group a pre-reading guide to accompany the evaluation report they will discuss. The pre-reading guide reminds invitees about the time and location of the meeting, offers guidance for pre-reading the report, and encourages participants to come prepared to the study group meeting.

Sample Pre-Reading Guide

Thank you for agreeing to be a member of the Study Group on the Districtwide Writer's Workshop Professional Learning Program Evaluation. As a study group member, we encourage you to consider sharing what you learn with others. Our meeting will be held in the Main Office Conference Room on Tuesday, May 16, at 3:45 p.m. at Perry High School. The meeting is scheduled to last until 5:00 p.m. Please come prepared to discuss the evaluation results as a member of both the large and small groups.

Before attending the meeting, take a few minutes and send the following information to _____ by _____ so we know who is attending the meeting. Thank you.

Name:

Role:

E-mail:

Relationship to the Districtwide Writer's Workshop Professional Learning Program:

Reason for volunteering to be a member of the Study Group:

Send this information to ___ (name and e-mail) _____ by ____(date)_____.

Suggestions for Reading the Report

As you read the report, consider using these codes and mark the text:

  ++ Strongly agree

  + Agree

  ?? Not clear to me

  ! Disagree

  !! Strongly disagree

Jot down questions you want to ask the following people. Mark the appropriate column to indicate whom you want to answer the questions.

Questions to Ask	District Staff	Evaluator	Program Staff	Program Participants	Policy Makers	Other Study Group Members

You may submit your questions in advance or bring a copy of these questions to the meeting.

Study Group Protocol

Step 3: Launch the meeting.

Facilitator introduces himself or herself.

Step 4: Introduce participants.

Members introduce themselves and state their interest in the program.

Step 5: Set agreements.

Facilitator and members make agreements for the conversation like the ones below.

- We will focus on the report and not our personal opinions or hunches.
- We will focus on the issues, not people.
- We will not find fault, but rather find possibilities.
- We will listen fully to each other's comments.
- We will approach this discussion with an inquisitive mind rather than a fix-it mind-set. That is, we want to understand rather than to act. We may choose to act after we fully understand. Understanding is the focus of this meeting.
- We will refer frequently to the report when we speak, pausing to let each member find the right page before we ask questions or make comments.

Step 6: Guide the discussion.

Facilitator guides the discussion using the questions below.

1. What did the report tell us?

2. What did you learn about the program that you didn't know?

3. What data sources were most influential to you?

4. What aspects of the report did you strongly agree with?

5. What aspects of the report did you disagree with?

6. What questions do you have about the report? Let's try to get answers to those questions.

7. What did you learn today about the evaluation and the program?

8. Who else needs to know about this report?

9. How do you plan to share what you learned today with your colleagues?

10. What might be some next steps for the program staff?

Table 10.6 Text Response Protocol for Reviewing Evaluation Reports

---

Follow steps 1–5 in Table 10.5.

Step 6: Guide discussion.

Facilitator asks participants to jot down five to ten ideas, each on separate index cards, that they found to be significant in the report and on the reverse side of the card a few words about why each idea is significant. (Allow about 10 minutes for individual review of the report, the codes, and writing the ideas.)

Step 7: Share significant ideas.

Facilitator asks participants to meet with three different people, each for 4 minutes, during which they each share one of their significant ideas and the reasons for selecting it. (Allow about 15 minutes for the three rounds and moving to find new partners each time.)

Step 8: Summarize significant ideas.

Facilitator asks participants to cluster their significant ideas together. One or two participants might begin by clustering theirs into groups on a wall using tape or pins to post their index cards. Others follow, creating new clusters as needed. Ideas that don't fit into any existing cluster are posted separately. After all cards are clustered, the facilitator assigns a small group of participants to each cluster to take responsibility for labeling the cluster and writing a single, succinct summary statement of the ideas within the cluster. (Allow about 10 minutes for clustering and 10 minutes for labeling and summarizing.)

Step 9: Share summary statements.

Facilitator asks each group to read its summary statement.

Step 10: Respond to questions.

Facilitator invites questions from the participants and encourages program staff or participants to respond.

Evaluators have a responsibility to encourage, support, and facilitate dissemination of evaluation results, yet they work collaboratively with primary stakeholders in coordinating dissemination. The *Program Evaluation Standards* in Appendix B, P5 Transparency and Disclosure states, "Evaluations should provide complete descriptions of findings, limitations, and conclusions to all stakeholders, unless doing so would violate legal and propriety obligations" (Yarbrough, Shulha, Hopson, & Caruthers, 2011). In addition, evaluators who plan to use information from the report to inform others about the evaluation process or as references for future work will want to ask permission to share the report with others. They must protect the identity of the school or district if they use the information to advance the field of evaluation.

USING EVALUATION RESULTS

As noted earlier, the completion of the evaluation report is not equivalent to its use, nor is dissemination of the results considered use of the results. Patton, the father of utilization-focused evaluation, joins a list of other renowned evaluators in advocating for use of evaluation results. To him, use of evaluation is both an ethical and management issue. "How evaluations are used affects the spending

of billions of dollars to fight problems of poverty, disease, ignorance, joblessness, mental anguish, crime, hunger, and inequality. How are programs that combat these societal ills to be judged? How does one distinguish effective from ineffective programs? And how can evaluation be conducted in ways that lead to use? How do we avoid producing reports that gather dust on bookshelves, unread and unused?" (2008, p. 4)

Use, according to Patton (2008), is engagement of stakeholders in ways that foster their understanding of, perceived value of, and action on the evaluation results. He categorizes use into several areas. Those areas practitioner evaluators are most concerned about include instrumental, conceptual use, or process use. Instrumental use is the direct use of evaluation results to make decisions about the program; develop a new process, policy, or action; or solve a problem related to the program. In the evaluation of the writer's workshop professional learning program, an instrumental use might be to support more classroom coaching for teachers who had lower implementation scores. Instrumental uses have a clear, identifiable action that follows from the recommendations or the evaluation results. Conceptual use influences how people, often those not immediately involved in the program, perceive the program, related policies, or processes, yet there is no direct use of the results to inform decisions about the program. In the evaluation of an instructional coaching program, a local school board in a neighboring district that had been questioning the district's proposal to implement coaching, better understood how coaching can impact teaching quality and student achievement. Process use is a change in the perceived value of evaluation or the evaluation process as a means for improvement. The results of process use are often related to what is evaluated or how evaluation occurs within an organization and may lead to program changes in terms of the extent or types of evaluation that occur. The evaluation process is the focus of this kind of use.

Patton (2008, 2015) identifies other types of uses for evaluations, some having a longer-term effect, some being more political in nature, and some being representations of misuses. A longer-term use of an evaluation might be in providing information that shapes future professional learning programs or changes the policy discourse related to the role of professional learning in schools. Political uses include mandatory compliance evaluations that are done because they are required and considered perfunctory responsibilities of program managers. Some political uses can elevate and legitimize programs, justify existing programs or approaches to addressing problems, or create a supportive environment for evaluation as a worthwhile investment. Misuses include using evaluation to justify an established position or suppress different ones, incomplete or inaccurate evaluations, or overuse of evaluation.

The best measure of use is the direct engagement of stakeholders in all aspects of the evaluation process. Practitioner evaluators are in the best position to support and manage engagement of stakeholders in the evaluation process. However, there are some potential ethical and political cautions to raise for evaluators or practitioner evaluators. One is involving only the key stakeholders or those who have a specific interest in the success of the program, such as the program director or staff. Another is limiting opportunities for engagement to those whose views are different or who have been underserved by the program. Evaluators must be thoughtful, deliberate, and unbiased in serving the

purpose of the evaluation and ensuring that the purpose is not satisfying one of the misuses. Evaluators must also understand and monitor their own values and how they influence their evaluation. Engaging a diverse, representative team of stakeholders and program participants as a collaboration team is a good way to increase use and avoid issues related to bias.

Reporting, disseminating, and using evaluation results requires evaluators to engage closely with primary stakeholders in all aspects of this step of the evaluation process. Practitioner evaluators and stakeholders of professional learning programs seek lessons learned from their work and to apply their learning to the program being evaluated and other professional learning programs to strengthen them. As the field of professional learning continues to grow and establish a firmer foundation based on evidence, every evaluation offers an opportunity to contribute knowledge to that foundation. Building on the successes of current professional learning and avoiding, when possible, past challenges, professional learning leaders will be able to design, implement, and evaluate more professional learning that has greater positive effects on educators and their students.

The rubric in Table 10.7 will guide evaluators in determining if their reporting, disseminating, and use of evaluation results meets high-level expectations.

Table 10.7   Reporting, Disseminating, and Using Evaluation Results Rubric

Reporting, Disseminating, and Using Evaluation Results	Incomplete Reporting, Disseminating, and Using Evaluation Results	Partially Complete Reporting, Disseminating, and Using Evaluation Results	Complete Reporting, Disseminating, and Using Evaluation Results
Choosing reporting formats	Evaluator selects a reporting format that aligns with the requests of the primary stakeholders.	Evaluator, working with primary stakeholders, selects reporting formats that are appropriate for the various audiences they intend the evaluation results to reach, including primary and secondary stakeholders, and participants.	Evaluator, working with representative stakeholders, selects reporting formats that are appropriate for the various audiences the evaluation results should reach, including primary and secondary stakeholders, participants, the public, policy makers, other program directors, and others beyond the school or school system.
Developing the report	Evaluator writes the evaluation reports and shares them with primary stakeholders.	Evaluator, using input from primary stakeholders about the contents and structure of the reports, writes the evaluation reports, shares them with various audiences for input, and revises them before submitting them to primary stakeholders.	Evaluator, using input from representative stakeholders about the contents and structure of the reports, writes the evaluation reports, shares them with representatives of various audiences for feedback on clarity, precision, accuracy, completeness, tone, and quality of presentation, and revises them before submitting them to primary stakeholders.

Reporting, Disseminating, and Using Evaluation Results	Incomplete Reporting, Disseminating, and Using Evaluation Results	Partially Complete Reporting, Disseminating, and Using Evaluation Results	Complete Reporting, Disseminating, and Using Evaluation Results
Selecting dissemination methods	Evaluator encourages primary stakeholders to disseminate the evaluation results in multiple ways to primary and secondary stakeholders and participants.	Evaluator facilitates discussion with representative stakeholders about a variety of methods for disseminating the evaluation results to primary and secondary stakeholders, participants, the public, policy makers, other program directors, and others beyond the school or school system.	Evaluator facilitates discussion with representative stakeholders about a variety of methods for disseminating the evaluation results and assists stakeholders in formulating a plan to disseminate the report to primary and secondary stakeholders, participants, the public, policy makers, other program directors, and others beyond the school or school system.
Disseminating results	Primary stakeholders, without support from the evaluator, disseminate evaluation results to various audiences.	Evaluator co-presents, co-facilitates, and/or supports representative stakeholders to execute their plan for disseminating evaluation results to identified audiences.	Evaluator assists representative stakeholders to design or select protocols or structures to use in disseminating evaluation results and co-presents, co-facilitates, and/or supports representative stakeholders to execute their plan for disseminating evaluation results to identified audiences.
Facilitating use	The evaluator encourages primary stakeholders to use the evaluation results.	Evaluator facilitates discussion with representative stakeholders about multiple uses for the evaluation results.	Evaluator facilitates discussion with representative stakeholders about multiple instrumental, conceptual, and process uses for the evaluation results and seeks permission to use the results in his or her own work, if granted and appropriate, to advance both the field of professional learning and evaluation.

Planning Phase

- Assess evaluability
- Formulate evaluation questions
- Construct the evaluation framework

Conducting Phase

- Collect data
- Organize, analyze, and display data
- Interpret data

Reporting Phase

- Report, disseminate, and use findings
- Evaluate the evaluation

Evaluate the Evaluation

11

The work of evaluators is not finished when the evaluation results are disseminated. It is at this point when evaluators step back from their work and evaluate the evaluation. Daniel Stufflebeam and Anthony Shinkfield (2007) describes meta-evaluation as

> an evaluation to help detect and address problems, ensure quality, and reveal an evaluation's strengths and limitations. It is the process of delineating, obtaining, and applying descriptive information and judgmental information—about the utility, feasibility, propriety, and accuracy of an evaluation and its systematic nature, competent execution, integrity and honesty, respectfulness, and social responsibility—to guide the evaluation and report its strengths and weaknesses. Meta-evaluation is a professional evaluation of evaluators. (p. 705)

This meta-evaluation step gives evaluators an opportunity to (1) assess their work in light of externally established criteria for quality such as the *Program Evaluation Standards* in Appendix B; (2) seek an external review of the evaluation; and/or (3) reflect on their decisions and actions as evaluators, how they executed the evaluation, and how they interacted with stakeholders and participants. The intent of this step is to learn how to improve their work as evaluators and ensure that the work they have done is credible and valid. This practice is the hallmark of a reflective practitioner and allows evaluators to model evaluation behaviors as a routine part of their work and to engage in continual improvement.

At this stage, the evaluator seeks answers to these questions:

- How credible is the evaluation of the professional learning program?
- How valid are the evaluation results?

- What is the overall effectiveness and efficiency of this evaluation?
- What are the strengths and limitations of this evaluation?
- How well does the evaluation meet the program evaluation standards?
- What can we learn about evaluation process, our skills as evaluators, and our decisions and execution of the process that will improve future evaluations?

Professional evaluators focus on the first two opportunities, and practitioner evaluators concentrate their evaluation of the evaluation on the second and third. When the evaluator or evaluation team wants to strengthen their work, they may seek one or more **critical friends** who will review the evaluation planning, conducting, and reporting documents to offer input on the work. This may occur in the process of the evaluation so that the evaluator may adjust and improve the quality of the evaluation. For example, when developing an evaluation framework, the evaluator may ask others with experience in evaluation to review and comment on it before it is finalized. This same process might occur at several other steps of the process as well, such as during the data organization, analysis, and display step and the interpretation step. When the evaluator works with a team of others to conduct the evaluation, they collectively may serve as each other's critical friend. Using standards such as the program evaluation standards as criteria strengthens the review of the evaluation process. Donna Mertens and Amy Wilson (2012) recommend that evaluations of the evaluation by an external reviewer occur at three times during the evaluation process: (1) "after planning and before implementation"; (2) "midway through the evaluation"; and (3) "as the study nears an end" (p. 515). They recommend the use of a meta-evaluation framework presented in Table 11.1 to plan the meta-evaluation.

Practitioner evaluators may invite primary or representative stakeholders and participants to join in a review of the full eight steps of the evaluation process to share their perspectives. They may be more interested in focusing the meta-evaluation step on their work as evaluators and their engagement in the evaluation process. Doing so acknowledges that every experience is an opportunity to learn, models the importance of continuous improvement, and strengthens evaluators' future work. The process of conducting an evaluation of the evaluation is beneficial to stakeholders who requested or will use the

Table 11.1 Meta-evaluation Plan

At what point in the evaluation process will the review occur?	Who will review the evaluation work to date?	When will the review to occur?	What resources are needed?

Adapted from Mertens, D. M., & Wilson, A. T. (2012). *Program evaluation theory and practice: A comprehensive guide*. New York, NY: Guilford.

evaluation as well. It gives them time to reflect on the value of evaluation as a means for improvement, clarify what they learned, and offer insights about how evaluation can strengthen future professional learning decisions and programs.

There is no "right" way to conduct an evaluation of the evaluation. They require criteria for judging the quality of the evaluation work, clarity about who will be engaged, and a plan for conducting them. The process may be formal, as might be required in an external evaluation by a professional evaluator with the intent to publish the results or it may be informal such as one in which practitioner evaluators reflect on their work.

Stufflebeam (2007), in the *Program Evaluations Metaevaluation Checklist*, suggests that meta-evaluations can be guided by the actions included in Table 11.2.

Mertens and Wilson (2012) report on a study of meta-evaluations conducted by Carl Hanssen, Frances Lawrenz, and Diane Dunet (2008). They used three questions to guide their study of meta-evaluations:

1. "What are the strengths and weaknesses of the evaluation process, including each of its components in terms of producing its intended results? How can the evaluation process be improved?

2. How efficacious is the evaluation process for producing its intended results?

3. To what degree does the evaluation framework enable an evaluator to produce an evaluation that satisfied accepted program evaluation standards?" (p. 516).

Practitioner evaluators might employ one or more approaches for evaluating their evaluations. One strategy is to create a survey to administer to those involved in any aspect of the evaluation that seeks perspectives on various aspects of the evaluation process, opportunities for engagement, and quality of

Table 11.2   Stufflebeam's (2007) Meta-evaluation Recommendations

A12 Meta-evaluation
• Budget appropriately and sufficiently for conducting an internal meta-evaluation and, as feasible, an external meta-evaluation
• Designate or define the standards the evaluators used to guide and assess their evaluation
• Record the full range of information needed to judge the evaluation against the employed standards
• As feasible and appropriate, contract for an independent meta-evaluation
• Evaluate all important aspects of the evaluation, including the instrumentation, data collection, data handling, coding, analysis, synthesis, and reporting
• Obtain and report both formative and summative meta-evaluations to the right-to-know audiences

reporting and disseminating results. Another approach might be to conduct focus groups with representatives from the stakeholder groups to gather input on the evaluation process. Yet another approach is to have primary stakeholders engage in a discussion with the evaluator or evaluation team focused on the strengths, limitations, and opportunities for upgrading the evaluation process. Evaluators may want to add questions to the dissemination study group protocol about the value of the evaluation and the overall evaluation processes employed. Evaluating the evaluation minimally engages primary stakeholders, including the professional learning program director and other leaders involved in the evaluation, including decision and policy makers who used the evaluation results in offering perspectives about the evaluation processes uses. Evaluators may also want to seek input from professional learning program participants involved in the evaluation to assess the data-collection methods used and their perceived benefit of the evaluation process. Table 11.3, "Questions to Guide Meta-evaluation Discussions," might guide an evaluator or evaluation team in framing evaluating evaluation discussions.

Useful Resource for Meta-Evaluation

Stufflebeam, D. L. (2007). Program evaluations metaevaluation checklist. https://wmich.edu/sites/default/files/attachments/u350/2014/program_metaeval_short.pdf

---

When evaluators seek to improve their own work, increase the use of evaluation within an organization, and build the capacity of others to engage in **evaluation think**, they contribute to a greater purpose. Through their work, they convey the importance of evaluation as a process for improvement and ultimately for increasing the focus on results.

After an extensive or even brief evaluation study, evaluators and evaluation teams may not have the energy or motivation to engage in this last step. Yet this last step of the eight-step evaluation process is the opportunity to grow as professional evaluators, model continuous improvement, strengthen evaluators' capacity, and increase the value of evaluation within education systems.

Table 11.3   Questions to Guide Meta-evaluation Discussions

Results

- How valid and credible are the evaluation results?
- How adequately do the data provided support conclusions drawn from the evaluation?
- How well does the evaluation meet program evaluation standards or other criteria established as indicators of quality of the evaluation?

Resources

- How sufficient were the time, personnel, and money allocated for this evaluation adequate to conduct the evaluation as it was designed?

Design

- How well did the evaluation framework align with the evaluation question(s) and provide the appropriate data to answer each question(s)?
- How were appropriate stakeholders involved in the design of this evaluation?
- How did the evaluation address the questions program stakeholders wanted and needed answered?
- How appropriate, efficient, and effective were the data-collection procedures?

Analysis/Findings/Interpretation of Data

- How appropriate were the data-analysis methods for the type of evaluation conducted?
- How clearly were the data displayed? How well did the data displays facilitate use of the data to formulate findings and support interpretation?
- How certain are we that the findings are credible, unbiased, and drawn from rigorous analysis of the data?
- How were multiple, appropriate stakeholders involved in the analysis and interpretation of the data and in formulating recommendations?
- How well do the recommendation flow from the data analysis and findings and how clear, concrete, actionable, timely, and reasonable are the recommendations based on the evaluation findings and interpretation?

Reporting

- How clearly and appropriately are the findings presented for the various audiences?
- To what degree do the intended users find the evaluation results to be useful, informative, and illuminating to guide decisions about the professional learning program?
- What opportunities did stakeholders have to ask questions about the evaluation results?
- In what ways have the evaluation reports been used? What plans are in place to act on the evaluation's recommendations or others that resulted from stakeholders?
- What program changes have occurred or are being planned as a result of this evaluation?

Evaluator

- How professional, ethical, and objective was the evaluator?
- To what degree did the evaluator uphold the *Program Evaluation Standards* and the Guiding Principles for Evaluators?
- How did the evaluator demonstrate the ability to be collaborative, culturally sensitive, and responsive to the needs of the program's manager, primary stakeholders, secondary stakeholders, and the participants?
- How did the evaluator engage in the evaluation of the evaluation?
- How has the evaluator made public the learnings he or she gained from this evaluation experience?

The evaluator might use the rubric in Table 11.4 to assess the effectiveness of her efforts to evaluate the evaluation.

Table 11.4 Evaluate the Evaluation Rubric

Evaluate the Evaluation	Incomplete Evaluation of the Evaluation	Partially Complete Evaluation of the Evaluation	Complete Evaluation of the Evaluation
Establishing criteria for the evaluation of the evaluation	Evaluator and/or evaluation team establishes no criteria for the evaluation of the evaluation.	Evaluator and/or evaluation team identifies areas of focus without specific criteria to guide the evaluation of the evaluation.	Evaluator and/or evaluation team identifies the criteria, such as *Program Evaluation Standards* or others, to use to guide the evaluation of the evaluation.
Selecting or developing a protocol or structure for evaluating the evaluation	Evaluator and/or evaluation team uses no protocol or structure to guide the evaluation of the evaluation.	Evaluator and/or evaluation team selects or designs a protocol or structure to guide the evaluation of the evaluation.	Evaluator and/or evaluation team selects or designs a protocol or structure to guide the evaluation of the evaluation that ensures gathering input from multiple, diverse perspectives and is focused on strengthening the evaluation process.
Engaging stakeholders in the evaluation of the evaluation	Evaluator and/or evaluation team conducts the evaluation of the evaluation without input from others.	Evaluator and/or evaluation team involves primary stakeholders, participants, and critical friends in the evaluation of the evaluation.	Evaluator and/or evaluation team involves representative stakeholders, participants, and external critical friends in the evaluation of the evaluation.
Identifying learnings from the evaluation of the evaluation	Evaluator and/or evaluation team fails to articulate explicit learnings from the evaluation of the evaluation.	Evaluator and/or evaluation team summarizes the evaluation of the evaluation, yet does not articulate explicit, actionable learning to apply in future evaluations.	Evaluator and/or evaluation team articulates explicit, actionable learnings drawn from the evaluation of the evaluation to strengthen future evaluations and minimize challenges.
Applying learnings to future work	Evaluator and/or evaluation team neglects to plan how to integrate learnings into future evaluations.	Evaluator and/or evaluation team states their intent to apply what they learned in the future without a specific plan to do so.	Evaluator and/or evaluation team formulates a plan to implement the learnings from the evaluation of the evaluation into future work as an evaluator.

Shifting Perspectives About Evaluating Professional Learning

12

Evaluating a professional learning program begins with a commitment to continuous improvement and to impacting educator and student success. It is in this context that the evaluation of professional learning becomes necessary and beneficial. When conducted as a routine part of any program, evaluation provides valuable information to help program managers make decisions so that the program positively impacts its clients. Table 12.1 describes the shift in thinking and practice the first edition of this book called for to move evaluation into a more favorable light. Few changes are needed in the list. What was needed nearly 20 years ago continues to be relevant today in the third edition. There continues to be a need to incorporate evaluation as routine practice for professional learning leaders.

Yet with the increase in accountability to quality, equity, effectiveness, and impact of professional learning, educators continue to face common challenges. Some of those challenges are described below with suggestions for circumventing them. Educators have more technology and accountability to leverage improvement in their evaluation practice, yet their willingness and engagement are lagging. New efforts to bring manageable evaluation processes to districts through rapid-cycle evaluation and processes of continuous improvement using the Edward Deming Plan-Do-Study-Act cycle are beginning to be more evident in schools and school systems. As districts step up to the challenge embedded within *ESSA* and state accountability systems, their opportunities to employ evaluation think and the eight-step evaluation process will increase.

Those who lead professional learning have a responsibility to use evaluation to continuously improve both the overall system of professional learning and its components. **Comprehensive professional learning systems** include a clear vision, professional learning standards, definition, assumptions, and

Table 12.1 Paradigm Shift in Evaluating Professional Learning

From evaluation that is	To evaluation that is
Externally driven and designed	Internally driven and designed
Summative only	Needs, planning, formative, and summative
Event focused	Program focused
Looking for answers/solutions from others	Discovering or creating solutions and alternatives with others
Feared by stakeholders and participants	Embraced by stakeholders and participants
Occasional	Continual
Filed/shelved by stakeholders	Used by stakeholders
Done as an afterthought	Planned from the beginning of the program inception
Documentation of program activities	Evaluation of merit, worth, impact, and value of a program
Process focused	Results focused
A report of evaluation results	A reflective dialogue about and use of the evaluation results

> Professional learning that increases educator effectiveness and results for all students uses a variety of sources and types of student, educator, and system data to plan, assess, and evaluate professional learning (Learning Forward, 2011).

well-orchestrated operational processes that include roles and responsibilities, decision-making authority, ongoing evaluation, and resource management (Killion, 2013). Evaluation is an essential component of a professional learning system designed to enhance and support the capacity of the education workforce to reach high levels of performance and contribute to the success of their immediate clients (Killion, 2013).

The standards for professional learning also call for evaluation of professional learning. Yet many professional learning leaders approach the work of evaluating professional learning as an option or second thought rather than a core responsibility. In their description of the core responsibilities of central office learning leaders, Joellen Killion and Cindy Harrison (2016) emphasize the significance of evaluation as a part of several roles. Learning system designers, they say, conduct "evaluation of the learning experience, the results, and the return on investment" (p. 46). Program managers, another role of learning leaders, are responsible for "evaluating the systemwide effectiveness of the professional learning and assisting other leaders, including leadership teams at schools, to evaluate the effectiveness of local, school-based professional learning" (p. 47). Facilitators, they add, "draw from a wide repertoire of processes, tactics, and strategies. They help groups clarify their purpose and task; gather,

organize, analyze, and evaluate needed data; determine a course of action; identify and solve problems; generate and evaluate solutions; make decisions; communicate with the larger community they represent; and assume responsibility for the outcome of the team's work" (p. 49). Change agents, they add, "use skills in needs assessment; data gathering, analysis, and interpretation; planning; evaluation; resource acquisition; and forecasting to plan, initiate, implement, and assess change efforts" (p. 51). Each aspect of the role of learning leaders, whether they are in schools, school systems, state or ministry departments of education, or other private or public education agencies, has a responsibility to evaluate the professional learning they provide.

Increasingly, practitioner evaluators are ready to take up the work of evaluating professional learning; however, they wonder where to begin and how to overcome what they perceive to be major obstacles in the way. This chapter offers some guidance on both.

JUMP IN

There are multiple places to start the work of evaluating professional learning. Two logical beginning points are assessing the overall quality of professional learning and evaluating the impact of existing programs of professional learning. Standards for professional learning and evaluation, state policies on professional learning, *ESSA*, and other guidance and regulatory documents call for some form of evaluation of professional learning. While assessing the quality of professional learning is not measuring its impact, it provides helpful information for strengthening the comprehensive professional learning system, educator access to professional learning, and the perception of its capacity to meet educator needs in its design, opportunity, and reach. No measure of quality is a sufficient substitute for a measure of impact, yet it is a helpful place to begin a needs or problem evaluation to identify what changes are necessary in the current professional learning system to increase the likelihood of impact. Professional learning that does not meet the needs, is not designed to promote deep-level learning, and is challenged with insufficient workplace support is unlikely to have an impact on educator practice and their clients.

The second and easily a parallel place to begin is to evaluate existing professional learning programs or new ones. Every school or school system has a set of standing professional learning programs. They may not be constructed as a program as defined in this book or meet evaluability criteria, yet practitioners might fill in the missing design components to evaluate their impact. Districts routinely have professional learning programs for aspiring principals, teacher leaders, coaching, technology integration, personalized learning, instructional strategies, or many other areas. Many districts have, for instance, programs to orient and induct new staff members, which are often accompanied by mentoring. Practitioner evaluators might explore how each activity they conduct to contribute to the success of new employees adds to their overall outcomes of retention, success, and sense of support. Using the eight-step

evaluation process helps those who contribute to the overall outcomes know what part they play in achieving them, promotes gathering data to answer the evaluation questions, and ultimately helps them know if their actions are adding up to the results they intend. They will quickly move to data-informed improvements in their newly constructed program of professional learning and most likely strong results for participants and their clients.

BRING A COLLEAGUE

Evaluation done in teams is more enjoyable and often a richer experience than evaluation done alone. It can be a form of professional learning for the team that uses an action research approach. Working together with one or more colleagues who are interested in learning how to evaluate professional learning more effectively can be the start of a community of practice that aims to solve the problem of how to evaluate professional learning more effectively. Team members might commit to joining a team to be a part of a single evaluation effort or to have team members support their individual evaluations. A novice evaluator or one who wants to continue to refine his or her expertise might use the team as a group of critical friends, or as Scriven (2009) suggests "**smart enemies**," which may be more honest than a group of friends. A critical friend can provide honest and rigorous reviews of another colleague's work, especially if the criteria are clear and shared. They can also be learning partners with the practitioner evaluator. Studying *Assessing Impact: Evaluating Professional Learning* as a foundation for their collaborative work develops their expertise and supports their application of the evaluation process. Their community members help solve knotty problems encountered along the way, providing compliments, suggestions, wonderings, and upgrades while learning from the work of others.

One example of such a community of practice occurred in Denver several years ago when a group of school district and community agency leaders came together, facilitated by this author, to learn about evaluation and to conduct parallel evaluations with continuous input and support from the community. They met together over a year, began with a brief training on the eight-step evaluation process, and proceeded to develop and implement their own program evaluation. At each subsequent meeting members brought their work for review and comment by community of practice members. Sharing their work reinforced the complexity of evaluation, yet the support of the community of practice members facilitated problem solving, fueled members' energy and commitment, and produced multiple successful practitioner evaluations of programs that existed and evaluation frameworks for emerging programs. Another example is Learning Forward's Academy program in which members seek solutions to problems of practice, implement them, and evaluate their effectiveness. Throughout the Academy, members learn about the eight-step evaluation process; develop theories of change, logic models, and evaluation frameworks with the support of their team members; conduct their evaluations; and present their results to the team.

DANCE TO THE MUSIC

Evaluation, if done well, takes time, effort, and resources. It is not about being judged for punitive purposes, but rather about learning as an organization to achieve excellence. Rather than waiting for the resources to magically appear or the mandate to evaluate to come crashing down, professional learning leaders might step out and initiate the flash dance of leading learning organizations by engaging in continuous improvement through evaluation. Rarely is there sufficient time or resources for what educators believe is important, yet there is always a choice to invest in what matters most to ensure that educators are engaging in learning to build their capacity to serve students. It takes one early adopter to start a movement. Modeling the value and process of evaluation can be enough to help others realize the opportunity evaluation provides them to engage in continuous learning.

SHIFT PERCEPTION

Evaluation is not about being judged for punitive purposes, but rather about learning as an organization to engage in continuous improvement to achieve excellence. Rather than viewing evaluation as a process that instills fear and inspection, professional learning leaders can shift their perception to seeing evaluation as a learning experience. Learning, after all, is the primary purpose of professional learning within an organization—learning to perform at higher levels, becoming more creative, resourceful, imaginative, efficient, and effective in the workplace. Evaluation provides the data to inform decisions, to maximize resources and effort—to make the changes in individual and collective capacity and the systems and structures to support the desired outcomes. Evaluators can use Table 12.1 as a starting point for examining their current and desired perceptions about evaluation.

TAP WHAT EXISTS

While the amount of data available in schools and school systems has increased exponentially with the advent of data warehouses and management systems collecting multiple forms of data from multiple sources, professional learning leaders continue to grapple with access to data. The logic of not having access to data is wearing thin as a reason to delay evaluation of professional learning. What is perhaps a more reasonable obstacle is access to data through data walls that protect identities and privacy of educators and students. These challenges can be overcome with evaluation designs that use data from groups, clusters, or pools of educators or students, perhaps disaggregated by some demographic factors such as type of school, years of experience, or content or level of school that remove the potential for breaching anonymity. Before imagining new forms or sources of data, professional learning leaders

can look first to what is available and can be used to inform evaluations. This means that practitioner evaluators consider using more approximate measures rather than direct or authentic measures of variables within evaluation questions, such as existing work products, student work, records, and surveys as evidence of implementation rather than observations, which allows the work of evaluation to continue. Waiting for the perfect conditions means delaying the opportunity to grow and learn. And, in the process of evaluation, new more useful methods for collecting data might be created and integrated into existing data-management systems.

Professional learning leaders might also examine existing processes that integrate evaluation as a necessary component. School improvement plans, strategic plans, grant-funded programs, and federal or state programs include evaluation as a necessary component. Professional learning leaders can use these required evaluations as opportunities to apply the eight-step evaluation process to expand practice and expertise in evaluation.

START SMALL, DREAM BIG

If evaluation is not a routine part of a professional learning leader's work, finding both the courage to begin and the time, fiscal, and physical resources to begin can be overwhelming. Scaling evaluation too quickly and to every program immediately is unreasonable. Professional learning leaders can begin with small steps, creating the vision for the day when evaluation is integrated into the conversation of every need to be addresses and planning for the initiative to address it. When a few basic questions are introduced early on as problems are identified and solutions developed, the initiative's plan will be more evaluable from the beginning. These questions might include what changes in behavior are needed to achieve these outcomes, what constitutes success, what data will provide credible and valid evidence of success, and what is important to know about this initiative? Approaching any initiative planning through the lens of evaluation think strengthens the plan and implementation.

OWN IT

Evaluation is everyone's responsibility. From the time of infancy throughout the life span, humans engage in forming judgments. An infant knows that a comforting pat, a soothing voice, or warm touch is preferable to being cold and damp. A child develops a preference for certain flavors. A student likes some subjects better than others. An adult prefers the company of people with certain attributes. Yet choices based on one's own subjective preference is not the work of evaluators. Developing an objective, analytic approach to formulating judgments requires critical thinking, and critical thinking is developed over time with practice that is guided by applying criteria against which to assess practice. The program evaluation standards and the guidelines for evaluating education programs in Appendices B2 and B3 are such criteria. Adopting a professional goal to improve one's evaluation practice through applying the

eight-step process is one way to own the responsibility of eliminating subjective judgments based on opinion or insufficient evidence.

TAKE A COMPASS

There are many excellent resources and books on evaluating programs. The field of evaluation has existed for more than half a century, and scholars continue to enlighten practitioners with more guidance and resources to inform their work. Professional learning leaders need a compass to direct their work. The eight-step process, founded on solid research and practice, is an example of one compass to guide the work of practitioner evaluators who decide to embark on the evaluation journey. While the adventure might be fun as a discovery process with rules and destinations made up along the way, it will be more expedient and effective if it is guided by the experience of those who have gone before who can provide a stepwise process to shape the work so that it leads to success.

FINAL NOTE

Evaluation is about improvement. Evaluating professional learning enables professional learning program leaders, stakeholders, and participants to make data-informed decisions about the program. If the evaluation is done well, everyone benefits. If done poorly, it will be a waste of resources. The most useful evaluations result from a desire to improve both the program and its results, thoughtful planning, careful implementation, and use of the evaluation findings. "With data collected in formative and summative evaluations, leaders of the professional learning systems have evidence to make improvements. Second, they generate evidence to determine whether the system is working both to support effective professional learning planning, implementation, and evaluation and to improve educator effectiveness and student success. In addition, an evaluation can inform resource investments. For a comprehensive professional learning system to work smoothly and to meet its many goals, all components of the system must be finely tuned and coherent" (Killion, 2013, p. 47). Professional learning leaders who are committed to developing the capacity of educators so that they meet the learning needs of students must be simultaneously committed to improving the quality and impact of the professional learning in which educators engage.

Appendix A
ESSA Definition of Professional Development

DEFINITION

"(42) PROFESSIONAL DEVELOPMENT.—The term 'professional

development' means activities that—
"(A) are an integral part of school and local educational

agency strategies for providing educators (including teachers, principals, other school leaders, specialized instructional support personnel, paraprofessionals, and, as applicable, early childhood educators) with the knowledge and skills necessary to enable students to succeed in a well-rounded education and to meet the challenging State academic standards; and

"(B) are sustained (not stand-alone, 1-day, or short term workshops), intensive, collaborative, job-embedded, data-driven, and classroom-focused, and may include activities that—

"(i) improve and increase teachers'—
"(I) knowledge of the academic subjects the

teachers teach;
"(II) understanding of how students learn; and

S. 1177—296

"(III) ability to analyze student work and achievement from multiple sources, including how to adjust instructional strategies, assessments, and materials based on such analysis;
"(ii) are an integral part of broad schoolwide and

districtwide educational improvement plans;

"(iii) allow personalized plans for each educator to address the educator's specific needs identified in

observation or other feedback;

"(iv) improve classroom management skills;

"(v) support the recruitment, hiring, and training

of effective teachers, including teachers who became certified through State and local alternative routes to certification;

"(vi) advance teacher understanding of—

"(I) effective instructional strategies that are

evidence-based; and

"(II) strategies for improving student academic

achievement or substantially increasing the knowledge and teaching skills of teachers;

"(vii) are aligned with, and directly related to,

academic goals of the school or local educational agency;

"(viii) are developed with extensive participation of teachers, principals, other school leaders, parents, representatives of Indian tribes (as applicable), and administrators of schools to be served under this Act;

"(ix) are designed to give teachers of English learners, and other teachers and instructional staff, the knowledge and skills to provide instruction and appropriate language and academic support services to those children, including the appropriate use of curricula and assessments;

"(x) to the extent appropriate, provide training for teachers, principals, and other school leaders in the use of technology (including education about the harms of copyright piracy), so that technology and technology applications are effectively used in the classroom to improve teaching and learning in the curricula and academic subjects in which the teachers teach;

"(xi) as a whole, are regularly evaluated for their impact on increased teacher effectiveness and improved student academic achievement, with the findings of the evaluations used to improve the quality of professional development;

"(xii) are designed to give teachers of children with disabilities or children with developmental delays, and other teachers and instructional staff, the knowledge and skills to provide instruction and academic support services, to those children, including positive behavioral interventions and supports, multi-tier system of supports, and use of accommodations;

"(xiii) include instruction in the use of data and assessments to inform and instruct classroom practice;

S. 1177—297

"(xiv) include instruction in ways that teachers, principals, other school leaders, specialized instructional support personnel, and school administrators may work more effectively with parents and families;

"(xv) involve the forming of partnerships with institutions of higher education, including, as applicable, Tribal Colleges and Universities as defined in section 316(b) of the Higher Education Act of 1965 (20 U.S.C. 1059c(b)), to establish school-based teacher, principal, and other school leader training programs that provide prospective teachers, novice teachers, principals, and other school leaders with an opportunity to work under the guidance of experienced teachers, principals, other school leaders, and faculty of such institutions;

"(xvi) create programs to enable paraprofessionals (assisting teachers employed by a local educational agency receiving assistance under part A of title I) to obtain the education necessary for those paraprofessionals to become certified and licensed teachers;

"(xvii) provide follow-up training to teachers who have participated in activities described in this paragraph that are designed to ensure that the knowledge and skills learned by the teachers are implemented in the classroom; and

"(xviii) where practicable, provide jointly for school staff and other early childhood education program providers, to address the transition to elementary school, including issues related to school readiness."

S. 1177-3, 8002, 42

Appendix B

Standards to Guide Evaluation of Professional Learning Programs

APPENDIX B1. STANDARDS FROM PROFESSIONAL LEARNING

Learning communities: Professional learning that increases educator effectiveness and results for all students occurs within learning communities committed to continuous improvement, collective responsibility, and goal alignment.

Leadership: Professional learning that increases educator effectiveness and results for all students requires skillful leaders who develop capacity, advocate, and create support systems for professional learning.

Resources: educator effectiveness and results for all students requires prioritizing, monitoring, and coordinating resources for educator learning.

Data: Professional learning that increases educator effectiveness and results for all students uses a variety of sources and types of student, educator, and system data to plan, assess, and evaluate professional learning.

Learning designs: Professional learning that increases educator effectiveness and results for all students integrates theories, research, and models of human learning to achieve its intended outcomes.

Implementation: Professional learning that increases educator effectiveness and results for all students applies research on change and sustains support for implementation of professional learning for long term change.

Outcomes: Professional learning that increases educator effectiveness and results for all students aligns its outcomes with educator performance and student curriculum standards.

Used with permission. Learning Forward. (2011). *Standards for professional learning.* Oxford, OH: Author.

APPENDIX B2. PROGRAM EVALUATION STANDARDS STATEMENTS

Joint Commission on Evaluation in Education

Utility Standards

The utility standards are intended to increase the extent to which program stakeholders find evaluation processes and products valuable in meeting their needs.

- **U1 Evaluator Credibility** Evaluations should be conducted by qualified people who establish and maintain credibility in the evaluation context.
- **U2 Attention to Stakeholders** Evaluations should devote attention to the full range of individuals and groups invested in the program and affected by its evaluation.
- **U3 Negotiated Purposes** Evaluation purposes should be identified and continually negotiated based on the needs of stakeholders.
- **U4 Explicit Values** Evaluations should clarify and specify the individual and cultural values underpinning purposes, processes, and judgments.
- **U5 Relevant Information** Evaluation information should serve the identified and emergent needs of stakeholders.
- **U6 Meaningful Processes and Products** Evaluations should construct activities, descriptions, and judgments in ways that encourage participants to rediscover, reinterpret, or revise their understandings and behaviors.
- **U7 Timely and Appropriate Communicating and Reporting** Evaluations should attend to the continuing information needs of their multiple audiences.
- **U8 Concern for Consequences and Influence** Evaluations should promote responsible and adaptive use while guarding against unintended negative consequences and misuse.

Feasibility Standards

The feasibility standards are intended to increase evaluation effectiveness and efficiency.

- **F1 Project Management** Evaluations should use effective project management strategies.
- **F2 Practical Procedures** Evaluation procedures should be practical and responsive to the way the program operates.
- **F3 Contextual Viability** Evaluations should recognize, monitor, and balance the cultural and political interests and needs of individuals and groups.
- **F4 Resource Use** Evaluations should use resources effectively and efficiently.

Propriety Standards

The propriety standards support what is proper, fair, legal, right and just in evaluations.

- **P1 Responsive and Inclusive Orientation** Evaluations should be responsive to stakeholders and their communities.
- **P2 Formal Agreements** Evaluation agreements should be negotiated to make obligations explicit and take into account the needs, expectations, and cultural contexts of clients and other stakeholders.
- **P3 Human Rights and Respect** Evaluations should be designed and conducted to protect human and legal rights and maintain the dignity of participants and other stakeholders.
- **P4 Clarity and Fairness** Evaluations should be understandable and fair in addressing stakeholder needs and purposes.
- **P5 Transparency and Disclosure** Evaluations should provide complete descriptions of findings, limitations, and conclusions to all stakeholders, unless doing so would violate legal and propriety obligations.
- **P6 Conflicts of Interests** Evaluations should openly and honestly identify and address real or perceived conflicts of interests that may compromise the evaluation.
- **P7 Fiscal Responsibility** Evaluations should account for all expended resources and comply with sound fiscal procedures and processes.

Accuracy Standards

The accuracy standards are intended to increase the dependability and truthfulness of evaluation representations, propositions, and findings, especially those that support interpretations and judgments about quality.

- **A1 Justified Conclusions and Decisions** Evaluation conclusions and decisions should be explicitly justified in the cultures and contexts where they have consequences.
- **A2 Valid Information** Evaluation information should serve the intended purposes and support valid interpretations.
- **A3 Reliable Information** Evaluation procedures should yield sufficiently dependable and consistent information for the intended uses.
- **A4 Explicit Program and Context Descriptions** Evaluations should document programs and their contexts with appropriate detail and scope for the evaluation purposes.
- **A5 Information Management** Evaluations should employ systematic information collection, review, verification, and storage methods.
- **A6 Sound Designs and Analyses** Evaluations should employ technically adequate designs and analyses that are appropriate for the evaluation purposes.
- **A7 Explicit Evaluation Reasoning** Evaluation reasoning leading from information and analyses to findings, interpretations, conclusions, and judgments should be clearly and completely documented.

- **A8 Communication and Reporting** Evaluation communications should have adequate scope and guard against misconceptions, biases, distortions, and errors.

Evaluation Accountability Standards

The evaluation accountability standards encourage adequate documentation of evaluations and a metaevaluative perspective focused on improvement and accountability for evaluation processes and products.

- **E1 Evaluation Documentation** Evaluations should fully document their negotiated purposes and implemented designs, procedures, data, and outcomes.
- **E2 Internal Metaevaluation** Evaluators should use these and other applicable standards to examine the accountability of the evaluation design, procedures employed, information collected, and outcomes.
- **E3 External Metaevaluation** Program evaluation sponsors, clients, evaluators, and other stakeholders should encourage the conduct of external metaevaluations using these and other applicable standards.

Reprinted with permission from Yarbrough, D. B., Shulha, L. M., Hopson, R. K., & Caruthers, F. A. (2011). *The program evaluation standards: A guide for evaluators and evaluation users* (3rd ed.). Thousand Oaks, CA: Sage.

APPENDIX B3. AMERICAN EVALUATION ASSOCIATION GUIDING PRINCIPLES FOR EVALUATORS

Revisions reflected herein ratified by the AEA membership, July 2004

Preface: Assumptions Concerning Development of Principles

A. Evaluation is a profession composed of persons with varying interests, potentially encompassing but not limited to the evaluation of programs, products, personnel, policy, performance, proposals, technology, research, theory, and even of evaluation itself. These principles are broadly intended to cover all kinds of evaluation. For external evaluations of public programs, they nearly always apply. However, it is impossible to write guiding principles that neatly fit every context in which evaluators work, and some evaluators will work in contexts in which following a guideline cannot be done for good reason. The Guiding Principles are not intended to constrain such evaluators when this is the case. However, such exceptions should be made for good reason (e.g., legal prohibitions against releasing information to stakeholders), and evaluators who find themselves in such contexts should consult colleagues about how to proceed.

B. Based on differences in training, experience, and work settings, the profession of evaluation encompasses diverse perceptions about the primary purpose of evaluation. These include but are not limited to the following: bettering products, personnel, programs, organizations, governments, consumers and the public interest; contributing to informed decision making and more enlightened change; precipitating needed change; empowering all stakeholders by collecting data from them and engaging them in the evaluation process; and experiencing the excitement of new insights. Despite that diversity, the common ground is that evaluators aspire to construct and provide the best possible information that might bear on the value of whatever is being evaluated. The principles are intended to foster that primary aim.

C. The principles are intended to guide the professional practice of evaluators, and to inform evaluation clients and the general public about the principles they can expect to be upheld by professional evaluators. Of course, no statement of principles can anticipate all situations that arise in the practice of evaluation. However, principles are not just guidelines for reaction when something goes wrong or when a dilemma is found. Rather, principles should proactively guide the behaviors of professionals in everyday practice.

D. The purpose of documenting guiding principles is to foster continuing development of the profession of evaluation, and the socialization of its members. The principles are meant to stimulate discussion about the

proper practice and use of evaluation among members of the profession, sponsors of evaluation, and others interested in evaluation.

E. The five principles proposed in this document are not independent, but overlap in many ways. Conversely, sometimes these principles will conflict, so that evaluators will have to choose among them. At such times evaluators must use their own values and knowledge of the setting to determine the appropriate response. Whenever a course of action is unclear, evaluators should solicit the advice of fellow evaluators about how to resolve the problem before deciding how to proceed.

F. These principles are intended to supercede [sic] any previous work on standards, principles, or ethics adopted by AEA or its two predecessor organizations, the Evaluation Research Society and the Evaluation Network. These principles are the official position of AEA on these matters.

G. These principles are not intended to replace standards supported by evaluators or by the other disciplines in which evaluators participate.

H. Each principle is illustrated by a number of statements to amplify the meaning of the overarching principle, and to provide guidance for its application. These illustrations are not meant to include all possible applications of that principle, nor to be viewed as rules that provide the basis for sanctioning violators.

I. These principles were developed in the context of Western cultures, particularly the United States, and so may reflect the experiences of that context. The relevance of these principles may vary across other cultures, and across subcultures within the United States.

J. These principles are part of an evolving process of self-examination by the profession, and should be revisited on a regular basis. Mechanisms might include officially-sponsored reviews of principles at annual meetings, and other forums for harvesting experience with the principles and their application. On a regular basis, but at least every five years, these principles ought to be examined for possible review and revision. In order to maintain association-wide awareness and relevance, all AEA members are encouraged to participate in this process.

The Principles

A. **Systematic Inquiry:** Evaluators conduct systematic, data-based inquiries.

1. To ensure the accuracy and credibility of the evaluative information they produce, evaluators should adhere to the highest technical standards appropriate to the methods they use.

2. Evaluators should explore with the client the shortcomings and strengths both of the various evaluation questions and the various approaches that might be used for answering those questions.

3. Evaluators should communicate their methods and approaches accurately and in sufficient detail to allow others to understand, interpret and critique their work. They should make clear the limitations of an evaluation and its results. Evaluators should discuss in a contextually appropriate way those values, assumptions, theories, methods, results, and analyses significantly affecting the interpretation of the evaluative findings. These statements apply to all aspects of the evaluation, from its initial conceptualization to the eventual use of findings.

B. **Competence:** Evaluators provide competent performance to stakeholders.

1. Evaluators should possess (or ensure that the evaluation team possesses) the education, abilities, skills and experience appropriate to undertake the tasks proposed in the evaluation.

2. To ensure recognition, accurate interpretation and respect for diversity, evaluators should ensure that the members of the evaluation team collectively demonstrate cultural competence. Cultural competence would be reflected in evaluators seeking awareness of their own culturally-based assumptions, their understanding of the worldviews of culturally-different participants and stakeholders in the evaluation, and the use of appropriate evaluation strategies and skills in working with culturally different groups. Diversity may be in terms of race, ethnicity, gender, religion, socio-economics, or other factors pertinent to the evaluation context.

3. Evaluators should practice within the limits of their professional training and competence, and should decline to conduct evaluations that fall substantially outside those limits. When declining the commission or request is not feasible or appropriate, evaluators should make clear any significant limitations on the evaluation that might result. Evaluators should make every effort to gain the competence directly or through the assistance of others who possess the required expertise.

4. Evaluators should continually seek to maintain and improve their competencies, in order to provide the highest level of performance in their evaluations. This continuing professional development might include formal coursework and workshops, self-study, evaluations of one's own practice, and working with other evaluators to learn from their skills and expertise.

C. **Integrity/Honesty:** Evaluators display honesty and integrity in their own behavior, and attempt to ensure the honesty and integrity of the entire evaluation process.

1. Evaluators should negotiate honestly with clients and relevant stakeholders concerning the costs, tasks to be undertaken, limitations of methodology, scope of results likely to be obtained, and uses of data resulting from a specific evaluation. It is primarily the

evaluator's responsibility to initiate discussion and clarification of these matters, not the client's.

2. Before accepting an evaluation assignment, evaluators should disclose any roles or relationships they have that might pose a conflict of interest (or appearance of a conflict) with their role as an evaluator. If they proceed with the evaluation, the conflict(s) should be clearly articulated in reports of the evaluation results.

3. Evaluators should record all changes made in the originally negotiated project plans, and the reasons why the changes were made. If those changes would significantly affect the scope and likely results of the evaluation, the evaluator should inform the client and other important stakeholders in a timely fashion (barring good reason to the contrary, before proceeding with further work) of the changes and their likely impact.

4. Evaluators should be explicit about their own, their clients', and other stakeholders' interests and values concerning the conduct and outcomes of an evaluation.

5. Evaluators should not misrepresent their procedures, data, or findings. Within reasonable limits, they should attempt to prevent or correct misuse of their work by others.

6. If evaluators determine that certain procedures or activities are likely to produce misleading evaluative information or conclusions, they have the responsibility to communicate their concerns and the reasons for them. If discussions with the client do not resolve these concerns, the evaluator should decline to conduct the evaluation. If declining the assignment is unfeasible or inappropriate, the evaluator should consult colleagues or relevant stakeholders about other proper ways to proceed. (Options might include discussions at a higher level, a dissenting cover letter or appendix, or refusal to sign the final document.)

7. Evaluators should disclose all sources of financial support for an evaluation, and the source of the request for the evaluation.

D. **Respect for People:** Evaluators respect the security, dignity, and self-worth of respondents, program participants, clients, and other evaluation stakeholders.

1. Evaluators should seek a comprehensive understanding of the important contextual elements of the evaluation. Contextual factors that may influence the results of a study include geographic location, timing, political and social climate, economic conditions, and other relevant activities in progress at the same time.

2. Evaluators should abide by current professional ethics, standards, and regulations regarding risks, harms, and burdens that might befall those participating in the evaluation; regarding informed consent for participation in evaluation; and regarding informing participants and clients about the scope and limits of confidentiality.

3. Because justified negative or critical conclusions from an evaluation must be explicitly stated, evaluations sometimes produce results that harm client or stakeholder interests. Under this circumstance, evaluators should seek to maximize the benefits and reduce any unnecessary harms that might occur, provided this will not compromise the integrity of the evaluation findings. Evaluators should carefully judge when the benefits from doing the evaluation or in performing certain evaluation procedures should be foregone because of the risks or harms. To the extent possible, these issues should be anticipated during the negotiation of the evaluation.

4. Knowing that evaluations may negatively affect the interests of some stakeholders, evaluators should conduct the evaluation and communicate its results in a way that clearly respects the stakeholders' dignity and self-worth.

5. Where feasible, evaluators should attempt to foster social equity in evaluation, so that those who give to the evaluation may benefit in return. For example, evaluators should seek to ensure that those who bear the burdens of contributing data and incurring any risks do so willingly, and that they have full knowledge of and opportunity to obtain any benefits of the evaluation. Program participants should be informed that their eligibility to receive services does not hinge on their participation in the evaluation.

6. Evaluators have the responsibility to understand and respect differences among participants, such as differences in their culture, religion, gender, disability, age, sexual orientation, and ethnicity, and to account for potential implications of these differences when planning, conducting, analyzing, and reporting evaluations.

E. **Responsibilities for General and Public Welfare:** Evaluators articulate and take into account the diversity of general and public interests and values that may be related to the evaluation.

1. When planning and reporting evaluations, evaluators should include relevant perspectives and interests of the full range of stakeholders.

2. Evaluators should consider not only the immediate operations and outcomes of whatever is being evaluated, but also its broad assumptions, implications, and potential side effects.

3. Freedom of information is essential in a democracy. Evaluators should allow all relevant stakeholders access to evaluative information in forms that respect people and honor promises of confidentiality. Evaluators should actively disseminate information to stakeholders as resources allow. Communications that are tailored to a given stakeholder should include all results that may bear on interests of that stakeholder and refer to any other tailored communications to other stakeholders. In all cases, evaluators should strive to present results clearly and simply so that clients and other stakeholders can easily understand the evaluation process and results.

4. Evaluators should maintain a balance between client needs and other needs. Evaluators necessarily have a special relationship with the client who funds or requests the evaluation. By virtue of that relationship, evaluators must strive to meet legitimate client needs whenever it is feasible and appropriate to do so. However, that relationship can also place evaluators in difficult dilemmas when client interests conflict with other interests, or when client interests conflict with the obligation of evaluators for systematic inquiry, competence, integrity, and respect for people. In these cases, evaluators should explicitly identify and discuss the conflicts with the client and relevant stakeholders, resolve them when possible, determine whether continued work on the evaluation is advisable if the conflicts cannot be resolved, and make clear any significant limitations on the evaluation that might result if the conflict is not resolved.

5. Evaluators have obligations that encompass the public interest and good. These obligations are especially important when evaluators are supported by publicly-generated funds; but clear threats to the public good should never be ignored in any evaluation. Because the public interest and good are rarely the same as the interests of any particular group (including those of the client or funder), evaluators will usually have to go beyond analysis of particular stakeholder interests and consider the welfare of society as a whole.

Background

In 1986, the Evaluation Network (ENet) and the Evaluation Research Society (ERS) merged to create the American Evaluation Association. ERS had previously adopted a set of standards for program evaluation (published in *New Directions for Program Evaluation* in 1982); and both organizations had lent support to work of other organizations about evaluation guidelines. However, none of these standards or guidelines were officially adopted by AEA, nor were any other ethics, standards, or guiding principles put into place. Over the ensuing years, the need for such guiding principles was discussed by both the AEA Board and the AEA membership. Under the presidency of David Cordray in 1992, the AEA Board appointed a temporary committee chaired by Peter Rossi to examine whether AEA should address this matter in more detail. That committee issued a report to the AEA Board on November 4, 1992, recommending that AEA should pursue this matter further. The Board followed that recommendation, and on that date created a Task Force to develop a draft of **guiding principles for evaluators**. The task force members were:

William Shadish, Memphis State University (Chair)

Dianna Newman, University of Albany/SUNY

Mary Ann Scheirer, Private Practice

Chris Wye, National Academy of Public Administration

The AEA Board specifically instructed the Task Force to develop general guiding principles rather than specific standards of practice. Their report, issued in 1994, summarized the Task Force's response to the charge.

Process of Development. Task Force members reviewed relevant documents from other professional societies, and then independently prepared and circulated drafts of material for use in this report. Initial and subsequent drafts (compiled by the Task Force chair) were discussed during conference calls, with revisions occurring after each call. Progress reports were presented at every AEA board meeting during 1993. In addition, a draft of the guidelines was mailed to all AEA members in September 1993 requesting feedback; and three symposia at the 1993 AEA annual conference were used to discuss and obtain further feedback. The Task Force considered all this feedback in a December 1993 conference call, and prepared a final draft in January 1994. This draft was presented and approved for membership vote at the January 1994 AEA board meeting.

Resulting Principles. Given the diversity of interests and employment settings represented on the Task Force, it is noteworthy that Task Force members reached substantial agreement about the following five principles. The order of these principles does not imply priority among them; priority will vary by situation and evaluator role.

- A. **Systematic Inquiry:** Evaluators conduct systematic, data-based inquiries about whatever is being evaluated.

- B. **Competence:** Evaluators provide competent performance to stakeholders.

- C. **Integrity/Honesty:** Evaluators ensure the honesty and integrity of the entire evaluation process.

- D. **Respect for People:** Evaluators respect the security, dignity, and self-worth of the respondents, program participants, clients, and other stakeholders with whom they interact.

- E. **Responsibilities for General and Public Welfare:** Evaluators articulate and take into account the diversity of interests and values that may be related to the general and public welfare.

Recommendation for Continued Work. The Task Force also recommended that the AEA Board establish and support a mechanism for the continued development and dissemination of the Guiding Principles, to include formal reviews at least every five years. The Principles were reviewed in 1999 through an EvalTalk survey, a panel review, and a comparison to the ethical principles of the Canadian and Australasian Evaluation Societies. The 2000 Board affirmed this work and expanded dissemination of the Principles; however, the document was left unchanged.

Process of the 2002–2003 Review and Revision. In January 2002 the AEA Board charged its standing Ethics Committee with developing and

implementing a process for reviewing the Guiding Principles that would give AEA's full membership multiple opportunities for comment. At its Spring 2002 meeting, the AEA Board approved the process, carried out during the ensuing months. It consisted of an online survey of the membership that drew 413 responses, a "Town Meeting" attended by approximately 40 members at the Evaluation 2002 Conference, and a compilation of stories about evaluators' experiences relative to ethical concerns told by AEA members and drawn from the *American Journal of Evaluation*. Detailed findings of all three sources of input were reported to the AEA Board in *A Review of AEA's Guiding Principles for Evaluators*, submitted January 18, 2003.

In 2003 the Ethics Committee continued to welcome input and specifically solicited it from AEA's Diversity Committee, Building Diversity Initiative, and Multi-Ethnic Issues Topical Interest Group. The first revision reflected the Committee's consensus response to the sum of member input throughout 2002 and 2003. It was submitted to AEA's past presidents, current board members, and the original framers of the Guiding Principles for comment. Twelve reviews were received and incorporated into a second revision, presented at the 2003 annual conference. Consensus opinions of approximately 25 members attending a Town Meeting are reflected in this, the third and final revision that was approved by the Board in February 2004 for submission to the membership for ratification. The revisions were ratified by the membership in July of 2004.

The 2002 Ethics Committee members were:

Doris Redfield, Appalachia Educational Laboratory (Chair)

Deborah Bonnet, Lumina Foundation for Education

Katherine Ryan, University of Illinois at Urbana–Champaign

Anna Madison, University of Massachusetts, Boston

In 2003 the membership was expanded for the duration of the revision process:

Deborah Bonnet, Lumina Foundation for Education (Chair)

Doris Redfield, Appalachia Educational Laboratory

Katherine Ryan, University of Illinois at Urbana–Champaign

Gail Barrington, Barrington Research Group, Inc.

Elmima Johnson, National Science Foundation

American Evaluation Association. (2004). *Guiding Principles For Evaluators.* Retrieved from Www.eval .org/Publications/Guidingprinciplesprintable.asp

Appendix C

Logic Model Templates

Logic models can be simple or more complex. The templates included here provide three examples, from simple to complex, to consider for developing a logic model.

LOGIC MODEL TEMPLATE 1

Professional Learning Program Goal(s):

Inputs/Resources	Activities/Components	Outputs	Outcomes
What resources, fiscal support, personnel, facilities, equipment, time, and technology do we need to accomplish the activities designed for this professional learning program?	What is the sequence of actions we will take to achieve the outcomes of this professional learning program?	What products, services, documents, or artifacts will we produce as we are engaged in the activities of this professional learning program?	What changes are we expecting in participants, their clients, or others associated with the professional learning program?

LOGIC MODEL TEMPLATE 2

Professional Learning Program Goal(s):

Inputs/ Resources	Activities/ Components	Outputs	Initial Outcomes	Intermediate Outcomes	Intended Results
What resources, fiscal support, personnel, facilities, equipment, time, and technology do we need to accomplish the activities designed for this professional learning program?	What is the sequence of actions we will take to achieve the outcomes of this professional learning program?	What products, services, documents, or artifacts will we produce as we are engaged in the activities of this professional learning program?	What are the initial changes in program participants we expect to see that, if present, will increase the likelihood of more substantial changes over time? (Usually changes in knowledge, skills, and attitudes)	What are the intermediate changes in program participants we expect to see that, if present, will increase the likelihood of impact on their clients? (Usually changes in aspirations and behaviors)	What are the changes in clients of program participants? Does the degree of change vary over time?

LOGIC MODEL TEMPLATE 3

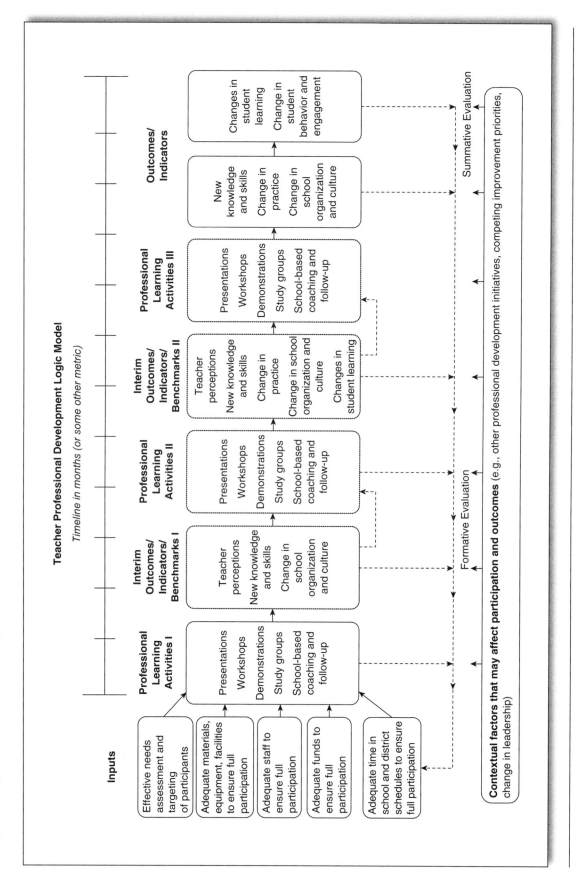

Teacher Professional Development Logic Model

Timeline in months (or some other metric)

Inputs

Effective needs assessment and targeting of participants

Adequate materials, equipment, facilities to ensure full participation

Adequate staff to ensure full participation

Adequate funds to ensure full participation

Adequate time in school and district schedules to ensure full participation

Professional Learning Activities I

Presentations
Workshops
Demonstrations
Study groups
School-based coaching and follow-up

Interim Outcomes/ Indicators/ Benchmarks I

Teacher perceptions
New knowledge and skills
Change in school organization and culture

Professional Learning Activities II

Presentations
Workshops
Demonstrations
Study groups
School-based coaching and follow-up

Interim Outcomes/ Indicators/ Benchmarks II

Teacher perceptions
New knowledge and skills
Change in practice
Change in school organization and culture
Changes in student learning

Professional Learning Activities III

Presentations
Workshops
Demonstrations
Study groups
School-based coaching and follow-up

Outcomes/ Indicators

New knowledge and skills
Change in practice
Change in school organization and culture

Changes in student learning

Change in student behavior and engagement

Formative Evaluation

Summative Evaluation

Contextual factors that may affect participation and outcomes (e.g., other professional development initiatives, competing improvement priorities, change in leadership)

Reprinted with permission: Haslam, M. B. (2010). *Teacher professional development evaluation guide.* Oxford, OH: National Staff Development Council. https://learningforward.org/docs/pdf/evaluationguide.pdf

Appendix D

Sample Logic Models

LOGIC MODELS FROM METRO NASHVILLE PUBLIC SCHOOLS AND AEL COLLABORATIVE INQUIRY PROFESSIONAL LEARNING PROGRAM

Lack of structures, protocols, processes, common language, especially for collaborative inquiry

Activities

- Professional development protocols and processes
- Read the selected sections in the book, *Got Data? Now What?* (Lipton & Wellman, 2012)
- Team members gain understanding of collaborative inquiry processes by engaging in ongoing professional development
- Define the communication norms
- Brain-storming session on terminology/labels to determine a common language
- Post/display data to start collaborative conversations
- Introduce collaborative learning cycle and protocols
- Discuss 7 actions of high performing groups

Short	Intermediate	Long
Team members have the ability to use collaborative inquiry to plan rigorous, motivating lessons to engage students.	Team members model collaborative inquiry processes during classroom instruction.	Team members use collaborative inquiry for improved instruction and student engagement.
Team members understand and articulate how to implement collaborative inquiry protocols in data meetings.	Team members establish/have consistent use of norms through schoolwide communication.	Team members use data more efficiently through the collaborative inquiry process to raise student achievement.
Team members to practice communication norms for professional learning communities.	Team members establish a consistent use of common language to contribute to the collaborative inquiry process.	Team members use a common language to communicate in a timely, clear, and reliable and consistent way to create a two-way manner.
Team members practice applying common language in professional learning communities.	Team members demonstrate and value trust in the collaborative inquiry process through actively engaging in data meetings.	Team members are focused using collaborative inquiry protocols embedded in schoolwide collaborative culture.

Lack of trust in the process (collaborative inquiry) and people; psychological safety

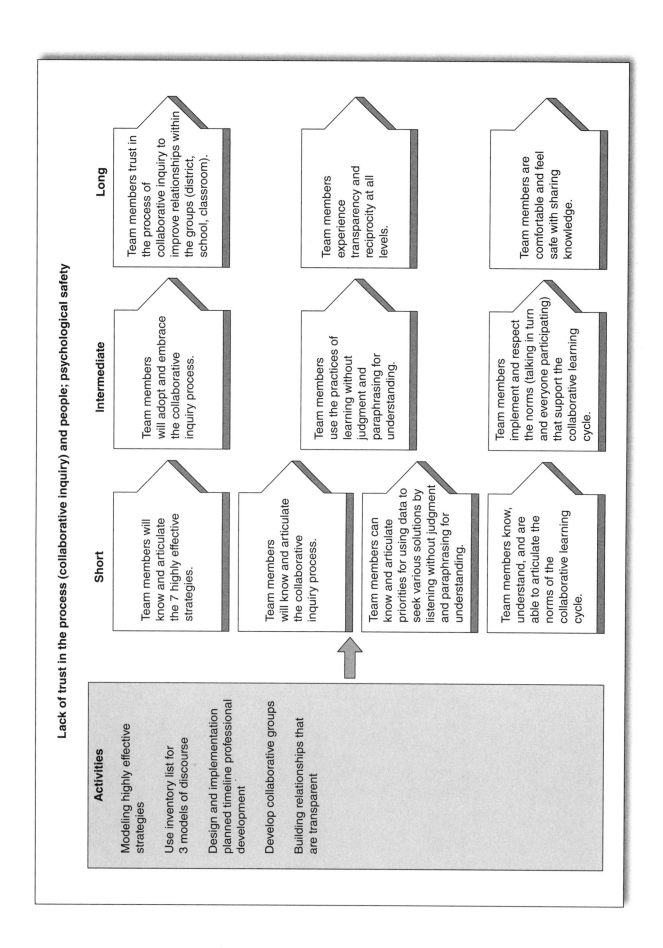

Activities	Short	Intermediate	Long
Modeling highly effective strategies	Team members will know and articulate the 7 highly effective strategies.	Team members will adopt and embrace the collaborative inquiry process.	Team members trust in the process of collaborative inquiry to improve relationships within the groups (district, school, classroom).
Use inventory list for 3 models of discourse	Team members will know and articulate the collaborative inquiry process.	Team members use the practices of learning without judgment and paraphrasing for understanding.	Team members experience transparency and reciprocity at all levels.
Design and implementation planned timeline professional development	Team members can know and articulate priorities for using data to seek various solutions by listening without judgment and paraphrasing for understanding.	Team members implement and respect the norms (talking in turn and everyone participating) that support the collaborative learning cycle.	Team members are comfortable and feel safe with sharing knowledge.
Develop collaborative groups	Team members know, understand, and are able to articulate the norms of the collaborative learning cycle.		
Building relationships that are transparent			

Lack of direction, follow-through, role definition within collaborative inquiry for new initiatives

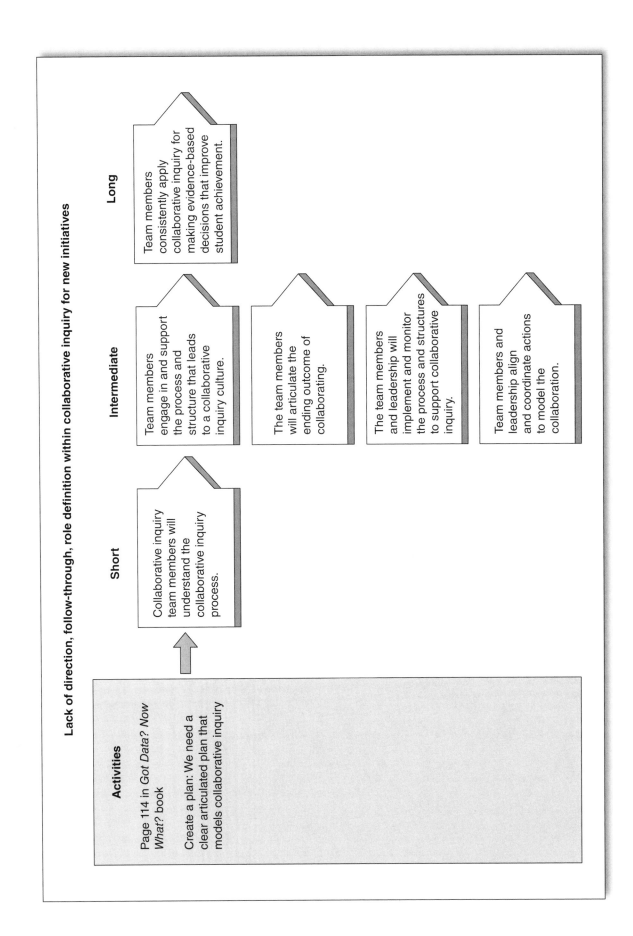

Short

Collaborative inquiry team members will understand the collaborative inquiry process.

Intermediate

Team members engage in and support the process and structure that leads to a collaborative inquiry culture.

The team members will articulate the ending outcome of collaborating.

The team members and leadership will implement and monitor the process and structures to support collaborative inquiry.

Team members and leadership align and coordinate actions to model the collaboration.

Long

Team members consistently apply collaborative inquiry for making evidence-based decisions that improve student achievement.

Activities

Page 114 in *Got Data? Now What?* book

Create a plan: We need a clear articulated plan that models collaborative inquiry

Appendix E
Sample Evaluation Planning Tools

This appendix contains samples of professional learning program evaluation tools. Appendix E.1 contains the theory of change, assumptions, logic model, and evaluation framework for a technology integration professional learning program.

TECHNOLOGY INTEGRATION THEORY OF CHANGE AND ASSUMPTIONS

THEORY OF CHANGE FOR TECHNOLOGY INTEGRATION A SAMPLE

| 1. Key leaders hold vision for project. | 2. Leaders develop partnerships and plan for project. | 3. Technology resources are readily available for teachers and students. | 4. Teachers receive professional development that includes training, curriculum development, and support. | 5. Teachers change classroom instructional practices. | 6. Teachers provide inquiry and exploration-based student learning activities. | 7. Student engage in learning. | 8. Student achievement increases. |

This theory of change is based on the following assumptions:

- Thorough planning conributes to program's success.
- Integrating technology advances student learning.
- To change instructional practice, teachers require opportunities to gain new knowledge and skills and appropriate resources.
- Implementing new teaching practices improves student achievement.
- When students are engaged in learning, they achieve.

Used with permission from Learning Forward.

Killion, J. (2003). 8 smooth steps: Solid footwork makes evaluation of staff development programs a song. *JSD, 24*(4), 15–26.

TECHNOLOGY INTEGRATION LOGIC MODEL

Inputs	Activities ➞	Initial Outcomes ➞	Intermediate Outcomes ➞	Intended Results
• Technology hardware, software, and infrastructure	Teachers and principals receive training on technology integration in mathematics.	Teachers and principals develop an understanding of how technology can enhance students' mathematics learning, engage students more actively in learning, differentiate learning and assessment. **Knowledge**	Teachers integrate technology into their mathematics instruction. **Behavior and aspiration**	Student achievement in mathematics increases by 10% by the year 2005.
• Trainers	Technology resources are deployed in mathematics classrooms.	Teachers learn strategies for integrating technology into mathematics instruction. **Skill**	Teachers integrating technology into their classroom instruction on a regular basis.	
• Planning time for integrating technology into mathematics lessons	Teachers are coached on integrating technology into their mathematics curriculum.	Teachers' comfort with integrating technology increases and they design opportunities for students to use technology for learning. **Attitude and behavior**	Students use technology to gather information, construct understanding, and engage more actively in learning. **Behavior and aspiration**	
• Time for conferring with coaches	Principals are trained in how to support teachers as they integrate technology into their classroom and how to serve as a leader for technology in their schools.	In instructional conferences, principals provide support to teachers in integrating technology into their classrooms. **Behavior**	Teachers' attitudes about technology improve. **Attitude** Students' attitudes about technology improve. **Attitude**	

Killion, J. (2003). 8 smooth steps: Solid footwork makes evaluation of staff development programs a song. *JSD, 24*(4), 15–26.

TECHNOLOGY INTEGRATION
EVALUATION FRAMEWORK

Evaluation Questions	Data/ Evidence Needed	Data Source	Data Collection Method	Data Analysis Method	Timeline	Responsible Person(s)
How frequently are teachers integrating technology into their mathematics lessons?	Teacher behavior	Teacher self-report	Survey	Count	Administer survey in May	Technology coordinator
		Principal observations	Logs	Count with description	Principal observations October through May	Principal
		Lesson plans	Artifacts	Quality analysis	Collect artifacts February and May	Technology coordinator
How do students use technology in mathematics?	Student behavior	Student self-report	Interviews	Patterns	Conduct student interviews in May	Graduate students
		Classroom assignments	Artifacts	Quality analysis	Collect artifacts in February and May	Technology coordinator
		Samples of student work	Artifacts	Quality analysis		
Is student achievement in mathematics increasing as expected? (10% on state tests by 2005)	Student knowledge and skills	State test	Artifacts	Comparing	April	Districting testing coordinator
		Classroom tests	Artifacts	Comparing	October–June	Teachers
		Student grades	Artifacts	Comparing	June	District testing coordinator

Used with permission from Learning Forward.

Killion, J. (2003). 8 smooth steps: Solid footwork makes evaluation of staff development programs a song. *JSD, 24*(4), 15–26.

Appendix F

Sample Evaluation
Planning Tool Templates

KASAB PLANNING TOOL

Professional learning program goal:

Professional learning program outcomes for educators:

Professional learning program outcomes for students:

Outcome Area	Students	Teacher	Principal/ Administrator	Central Office	Organization
Knowledge					
Attitudes					
Skills					
Aspirations					
Behaviors					

LOGIC MODEL PLANNING GUIDE

Professional learning program goal:

Professional learning program outcomes for educators:

Professional learning program outcomes for students:

Inputs	Activities	Initial Outcomes	Intermediate Outcomes	Final Outcomes/ Results

Conditions to consider:

EVALUATION FRAMEWORK TEMPLATE

Types of Changes (KASAB/ Outcomes)	Formative and Summative Evaluation Questions	Data Source	Data-Collection Method	Data-Analysis Method	Timeline	Responsible Party

Appendix G
Sample Data-Collection Instruments

This section contains sample **data-collection instruments** that can be used as models for developing one appropriate to professional learning program evaluations. Developing instruments is a process that requires clear definitions of the constructs to measure, thoughtful item development, and multiple revisions based on field-testing evidence.

EXHIBIT 1: TEACHER INTERVIEW PROTOCOL

Metro Nashville Public Schools and Appalachia Regional Laboratory Collaborative Inquiry Professional Learning Program (www.mnpscollaboration.org)

Interviewer _____ School _____ Date _____

Interviewee Gender _____ Grades teaching _____ Subjects _____
Years in teaching _____

Welcome Script

Thank you for agreeing to be interviewed to talk about collaborative inquiry. My name is [insert name], and [insert name] is here with me today. I am with [name department], and [insert name], is with [name department].

Overview of Topic

The interview will last about 30 minutes, and we will be having the same interview with other teachers in your school. We will use the information we gather from these discussions to learn what teachers think about collaborative inquiry, what support is needed to implement collaborative inquiry, and how collaborative inquiry is affecting instruction and student learning.

Ground Rules

There are no right or wrong answers to any of the questions I will ask . . . I am interested in your honest thoughts and opinions. If it is okay with you, we would like to record today's session. Your names will not be used in reports. Even if we use a quote from today's interview in a report, your name will not be associated with it. Is this okay? [If not, rely on note taking.] Do you have any questions? If not, let's get started.

So to be sure we are talking about the same thing, let's define Collaborative Inquiry as a data-based team process that consciously uses the collaborative learning cycle (activating and engaging, exploring and discovering, and organizing and integrating) and the qualities of effective teams (fostering a culture of trust, maintaining a clear focus, taking collective responsibility, and data-informed decision making).

1. Are you implementing CI practices?	_____ YES _____ NO
If not, why not? (Check each that applies) (then go to Question #3)	____ not trained/prepared ____ no time ____ not comfortable with ____ disinterest ____ other _____
If yes, in what ways? (Clarify if only in team meetings—or if also in the classroom)	

2. (If in instruction) In what subjects are you implementing it? What grades?	List:
With which students? (Check all that apply)	____ whole class ____ small group ____ individual students
3. Is your team meeting regularly?	_____ YES _____ NO
If not, why not? (Check all that apply)	____ inadequate time ____ teacher disinterest ____ other _____
4. Is your team implementing CI practices?	_____ YES _____ NO
If yes, which CI tools is the team using? (Check all that apply)	____ IC map ____ *Got Data? Now What?* inventories and protocols ____ other _____
5. Are you able to access the services of an instructional coach or data coach to help in the CI process? (Check all that apply)	Data coach ____ as often as I request? ____ on a regularly scheduled basis? ____ only with my team? Instructional coach ____ as often as I request? ____ on a regularly scheduled basis? ____ only with my team?
6. Does your team have adequate access to the data you need?	_____ YES _____ NO
If not, what do you lack?	
7. Has your team changed as a result of CI implementation?	_____ NO _____ YES
8. If yes, check all that apply	____ team fosters a culture of trust ____ team maintains a clear focus ____ team assumes collective responsibility for the team ____ team uses relevant data to drive decision making ____ other changes?_____
9. Which of the following does your school support? (Mark a Y or N for each)	____ continuing preparation for you in implementing CI ____ time for the team to collaborate ____ positive feedback on implementing CI ____ principal's attention to supports and barriers to CI ____ accessibility of a CI-trained data coach ____ accessibility of a CI-trained instructional coach
For each No, is that support important for implementing CI?	

(Continued)

(Continued)

10. Which of the following characterize CI implementation in your school? (Mark each: 1 = not yet, 2 = to a degree, 3 = for the most part)	____ we have a common definition of CI ____ we are able to trust each other in my team ____ our teachers have a positive feeling about CI ____ our teachers believe in CI ____ our principal believes in CI ____ our data coach believes in CI ____ our instructional coaches believe in CI ____ other _____
11. What else should I know about your team's implementation of CI (or not)? About yours?	
12. What else should I know about your school's implementation of CI?	

Used with permission. Wilkerson, S., & Johnson. M. (2016). *MNPS (Team or Coach) Focus Group Protocol.* Created for Metropolitan Nashville Public Schools under REL Appalachia 2011–2016 contract. For more information, go to http://www.magnoliaconsulting .org/ or www.mnpscollaboration.org.

EXHIBIT 2: PROFESSIONAL LEARNING SURVEY

Survey of Professional Learning for All Employees

Role: _____

Mark the level of agreement with each statement based on your role.	Always	Frequently	Sometimes	Seldom	Never	Don't Know/ NA
The budget allocated for professional learning at the division level allows us to meet the division's professional learning needs.	5	4	3	2	1	0
The budget allocated for professional learning at the school level allows us to meet the school's professional learning needs.	5	4	3	2	1	0
Time available for professional learning allows us to meet our professional learning needs.	5	4	3	2	1	0
Expectations about staff involvement in professional learning are clear to all employees.	5	4	3	2	1	0
There is widespread understanding among staff members about the role of professional learning in the division and the schools.	5	4	3	2	1	0
The division and schools evaluate their professional learning programs.	5	4	3	2	1	0
It is easy to access professional learning services within the division.	5	4	3	2	1	0
Division-based professional learning providers are prepared and qualified in their roles.	5	4	3	2	1	0
Division professional learning providers respond to schools' individual professional learning needs.	5	4	3	2	1	0
Staff members have frequent opportunities for collaboration and shared work.	5	4	3	2	1	0
All employees have opportunity to Expand job-specific skills.	5	4	3	2	1	0
Professional learning programs offered at the division and school level are responsive to the characteristics of adult learners.	5	4	3	2	1	0
The division supports continuous improvement, risk-taking, and implementation of new practices.	5	4	3	2	1	0
Professional learning plans for different purposes (individual, team, school, division) are evident and aligned to goals.	5	4	3	2	1	0
There is follow-up support to ensure transfer of new learning with fidelity.	5	4	3	2	1	0
Professional learning opportunities are available outside of the division.	5	4	3	2	1	0
Professional learning programs are differentiated to address various levels of staff experience, learning need, and learning preference.	5	4	3	2	1	0

(Killion, 2001)

EXHIBIT 3:
SHELTERED INSTRUCTION OBSERVATION PROTOCOL

SIOP - Level of Understanding and Degree of Implementation Survey

Name: _____

Subject area/Grade level: _____ **Date:** _____

NOTE: Please rate statements according to where you are in the learning process when you take the survey. It is important to put a code (name/number) so growth overtime can be monitored when the survey is completed again.

DIRECTIONS: Based on your current level of understanding and degree of implementation of Sheltered Instruction Observation Protocol (SIOP), please circle the appropriate responses.

	Level of Understanding					Degree of Implementation				
	Little/No			*Extensive*		*Never*			*Frequently*	
LESSON PREPARATION										
1. Content objectives	1	2	3	4	5	1	2	3	4	5
2. Language objectives	1	2	3	4	5	1	2	3	4	5
3. Content concepts	1	2	3	4	5	1	2	3	4	5
4. Supplementary materials	1	2	3	4	5	1	2	3	4	5
5. Adaptation of content	1	2	3	4	5	1	2	3	4	5
6. Meaningful activities	1	2	3	4	5	1	2	3	4	5
BUILDING BACKGROUND										
7. Concepts explicitly linked	1	2	3	4	5	1	2	3	4	5
8. Links explicitly made	1	2	3	4	5	1	2	3	4	5
9. Key vocabulary	1	2	3	4	5	1	2	3	4	5
COMPREHENSIBLE INPUT										
10. Speech	1	2	3	4	5	1	2	3	4	5
11. Clear explanation	1	2	3	4	5	1	2	3	4	5
12. A variety of techniques	1	2	3	4	5	1	2	3	4	5
STRATEGIES										
13. Students' use of learning strategies	1	2	3	4	5	1	2	3	4	5
14. Scaffolding techniques	1	2	3	4	5	1	2	3	4	5
15. Questions or tasks to promote higher-order thinking skills	1	2	3	4	5	1	2	3	4	5

INTERACTION

16.	Frequent opportunities for interaction	1	2	3	4	5	1	2	3	4	5
17.	Grouping configurations	1	2	3	4	5	1	2	3	4	5
18.	Sufficient wait time for student responses	1	2	3	4	5	1	2	3	4	5
19.	Students clarify key concepts in L1	1	2	3	4	5	1	2	3	4	5

PRACTICE AND APPLICATION

20.	Hands-on materials and/or manipulatives	1	2	3	4	5	1	2	3	4	5
21.	Apply content and language knowledge	1	2	3	4	5	1	2	3	4	5
22.	Integrate all language skills	1	2	3	4	5	1	2	3	4	5

LESSON DELIVERY

23.	Content objectives clearly supported	1	2	3	4	5	1	2	3	4	5
24.	Language objectives clearly supported	1	2	3	4	5	1	2	3	4	5
25.	Students engaged	1	2	3	4	5	1	2	3	4	5
26.	Pacing appropriate for students' ability level	1	2	3	4	5	1	2	3	4	5

REVIEW AND ASSESSMENT

27.	Review of key vocabulary	1	2	3	4	5	1	2	3	4	5
28.	Review of key content concepts	1	2	3	4	5	1	2	3	4	5
29.	Regular feedback to students on their output	1	2	3	4	5	1	2	3	4	5
30.	Assessment of student comprehension and learning of all lesson objectives	1	2	3	4	5	1	2	3	4	5

PLEASE RATE HOW YOU PERCEIVE YOUR OWN EFFECTIVENESS:

Minimum = 1   Maximum = 5

1.	Using the 30 instructional features of SIOP	1	2	3	4	5
2.	Collaborating with colleagues to reflect and improve effectiveness in teaching ELL students using SIOP	1	2	3	4	5
3.	Receiving feedback and support in systemically implementing SIOP to increase student achievement for ELL students	1	2	3	4	5

Used with permission of Linda Munger, Munger Education Associates.

Adapted from "The Sheltered Instruction Observation Protocol (SIOP)," by J. Echevarria & A. Graves, 2003, *Sheltered content instruction: Teaching English-language learners with diverse abilities* (p. 56). Boston, MA: Allyn & Bacon.

EXHIBIT 4:
SAMPLE SURVEY QUESTIONS

The following three pages display sample survey questions for three role groups on same construct—work in collaborative teams—extracted from the Teacher Data Use Surveys (Wayman, Wilkerson, Cho, Mandinach, & Supovitz, 2016) used in the evaluation of Metro Nashville Public School Collaborative Inquiry Professional Learning Program (www.mnpscollaboration.org)

Administrator Survey Items on Work in Collaborative Teams

15. How often do you participate in scheduled meetings to work in collaborative team(s) with your teachers? (Check only one.)
    - ☐ Less than once a month.
    - ☐ Once or twice a month.
    - ☐ Weekly or almost weekly.
    - ☐ A few times a week.
    - ☐ I do not participate in scheduled meetings to work in collaborative teams.

If you answered "I do not participate in scheduled meetings to work in collaborative teams" in question 15, please go to question 18.

16. As you think about your <u>collaborative team(s)</u>, please indicate how much you agree or disagree with the following statements:

Statement	Strongly disagree	Disagree	Agree	Strongly agree
a. Members of my team trust each other.	☐	☐	☐	☐
b. It's ok to discuss feelings and worries with other members of my team.	☐	☐	☐	☐
c. Members of my team respect colleagues who lead school improvement efforts.	☐	☐	☐	☐
d. Members of my team respect those colleagues who are experts in their craft.	☐	☐	☐	☐
e. As an administrator, I foster a trusting environment for discussing data in teams.	☐	☐	☐	☐

Items a–d are from University of Chicago Consortium on School Research. (2013). *Teacher Survey Codebook,* Chicago, IL: Author.

17. How often do collaborative team(s) in your school do the following?

Action	Never	Sometimes	Often	A lot
a. We approach an issue by looking at data.	☐	☐	☐	☐
b. We discuss our preconceived beliefs about an issue.	☐	☐	☐	☐
c. We identify questions that we will seek to answer using data.	☐	☐	☐	☐
d. We explore data by looking for patterns and trends.	☐	☐	☐	☐
e. We draw conclusions based on data.	☐	☐	☐	☐
f. We identify additional data to offer a clearer picture of the issue.	☐	☐	☐	☐
g. We use data to make links between instruction and student outcomes.	☐	☐	☐	☐
h. When we consider changes in practice, we predict possible student outcomes.	☐	☐	☐	☐
i. We revisit predictions made in previous meetings.	☐	☐	☐	☐
j. We identify actionable solutions based on our conclusions.	☐	☐	☐	☐

Used with permission. Wilkerson, S., & Johnson. M. (2016). *MNPS Collaborative Inquiry Interview Protocol for (Administrator, Teacher, or Instructional Support Staff)*. Created for Metropolitan Nashville Public Schools under REL Appalachia 2011–2016 contract. For more information, go to http://www.magnoliaconsulting.org/ or www.mnpscollaboration.org.

Teacher Survey Items on Work in Collaborative Teams

The following questions ask about your work in collaborative teams.

15. How often do you have scheduled meetings to work in collaborative team(s)? (Check only one.)
    - ☐ Less than once a month.
    - ☐ Once or twice a month.
    - ☐ Weekly or almost weekly.
    - ☐ A few times a week.
    - ☐ I do not have scheduled meetings to work in collaborative teams.

If you answered "I do not have scheduled meetings to work in collaborative teams" in question 15, please go to question 18.

16. As you think about your <u>collaborative team(s)</u>, please indicate how much you agree or disagree with the following statements:

Statement	Strongly disagree	Disagree	Agree	Strongly agree
a. Members of my team trust each other.	☐	☐	☐	☐
b. It's ok to discuss feelings and worries with other members of my team.	☐	☐	☐	☐
c. Members of my team respect colleagues who lead school improvement efforts.	☐	☐	☐	☐
d. Members of my team respect those colleagues who are experts in their craft.	☐	☐	☐	☐
e. My principal or assistant principal(s) fosters a trusting environment for discussing data in teams.	☐	☐	☐	☐

Items a–d are from University of Chicago Consortium on School Research. (2013). *Teacher Survey Codebook*, Chicago, IL: Author.

17. How often do you and your collaborative team(s) do the following?

Action	Never	Sometimes	Often	A lot
a. We approach an issue by looking at data.	☐	☐	☐	☐
b. We discuss our preconceived beliefs about an issue.	☐	☐	☐	☐
c. We identify questions that we will seek to answer using data.	☐	☐	☐	☐
d. We explore data by looking for patterns and trends.	☐	☐	☐	☐
e. We draw conclusions based on data.	☐	☐	☐	☐
f. We identify additional data to offer a clearer picture of the issue.	☐	☐	☐	☐
g. We use data to make links between instruction and student outcomes.	☐	☐	☐	☐
h. When we consider changes in practice, we predict possible student outcomes.	☐	☐	☐	☐
i. We revisit predictions made in previous meetings.	☐	☐	☐	☐
j. We identify actionable solutions based on our conclusions.	☐	☐	☐	☐

Used with permission. Wilkerson, S., & Johnson. M. (2016). *MNPS Collaborative Inquiry Interview Protocol for (Administrator, Teacher, or Instructional Support Staff)*. Created for Metropolitan Nashville Public Schools under REL Appalachia 2011–2016 contract. For more information, go to http://www.magnoliaconsulting.org/ or www.mnpscollaboration.org.

Instructional Support Staff Survey
Items on Work in Collaborative Teams

The following questions ask about your work in collaborative teams.

15. How often do you have scheduled meetings to work in collaborative team(s) with your teachers? (Check one only).
    ☐ Less than once a month.
    ☐ Once or twice a month.
    ☐ Weekly or almost weekly.
    ☐ A few times a week.
    ☐ I do not have scheduled meetings to work in collaborative teams.

If you answered "I do not have scheduled meetings to work in collaborative teams" in question 15, please go to question 18.

16. As you think about your <u>collaborative team(s)</u>, please indicate how much you agree or disagree with the following statements:

Statement	Strongly disagree	Disagree	Agree	Strongly agree
a. Members of my team trust each other.	☐	☐	☐	☐
b. It's ok to discuss feelings and worries with other members of my team.	☐	☐	☐	☐
c. Members of my team respect colleagues who lead school improvement efforts.	☐	☐	☐	☐
d. Members of my team respect those colleagues who are experts in their craft.	☐	☐	☐	☐
e. My principal or assistant principal(s) fosters a trusting environment for discussing data in teams	☐	☐	☐	☐

Items a–d are from University of Chicago Consortium on School Research. (2013). *Teacher Survey Codebook*, Chicago, IL: Author.

17. How often do you and your collaborative team(s) do the following?

Action	Never	Sometimes	Often	A lot
a. We approach an issue by looking at data.	☐	☐	☐	☐
b. We discuss our preconceived beliefs about an issue.	☐	☐	☐	☐
c. We identify questions that we will seek to answer using data.	☐	☐	☐	☐
d. We explore data by looking for patterns and trends.	☐	☐	☐	☐
e. We draw conclusions based on data.	☐	☐	☐	☐
f. We identify additional data to offer a clearer picture of the issue.	☐	☐	☐	☐
g. We use data to make links between instruction and student outcomes.	☐	☐	☐	☐
h. When we consider changes in practice, we predict possible student outcomes.	☐	☐	☐	☐
i. We revisit predictions made in previous meetings.	☐	☐	☐	☐
j. We identify actionable solutions based on our conclusions.	☐	☐	☐	☐

Used with permission. Wilkerson, S., & Johnson. M. (2016). *MNPS Collaborative Inquiry Interview Protocol for (Administrator, Teacher, or Instructional Support Staff)*. Created for Metropolitan Nashville Public Schools under REL Appalachia 2011–2016 contract. For more information, go to http://www.magnoliaconsulting.org/ or www.mnpscollaboration.org.

EXHIBIT 5: PROFESSIONAL LEARNING COMMUNITY OBSERVATION CHECKLIST

Use this document to collect and share feedback on learning teams. This tool can be used by the team, coach, or principal.

✓	PLC Actions	Notes
Organization		
	All members are present.	
	The team facilitator is using an agenda.	
	Team norms are posted and in use.	
	Student learning goals are either visible or explicitly stated.	
	The purpose of the PLC meeting is evident.	
	Team is using a protocol to structure the work.	
Engagement		
	All members are actively engaged.	
	Communication is positive, focused on results.	
	The facilitator helps the team accomplish its goal without being directive.	
	Team members contribute equitably.	
Work		
	Team is focusing on an identifiable curricular area.	
	Team is focusing on instruction.	
	Team is focusing on data.	
	Team is focusing on assessment.	
	Team is focusing on student work.	
	Team is focusing on meeting the needs of specific students.	
	Team members discuss action items, set the agenda for the next meeting.	
	Teams refer to the curriculum.	

Killion, J. (2013). *Comprehensive professional learning system: A workbook for states and districts.* Oxford, OH: Learning Forward.

EXHIBIT 6: INNOVATION CONFIGURATION MAP FOR LEARNING SCHOOL

This **innovation configuration map** is a portion of the full map that describes what teachers, teacher leaders, coaches, and principals do in a learning school. A learning school is a school that implements Learning Forward's definition of professional learning within collaborative learning teams. An innovation configuration map is an assessment tool for assessing practice to measure if it meets the expected or ideal level as expressed in Level 1. Variations from 2–6 (low) describe levels of practice that are at some stage of approaching ideal practice.

CONTINUOUS CYCLE OF IMPROVEMENT

Outcome 2: Learning teams use a cycle of continuous improvement to refine teaching quality and improve student learning.

DATA ANALYSIS

2.1: Learning teams engage in ongoing data analysis of teacher and student performance to determine school, educator, and student learning goals.

Level 1	Level 2	Level 3	Level 4	Level 5	Level 6
Analyze multiple types of data (achievement, process, demographic, and perception) at the school, team, and classroom levels throughout the school year to identify student strengths and weaknesses to set annual goals for student growth and teacher learning; analyze multiple types of data at the school, team, and classroom levels several times throughout the school year to measure progress toward annual goals for student and teacher learning, to set benchmark goals for teacher and student learning, and to make ongoing adjustments in both goals and strategies for attaining the goals.	Analyze student achievement and demographic data at the school, team, and classroom levels throughout the school year to identify student strengths and weaknesses to set annual goals for student growth and teacher learning; analyze student achievement and demographic data at the school, team, and classroom levels several times throughout the school year to measure progress toward annual goals for student and teacher learning, to set benchmark goals for teacher and student learning, and to make ongoing adjustments in both goals and strategies for attaining the goals.	Analyze student achievement data at the school, team, and classroom levels throughout the school year to identify student strengths and weaknesses to set annual goals for student growth and teacher learning; analyze student achievement data at the school, team, and classroom levels several times throughout the school year to measure progress toward annual goals for student and teacher learning, to set benchmark goals for teacher and student learning, and to make ongoing adjustments in both goals and strategies for attaining the goals.	Analyze student achievement data at the school level throughout the school year to identify student strengths and weaknesses to set annual goals for student growth and teacher learning; analyze student achievement data at the school, team, and classroom levels several times throughout the school year to measure progress toward annual goals for student and teacher learning, and to set benchmark goals for teacher and student learning.	Analyze student achievement data at the school level throughout the school year to identify student strengths and weaknesses to set annual goals for student growth and teacher learning; analyze student achievement data at the school, team, and classroom levels several times throughout the school year to measure progress toward annual goals for student and teacher learning.	Analyze student achievement data at the school level throughout the school year to identify student strengths and weaknesses to set annual goals for student growth.

STUDENT LEARNING GOALS

2.2: Learning teams set goals for student learning.

Level 1	Level 2	Level 3	Level 4	Level 5	Level 6
Write annual and benchmark SMART (specific, measurable, attainable, results-oriented, time-bound) goals for student achievement based on school, team, and classroom data to guide their planning and improvement efforts and revise those goals throughout the school year.	Write annual SMART (specific, measurable, attainable, results-oriented, time-bound) goals for student achievement based on school, team, and classroom data to guide their planning and improvement efforts and revise those goals throughout the school year.	Write annual SMART (specific, measurable, attainable, results-oriented, time-bound) goals for student achievement based on school, team, and classroom data to guide their planning and improvement efforts.	Receive annual SMART (specific, measurable, attainable, results-oriented, time-bound) goals for student achievement based on schoolwide data to guide their planning and improvement efforts.	Receive annual SMART (specific, measurable, attainable, results-oriented, time-bound) goals for student achievement based on districtwide data to guide their planning and improvement efforts.	Receive annual goals for student achievement based on districtwide data to guide their planning and improvement efforts.

EDUCATOR LEARNING GOALS

2.3: Learning teams write goals for educator learning aligned with student learning goals to guide professional learning.

Level 1	Level 2	Level 3	Level 4	Level 5	Level 6
Write annual and benchmark professional learning goals for the school and teams aligned with student learning goals and revise those goals throughout the school year.	Write annual and benchmark professional learning goals for the school and teams aligned with student learning goals.	Write annual professional learning goals for the school aligned with student learning goals.	Use district professional learning goals to guide adult learning within the school and team.	Use district professional learning goals to guide adult learning within the school.	Use topics rather than goals to guide professional learning within the school.

MULTIPLE DESIGNS

2.4: Learning teams select and implement multiple designs for professional learning aligned with NSDC's Standards for Staff Development to develop knowledge, attitudes, skills, aspirations, and behaviors necessary to support advanced levels of student learning.

Level 1	Level 2	Level 3	Level 4	Level 5	Level 6
Select, with broad-based input from teacher leaders and teachers, and implement multiple selected designs for team and whole-school professional learning that align with educator and student learning goals and support and encourage collaborative inquiry, problem solving, and learning among educators.	Select, with broad-based input from teacher leaders and teachers, and implement two selected designs for team and whole-school professional learning that align with educator and student learning goals and support and encourage collaborative inquiry, problem solving, and learning among educators.	Select, with broad-based input from teacher leaders and teachers, and implement a single design for team and whole-school professional learning that align with educator and student learning goals and support and encourage collaborative inquiry, problem solving, and learning among educators.	Implement multiple selected designs for team and whole-school professional learning aligned with student learning goals with limited input from teacher leaders and teachers.	Implement a single design for team and whole-school professional learning aligned with student learning goals with limited input from teacher leaders and teachers.	Implement designs for team- and whole-school professional learning selected by someone outside the school without input from teacher leaders and teachers.

INTERVENTIONS FOR STUDENT LEARNING

2.5: Learning teams select or develop research-based, coherent, classroom-centered interventions for student learning.

Level 1	Level 2	Level 3	Level 4	Level 5	Level 6
Select and/or develop research-based, coherent, classroom-centered interventions for student learning that align with team and student learning goals, focus on the school's instructional framework for teaching quality, and emphasize changes in teacher practice to promote student learning.	Select and/or develop research-based, coherent, classroom-centered interventions for student learning that align with team and student learning goals and focus on the school's instructional framework for teaching quality.	Select and/or develop research-based, coherent, classroom-centered interventions for student learning that align with team and student learning goals.	Select and/or develop classroom-centered interventions for student learning that align with team and student learning goals.	Select and/or develop school-centered interventions for student learning that align with team and student learning goals.	Select and/or develop nonclassroom- and nonschool-centered interventions for student learning.

JOB-EMBEDDED SUPPORT

2.6: The school leadership team, teacher leaders (coaches), and team members provide ongoing support at the classroom level to implement educator learning to increase student achievement.

Level 1	Level 2	Level 3	Level 4	Level 5	Level 6
Provide continuous job-embedded coaching and other forms of classroom-based support (e.g. peer observation, instructional, walk-throughs, demonstration lessons, etc.) to transfer educator learning to classroom and schoolwide practice to increase student achievement.	Provide periodic job-embedded coaching and other forms of classroom-based support (e.g. peer observation, instructional, walk-throughs, demonstration lessons, etc.) to transfer educator learning to classroom and schoolwide practice to increase student achievement.	Provide occasional job-embedded coaching and other forms of classroom-based support (e.g. peer observation, instructional, walk-throughs, demonstration lessons, etc.) to transfer educator learning to classroom and schoolwide practice to increase student achievement.	Provide one opportunity for job-embedded coaching and other forms of classroom-based support (e.g. peer observation, instructional, walk-throughs, demonstration lessons, etc.) to transfer educator learning to classroom and schoolwide practice to increase student achievement.	Provide no job-embedded coaching or other forms of classroom-based support (e.g. peer observation, instructional, walk-throughs, demonstration lessons, etc.) to transfer educator learning to classroom and schoolwide practice to increase student achievement.	

ONGOING EVALUATION

2.7: Learning teams evaluate the effectiveness of professional learning.

Level 1	Level 2	Level 3	Level 4	Level 5	Level 6
Assess regularly (multiple times per year) the effectiveness of professional learning in achieving identified educator and student learning goals, improving teaching, and assisting all students in meeting academic standards.	Assess semiannually the effectiveness of professional learning in achieving identified educator and student learning goals, improving teaching, and assisting all students in meeting academic standards.	Assess annually the effectiveness of professional learning in achieving identified educator and student learning goals, improving teaching, and assisting all students in meeting academic standards.	Assess over multiple years the effectiveness of professional learning in achieving identified educator and student learning goals, improving teaching, and assisting all students in meeting academic standards.	Conduct no assessment of the effectiveness of professional learning in achieving identified educator and student learning goals, improving teaching, and assisting all students in meeting academic standards.	

EXHIBIT 7: INNOVATION CONFIGURATION MAP FOR COLLABORATIVE INQUIRY

Component B: Assumes Collective Responsibility

IC Map Team: Charlene Dickerson, Craig Hammond, LeTicia Taylor

Component B: Assumes Collective Responsibility
The Team....

a	b	c	d	e
Communicates and meets routinely with consistent attendance by most members. A notification is provided when a team member is absent. Fosters a balance of advocacy and inquiry for one's own ideas and the ideas of others. Provides a summary of decisions, actions, and responsibilities agreed upon during the meeting. Agrees to follow through and monitor the progress of actionable items.	Communicates and meets routinely with consistent attendance by most members. A notification is provided when a team member is absent. Fosters a balance of advocacy and inquiry for one's own ideas and the ideas of others. Reaches decisions about future actions to take and assigns them to team members.	Communicates and meets routinely with consistent attendance by most members. Has active participation both verbally and physically by members. Reaches decisions about future actions to take.	Communicates and meets sporadically with team members missing the meeting without notifying others. Has disparate participation and discussion among its members, where 1-2 members attend or dominate the conversation. Fails to establish action items.	Fails to communicate and meet on a regular basis.

Used with permission. Johnson, M., & Wilkerson, S. (2016). *MNPS IC Map for Collaborative Inquiry*. Created for Metropolitan Nashville Public Schools under REL Appalachia 2011-2016 contract. For more information, go to www.mnpscollaboration.org or http://www.magnoliaconsulting.org/.

Component D: Uses the Collaborative Learning Cycle when investigating relevant data to guide decision making.

The IC Map Team: Mary Laurens Seely, Antoinette Williams, Ruth Gurich, Karen Flowers

Component D: Uses the collaborative learning cycle when investigating relevant data to guide decision making. The Team…..			
a	b	c	d
Activating and Engaging	**Activating and Engaging**	**Activating and Engaging**	**Activating and Engaging Exploring and Discovering Organizing and Integrating**
Identifies decision(s) to be made prior to collecting data and reframes it as a question.	Identifies decision(s) to be made prior to collecting data and reframes it as a question.	Collects data before discussing the decision(s) to be made.	Considers only opinions or data from one source that supports initial assupmtions and decision making.
Generates predictions based on what will be visible in the data and connects it to an underlying assumption about the data to be explored.	Generates predictions based on what will be visible in the data. Shares assumptions about the data to be explored, but they are not connected to the predictions..	Shares assumptions (beliefs about learners and learning) about the data to be explored.	
Exploring and Discovering	**Exploring and Discovering**	**Exploring and Discovering**	
Makes observations and asks questions about data from multiple sources, both quantitative and qualitative.	Makes observations from multiple sources, both quantitative and qualitative.	Begins discussions of data from multiple sources, both quantitative and qualitative.	
Uses data displays and a structured sequence (e.g., time to orient, initial talking points) for exploring and looking for patterns or trends emerging from the data.	Uses data displays to look for patterns or trends emerging from the data.	Looks for patterns or trends emerging from the data.	
Avoids making inferences or conclusions and explaining the data.			
Organizing and Integrating	**Organizing and Integrating**	**Organizing and Integrating**	
Analyzes data-based observations to generate multiple theories of causation about the data.	Analyzes data-based observations to generate multiple theories of causation about the data.	Analyzes data to generate multiple theories of causation about the data.	
Reaches consensus on causal theories to test and the multiple sources of data needed to monitor the progress.	Reaches consensus on causal theories to test and the multiple sources of data needed to monitor the progress.	Develops a plan to test the root cause theory.	
Develops a plan to test the root cause theory that has clear outcomes, measurable criteria for success, action steps, and a progressing monitoring process.	Develops a plan to test the root cause theory.		

Used with permission. Johnson, M., & Wilkerson, S. (2016). *MNPS IC Map for Collaborative Inquiry*. Created for Metropolitan Nashville Public Schools under REL Appalachia 2011-2016 contract. For more information, go to www.mnpscollaboration.org or http://www .magnoliaconsulting.org/.

EXHIBIT 8: INNOVATION CONFIGURATION MAP FOR WRITING PROGRAM, GADSDEN ELEMENTARY SCHOOL DISTRICT #32, SAN LUIS, ARIZONA

Implementing Change Among School Staff

The principal and other leaders do the following.

Desired outcome	LEVEL 1	LEVEL II	LEVEL III	LEVEL IV
Create atmosphere or context for change	Schedule time and place for staff reflection and collaborative work	Schedule time and place for staff reflection and collaborative work	Schedule time and place for staff reflection and collaborative work	Schedule time and place for staff reflection and collaborative work
	Provide learning environment	Provide learning environment	Provide learning environment	Provide learning environment
	Develop culture of learning	Develop culture of learning	Develop staff's skills of	
	Develop staff's skills of • collaboration • modes of conversation • conflict management • decision-making model Nurture leadership team skills. Activate leadership teams for learning. Monitor to ensure time is used well	Develop staff's skills of • collaboration • modes of conversation • conflict management • decision-making model Activate leadership teams for learning	• collaboration • modes of conversation • conflict management • decision-making models	
Develop and communicate a shared vision	Identify purpose or school mission Define values and staff beliefs Engage staff in studying data to identify needs for improvement Study and select new programs or practices to address the priority need for improvement Create an innovation configuration that represents and communicates the new practice, the vision of change Keep the vision visible Revisit the vision periodically	Identify purpose or school mission Engage staff in studying data to identify needs for improvement Select new programs or practices to address the priority need for improvement Create an innovation configuration that represents and communicates the new practice, the vision of change	Engage staff in studying data to identify needs for improvement Select new programs and practices to address the priority need for improvement	Engage staff in studying data to identify needs for improvement Adopt new programs and practices to address the need for improvement

Desired outcome	LEVEL I	LEVEL II	LEVEL III	LEVEL IV
Plan and provide resources	Gather staff information (stages of concern, level of understanding, innovation configuration) and relevant data Use six strategies to develop an implementation plan that will achieve the vision Identify resources needed and plan to access them: • currently available • needed as reflected in the vision Establish timelines	Gather staff information (stages of concern, level of understanding, innovation configuration) and relevant data Use six strategies to develop an implementation plan that will achieve the vision Identify resources needed and plan to access them: • currently available • needed as reflected in the vision	Use six strategies to develop an implementation plan that will achieve the vision Identify resources needed and plan to access them: • currently available • needed as reflected in the vision	Identify resources needed and plan to access them: • currently available • needed as reflected in the vision
Invest in professional development	Gather and analyze student data (AIMS, mandated and district assessments) and teacher data (stages of concern, level of understanding, innovation configuration) Use staff and student data to create adult learning activities Create vision-driven action plan for professional development Arrange for, schedule, and deliver adult learning activities Establish timelines	Gather and analyze student data (AIMS, mandated and district assessments) and teacher data (stages of concern, level of understanding, innovation configuration) Use staff and student data to create adult learning activities Create vision-driven professional development plan	Gather and analyze student data (AIMS, mandated and district assessments) and teacher data (stages of concern, level of understanding, innovation configuration) Create professional development plan	Create professional development plan
Check for progress	Gather staff information • stages of concern • level of understanding • innovation configuration Include staff in interpreting data and determining needs Develop a culture of continuous assessment Celebrate small and large successes publicly or privately Establish timelines	Gather staff information • stages of concern • level of understanding • innovation configuration Include staff in interpreting data and determining needs Develop a culture of continuous assessment	Gather staff information • stages of concern • level of understanding • innovation configuration Ask staff what they need for implementation of new practices	Ask staff what they need for implementation of new practices

(Continued)

(Continued)

Desired outcome	LEVEL I	LEVEL II	LEVEL III	LEVEL IV
Provide assistance	Schedule needed professional development • large-group • small-group • individuals Provide coaches or mentors Review time and activities for collaborative work Inventory resources, restock, or share Revisit action plan and revise as needed Celebrate small and large successes publicly or privately	Schedule needed professional development • large-group • small-group • individuals Provide coaches or mentors Review time and activities for collaborative work Inventory resources and restock	Schedule needed professional development • large-group • small-group • individuals Review time and activities for collaborative work Inventory resources and restock	Schedule needed professional development • large-group

EXHIBIT 8: FOCUS GROUP PROTOCOL

Team Focus Group Protocol

Meeting Data Date: Start Time: _____ End Time: _____ Meeting Location: Meeting Leaders:	Participant Data No. in Team: No. Attended: No. Female: No. Participated in CI Training:
Welcome Script Good morning, and welcome to our session. Thank you for joining us today to talk about collaborative inquiry in your school. My name is [insert name], and [insert name] is here with me today. I am with [name department], and [insert name], is with [name department]. **Overview of Topic** The purpose of our time together today is to talk about the collaborative inquiry work in your school. This discussion will last about 1 hour, and we will be having similar discussions with others who have been involved in the collaborative inquiry training. We will use the information we gather from these discussions to learn what teachers think about collaborative inquiry, what support is needed to implement collaborative inquiry, and how collaborative inquiry is affecting students. **Ground Rules** I will guide our discussion by asking questions, but I want each of you to feel free to elaborate on any points we cover or to bring up additional issues you think are important. There are no right or wrong answers to any of the questions I will ask . . . I am interested in your honest thoughts and opinions. I would like for us to have an open discussion, so please share your thoughts, even if they are different from what others have said. Also, I ask that we respect each other's views, even if they are different from our own. If it is okay with you all, we would like to record today's session to be sure we don't miss anything during our discussion. We will be using only first names today, and none of your names will be used in reports. Even if we use a quote from today's session in a report, your name will not be associated with it. Is this okay with everyone? [NOTE: Make sure everyone is comfortable with recording the discussion. If not, rely on note taking.] To help us stay on task today, I am asking that we all turn off our cell phones. If you can't turn off your phone and need to take a call, please do so as quickly and quietly as possible. Are there any questions? If not, let's get started.	
Start the Tape	
So we are all talking about the same thing, let's define Collaborative Inquiry is a data-based team process that consciously uses the collaborative learning cycle (activating and engaging, exploring and discovering, and organizing and integrating) and the qualities of effective teams (fostering a culture of trust, maintaining a clear focus, taking collective responsibility and data-informed decision making.	

Introductions	For us to get acquainted, let's begin by each person stating your first name, grade and subjects you teach, and how many years you have been teaching?
Q.1	On a scale of 1 to 10 with 1 being "not yet" and 10 being "fully," how would you rate Implementation of CI for your team? (Collect each person's response.) Give your honest rating and a one sentence reason for your rating.
Q.2	Has the team been meeting on a regular basis? How often?
Q.3	What resources is your team using? Are you using the IC Map? Other CI tools?
Q.4	How do you establish the agenda for each meeting? How do you ensure meetings incorporate CI practices?
Q.5	In your meetings, do members assume collective responsibility for the decisions and actions of the team? How is that demonstrated? Can you provide an example?
Q.6	Do the members of the team trust one another? How do you know trust is established? Have you had disagreements and how did you resolve them?
Q.7	What is an example of a decision the team has made based on the collaborative inquiry process and how did you carry it out?
Q.8	Have the team's decisions led to changes in instruction? What is an example? How did you report back to other team members on the change?
Q.9	What are barriers to the implementation of CI in your school?
Q.11	What additional support is needed to implement CI in your school? What support do you as a team need?
Q.12	Are you confident that CI will increase student success? What gives you confidence? What diminishes your confidence?
Q.13	What things about the implementation of CI have surprised you?
Q.14	How could the capacity of teachers to implement CI be improved?
Q.15	What else should we know about the implementation of CI for your school? Or for you?
Thank you very much for your time. You will receive information about the results of the evaluation but individuals and teams will remain confidential.	

Used with permission. Wilkerson, S., & Johnson. M. (2016). *MNPS (Team or Coach) Focus Group Protocol.* Created for Metropolitan Nashville Public Schools under REL Appalachia 2011–2016 contract. For more information, go to http://www.magnoliaconsulting .org/ or www.mnpscollaboration.org.

Appendix H
Step-by-Step Evaluation Guide

MAPPING AN EVALUATION STEP BY STEP

The questions below serve to guide the evaluator in following the eight-step process to plan and complete an evaluation of a professional learning program.

- What is the purpose of this evaluation?
- Who are the primary users/stakeholders of the evaluation results?
- What is their intended plan for using the results?

Step One: Assess Evaluability

1. What are the professional learning program's goals? Are they plausible, student focused, and results oriented?

2. What are the professional learning program's outcomes for educators' clients (students)?
   - Are they measurable?
   - Do they specify the intended change (knowledge, attitude, skill, aspiration, behavior)?
   - Are they plausible, student focused, and results oriented?

3. What are the professional learning program's outcomes for educators?
   - Are they measurable?
   - Do they specify the intended change (knowledge, attitude, skill, aspiration, behavior)?
   - Are they plausible and focused on educator behaviors/practices?

4. Have the standards for success been set for all outcomes?

5. What is the professional learning program's theory of change and the assumptions upon which it is based?

6. Is the professional learning program's logic model complete? In other words, what are the inputs, activities, initial outcomes, intermediate outcomes, and intended results of this program?

7. Do the program's theory of change and logic model make sense?

8. Do key stakeholders understand the program's theory of change?

9. Is this evaluation worth doing?

Step Two: Formulate Evaluation Questions

1. What are the evaluation questions?
   - Formative
   - Summative

2. How well do the evaluation questions reflect the interests of the primary stakeholders of the evaluation results?

3. How well do the evaluation questions align with the program's goals and purpose of the evaluation?

4. Are the evaluation questions
   - reasonable,
   - appropriate,
   - answerable,
   - specific about success indicators, and
   - specific about the measure of program success?

Step Three: Construct the Evaluation Framework

1. Determine the evaluator.
   - Who will conduct the evaluation?
     - Internal evaluator
     - External evaluator
     - Combination
   - Does the designated evaluator have the knowledge, skills, and resources to conduct the evaluation?

2. Decide how to answer the evaluation question(s).
   - What are the key constructs/variables (terms such as student achievement, improvement, increase, professional learning) that will be measured? How have they been defined so that they are clear and specific?
   - Do the evaluation questions require making a comparison to determine impact? If so, what are possible comparison groups? Which is the most appropriate comparison group for this evaluation?

        – Cohort

        – Individual

        – Group

        – Panel

        – Generic

3. Create a data plan.

- Who or what is expected to change as a result of this staff development program?
- What types of changes are expected as a result of this staff development program in the identified target audiences or organizational structures?

        – Knowledge

        – Attitude

        – Skill

        – Aspiration

        – Behavior

- What data can provide evidence that the changes intended have occurred?
- What data-collection methodologies are most appropriate for the needed data?
- What are the sources of data that will provide evidence of the intended change?
- How essential is it to have multiple data sources for this evaluation?
- When will the data be collected?
- Where will the data be collected?
- How will various data collected be analyzed?

4. Determine the cost.

- What resources are needed, including time, fiscal resources, and personnel, available to conduct this evaluation?
- If resources are not adequate, what aspects of the evaluation plan can be modified without compromising the integrity of the evaluation?
- If resources are inadequate, how will the evaluation be affected?
- Is the evaluation worth doing?

5. Establish responsibilities.

- Who is responsible for various parts of the evaluation?

6. Have primary stakeholders reviewed and approved the evaluation plan?

Step Four: Collect Data

1. How the instruments and procedures for data collection been field tested?

2. What revisions are necessary?

3. How will data collectors be trained?

4. After early data collection, do any data seem redundant? What are the advantages and disadvantages of continuing to collect these data? Is it appropriate to continue or to discontinue collecting these data?

5. After early data collection, what data seem to be missing? Is it essential to collect these missing data? How will a new data-collection methodology be implemented to collect these data?

6. What processes have been established to manage data collection and transfer?

7. What processes are established to ensure safekeeping and integrity of data?

8. If collecting quantitative data, what kinds of scores are needed to accurately reflect the data and to answer the evaluation questions?

Step Five: Organize, Analyze, and Display Data

1. How will data be sorted, grouped, and arranged before analysis?

2. How will missing data be handled?

3. What method of data analysis is needed to answer the evaluation questions?
   - Univariate analysis
   - Bivariate analysis
   - Multivariate analysis

3. How will data be displayed to facilitate interpretation and understanding?

4. How clearly and succinctly are the data summaries and descriptions transferred into findings?

5. How will stakeholders and participants be involved in the data-analysis process?

Step Six: Interpret Data

1. What do these data mean?

2. What interpretations and claims can be made from these data?

3. How well supported are the interpretations and claims?
   - Major findings
     - Strongly
     - Weakly

- Minor findings
  - Strongly
  - Weakly

4. What possible alternative interpretations have been considered?

5. Does this evaluation support claims of attribution or contribution?

6. Does this program have merit, worth, and significance?

7. What recommended actions can help the program stakeholders improve their program and its impact?

8. Are the recommendations logical, actionable, and appropriate?

9. How have representative stakeholders and participants with diverse perspectives been involved in the interpretation process and formulating recommendations?

Step Seven: Report, Disseminate, and Use Results

1. Will the evaluation have interim and/or final evaluation reports?

2. Who are the primary users of the evaluation report?

3. What components do the primary users want included in the evaluation report?

4. What format for reporting the results are most appropriate for the primary users of the evaluation report?

5. What other audiences are likely to want some version of the evaluation report?

6. What formats for reporting the results are appropriate for the other audiences?

7. How does the report demonstrate sensitivity the report sensitive to the human rights of participants?

8. How have other stakeholders and participants been involved in the reporting, disseminating, and using the evaluation results?

Step Eight: Evaluate the Evaluation

1. How will the effectiveness of the evaluation be assessed?

2. What questions will guide the evaluation of the evaluation?
   - Credibility

- Validity
- Significance
- Resources
- Design
- Findings
- Reporting
- Evaluator

3. What stakeholders will be involved in the evaluation of the evaluation? How will they be involved?

Glossary

Activities

Planned services a program provides to accomplish its outcomes.

Artifacts

Documents or products that exist within a district or school and that serve as a source of information about a program (e.g., attendance records, course syllabi, descriptions of professional learning programs, end-of-course evaluations on file).

Aspiration

Desire or internal motivation to engage in a particular practice; one type of change that can occur as a result of professional learning.

Attitude

Beliefs about the value of particular information or strategies; one type of change that can occur as the result of professional learning.

Attribution

The claim that a program is solely responsible for the changes that occurred in program participants or their clients and that nothing else could possibly have produced the results.

Backmapping process

A process for planning professional learning with the outcomes. This planning model is based on results and begins "with the end in mind."

Behavior

Consistent application of knowledge and skills, driven by attitudes and aspirations; regular practices; one type of change that can occur as a result of professional learning.

Black-box evaluation

Evaluation conducted without an articulated program theory of change and that does not provide information about what is occurring to contribute to the observed changes.

Case study

An evaluation design that studies the effects of a professional learning program on one or more participants in their natural setting and describes their experiences and changes.

Chi-square

A statistical process that is a simple and direct test of significant difference between groups when the observations can be classified into discrete categories and created as observed frequencies.

Claim

A conclusion about the professional learning program based on multiple forms of evidence or triangulated data; can be either major or minor claims of importance and strength.

Client

In the context of results-based professional learning, the clients are those who are being served by the educators participating in professional learning experiences, e.g., teacher; students; principal; teacher.

Clustering

A data-analysis method that puts discrete data into classes, categories, or groups on the basis of common features.

Cohort group comparison

Comparing the performance of a group prior to intervention to its performance after the intervention to determine whether change has occurred; it results in a single score for the entire group. For example, change in pre- and posttest scores indicates a change.

Comparing

A data-analysis method that examines the similarities and differences in features of individuals or the program before, during, or after the intervention.

Comparison group

A designated group that has not participated in the professional learning program against which the outcomes of those who do participate are compared to determine a program's impact.

Comprehensive professional learning system

A coherent organization and structure of professional learning that includes a clear vision, professional learning standards, definition, assumptions, and well-orchestrated operational processes that include roles and responsibilities, decision-making authority, ongoing evaluation, and resource management.

Construct

A concept being measured in an evaluation; because constructs are often general they require defining through specific characteristics or indicators that can

be measured; for example, improved teaching practice is a construct that requires definition in order to measure it.

Context

The conditions within which the program occurs; may be characterized by physical, social, psychological, environmental, or political factors.

Contribution

The claim that a program contributes to the impact of professional learning on student achievement when there is an assumption that other factors are also influencing these results.

Counting

The numerical description of data that allows comparison of the professional learning program to another program or to some standard of acceptable performance.

Covariation

A circumstance when changes in a variable always appear in relation to changes in another variable.

Critical friend

A colleague who serves as a reviewer, advisor, and critic of an evaluator's work.

Data

Discrete bits of information that become evidence through a process of analysis and interpretation.

Data collection

The method used to gather data from the appropriate sources; might include data-collection instruments, such as surveys, or other means such as observation, document analysis, focus groups, or interviews.

Data-collection instrument

An instrument (such as a test or survey) that provides a way for data to be gathered. Both existing and newly developed instruments are an option for evaluators and key stakeholders. Existing instruments are usually field tested, valid, and reliable. Sometimes they are normed and standardized. Developing an instrument allows for alignment with the constructs of the evaluation and appropriateness to context or population who will complete the instrument.

Data plan

The decisions related to identifying the desired information to answer the evaluation questions, its source, how to collect it, and how to analyze it.

Data source

The origin of the information desired to answer the evaluation questions; often participants in professional learning, their clients, or their work products or samples.

Decision makers

Individual and groups who have responsibility for the success of a program and typically include administrators, oversight committees, or management teams.

Describing

A data-analysis method based on narrative description of the professional learning program often including descriptive statistics such as mean, median, mode, and range.

Documentation

Records, documents, artifacts, and so on that exist within a system that are summarized, rather than analyzed, to explain or judge.

Documents

Artifacts or records within a system that can shed light on a professional learning program.

Empowerment evaluation

An evaluation in which the evaluator assumes the responsibility of building the capacity of stakeholders to conduct their own evaluations in the future or to use evaluation processes to objectively and rigorously analyze their own work.

Evaluand

The subject of an evaluation; in the evaluation of professional learning, it is the professional learning program.

Evaluability assessment

The analysis of a professional learning program's ability to be evaluated that is based on the design of the program, the utility of the evaluation, and the proposed logic of the program.

Evaluation of professional learning

Systematic, purposeful, standards-driven process of studying, reviewing, analyzing, and interpreting data about professional learning gathered from multiple sources to make judgments and informed decisions about the program.

Evaluation design

The overarching plan for conducting an evaluation, as in qualitative, experimental, quasi-experimental, case study, and so on.

Evaluation questions

A set of questions, developed by the evaluators and others, drawn from the program goals and objectives that define the focus of the evaluation.

Evaluation think

How individuals and teams look critically and analytically at their work to discover what is working and what is not, in order to redefine their work and

improve results; self-assessing what we learn, do, believe, value, and want; asking for evidence and scrutinizing our practices; generating information to make sound decisions.

Event

An isolated professional learning experience that is viewed as an individual occurrence that may or may not be a part of a larger program or the context in which it occurs.

Every Student Succeeds Act (ESSA)

Federal reauthorization of the Elementary and Secondary School Act of 1965 by the 114th Congress in December 2015.

Evidence

Data that serve to answer an evaluation question and to support findings about a program.

Examining outliers

A data-analysis method that looks at situations on the extreme ends of the data set to determine what information, if any, can be learned that does not appear in the data that tend more toward the mean.

Experimental design

A form of evaluation design in which participants are randomly assigned to one of two groups—one group of participants experiences the professional learning program and another group does not; the design minimizes threats to the validity of the conclusions.

Extant data

Records, artifacts, or documents that exist within a system and that might shed light on the professional learning program (e.g., performance records, policies, meeting agenda and minutes, annual reports).

External evaluator

Someone hired to conduct an evaluation who is not employed by the school or district where the evaluation is taking place and presumably with no vested interest in the outcome of the evaluation.

Factoring (or factor analysis)

A statistical analysis that breaks down the aggregates into their parts and allows the evaluator to determine how much each contributed to the results.

Finding

A statement that summarizes or describes the analyzed data.

Finding covariation

A data-analysis method that examines the interaction between two variables to determine whether changes in one relate to changes in another.

Focus group

Small, representative group of individuals who are selected to share their perspectives about a topic of interest. The questions are prepared in advance, the discussion is moderated by a facilitator, and responses are recorded and analyzed.

Formative evaluation

The analysis of how the professional learning program operates, its implementation, and potential barriers; formative evaluation is undertaken to improve the program's operation and likelihood of achieving its outcomes.

Glass-box evaluation

An evaluation conducted on a professional learning program that has a clearly articulated theory of change and that provides information on the sequence of changes occurring within the program that contribute to the program's outcome.

Guiding Principles for Evaluators

Statements developed by the American Evaluation Association to guide evaluators in every field and to inform evaluation clients and the public about the responsible practice of professional evaluators.

Impact

The effect of a program on its participants and their clients; for example, teacher professional learning and student learning.

Individual comparison

Comparing the performance of individuals after the intervention with their performance before the intervention; results in multiple scores that allow the evaluator to analyze how change affected individuals rather than the whole group.

Initial outcomes

Effects of a program's activities or services frequently characterized as changes in participant knowledge, attitudes, and skills.

Innovation configuration map

A sophisticated rating scale that delineates the critical components of a program and the continuum of *ideal* to *unacceptable* levels of performance of implementation for each component and that specifies the level of acceptable performance for each component.

Intermediate outcomes

Changes that occur in participants as a result of their participation in the professional learning program, frequently characterized as changes in aspiration and behavior.

Internal evaluator

Someone who is employed by the school or district where the evaluation is taking place and who agrees to conduct the evaluation with objectivity and rigor.

Intervention

The professional learning program designed and implemented to address the identified needs.

Interview

An oral data-collection method in which the evaluator typically uses prepared questions to ask respondents about their knowledge, attitude, skill, aspiration, and behaviors.

Knowledge

Conceptual understanding of information, theories, principles, and research; one type of change that can occur as a result of professional learning.

Log

A data-collection method used to document occurrences of particular behaviors, practices, or occurrences.

Logic model

A graphic display that uses a program's theory of change to depict the operation of a program by delineating its critical components, including resources, activities, initial outcomes, intermediate outcomes, and intended results.

Mean score

The average of a range of scores.

Merit

The intrinsic value of a program; how it is perceived by those it intends to help based on established criteria.

Meta-evaluation

A systematic process of evaluating an evaluation.

Mixed-method evaluation

An evaluation design that used two or more designs to measure the professional learning program such as case studies and quasi-experiment.

Mom test

A succinct two-sentence statement of the essence of an evaluation report.

Multiple-intervention evaluation

An evaluation methodology that compares multiple implementations of an intervention as one way to determine impact.

Multivariate analysis

Analysis of multiple variables to determine whether any relationship exists between or among them.

Naturalistic evaluation

An evaluation design that allows evaluators to study program activities and their effects on participants within the natural setting and without limitations established by established hypotheses.

No Child Left Behind Act of 2001

Federal legislation passed by the U.S. Congress in 2001 and signed into law in 2002 to replace the previous Elementary and Secondary School Act; the law has four pillars: stronger accountability for results, more freedom for states and communities, proven education methods, and more choices for parents.

Observation

A data-collection method in which an evaluator directly watches and notes behaviors most often used to measure skill or behavior.

Outliers

An unusual or abnormal case that differs from most other cases in the same situation.

Panel group comparison

Comparison of the performance of one intact group to another group at a later time assumed to be equivalent (e.g., the comparison of seventh-grade scores in one year to seventh-grade scores the next year).

Participants

The educators who engage in a professional learning program and whose knowledge, attitudes, skills, aspirations, and behaviors the professional learning program serves or supports.

Pearson's *r*

An inferential statistic that measures the relationship and the direction of the relationship between two variables.

Planning evaluation

An evaluation conducted before a professional learning program that is designed to determine the needs of potential participants their social conditions and the best way to address the needs.

Policy makers

Individuals or groups who hold decision-making authority over the professional learning program and may include funders, administrators, governance committees, and school boards.

Practitioner

An educator, either alone or with colleagues, who undertakes evaluation as a normative practice in his or her work.

Primary stakeholder

The person or group of people who commission the evaluation of professional learning or who will be the principal users of the evaluation results.

Professional learning program

A set of planned and implemented actions, guided by research, evidence, and standards of effective professional learning, accompanied by adequate resources, and directed toward the achievement of defined outcomes related to educator practice and its impact on student learning.

Professional learning versus professional development

Learning emphasizes the expected changes in educator knowledge, attitudes, skills, aspirations, and behaviors, while development emphasizes the activities to accomplish those changes.

Program Evaluation Standards

Statements that describe the attributes of high-quality program evaluation in education developed by the Joint Committee on Evaluation in Education to guide the ethical practice of evaluators.

Program goal

A statement of a desired state toward which a program is directed; the overall purpose of a program.

Program outcome

A statement of the specific, measurable change expected of or produced by the program.

Qualitative data

Data that are expressed in descriptions or characteristics. Qualitative data appear typically in words rather than numbers and are gathered in interviews, observations, document analysis, and the like.

Quantitative data

Data that are expressed in numbers and can be analyzed statistically. Quantitative data are numbers and are gathered from ratings, scores, and the like.

Quasi-experimental design

An evaluation design in which participants are assigned non-randomly to one of two groups, one which experiences the professional learning program and one which does not; the design which implements some controls to minimize threats to the validity of the conclusions.

Random assignment

Assignment of units of study—such as students, classrooms, or schools—to groups by the laws of chance, one that will receive the intervention (treatment group) and one or more that will not receive the intervention or that will receive an alternative intervention (comparison group).

Rapid Feedback Evaluation (RFE)

Small-scale evaluations that provide short-cycle, quick results for immediate decision making about a program; sometimes used when a full-scale evaluation might take too long.

Rating scale

Data-collection method used to measure behavior and performance; rating scales typically specify a continuum of strong to weak practices or list desirable practices.

Research

A systematic investigation, including research development, testing, and evaluation, designed to develop or contribute to generalizable knowledge.

Results

The effects of a professional learning program. In results-based professional learning, results are expressed in terms of changes in educator practice or behavior and in student achievement.

Rival explanation

A plausible explanation of the observed changes that differs from the desired explanation. Data-analysis methods work to disprove rival explanations so as to strengthen arguments for the desired explanation.

Rubric

An extended form of rating scale that delineates a progression of expected performance and a level of acceptable performance.

Scatterplots

A graph of the relationship between the frequency distributions of two sets of scores (one plotted on the X axis and one plotted on the Y axis) that represents the relationship among the scores.

Skills

The ability or capacity to use strategies and processes to apply knowledge; skills are one type of change that can occur as a result of professional learning.

Smart enemies

A term coined by Michael Scriven to describe a reviewer of an evaluation who is likely to provide an honest and rigorous critique of the evaluation.

Stakeholders

Individuals or groups with an interest in the professional learning program. They might be school or district staff, school board members, community members, education agency staff, other educators, or public or private funders.

Standard

The explicit criterion or criteria that define the program's acceptable performance.

Standard score

A recalculation of the raw score that provides equal-interval scales for comparison across students and tests for the purpose of mathematical calculations.

Standards for Professional Learning

Statements that describe the criteria of high-quality learning for educators designed to increase their effectiveness and student success; published by Learning Forward and adopted by multiple states, education agencies, and school systems to guide the design, implementation, and evaluation of professional learning.

Stanines

Rough approximation of an individual's performance relative to the performance of others in the group; stanine scores range from 1 to 9, with 1 being the lowest.

Summative evaluation

The evaluation of a professional learning program conducted at the end of the program or significant benchmark points to provide information about how well the program met its intended outcomes.

Survey

A data collection method to gather information from a defined group or sample usually by means of written questionnaires.

Tests

Data-collection method using instruments or tasks to measure knowledge, attitude, aspiration, and, to a limited degree, skill.

Theory of action

A description of the actions that activate the theory of change.

Theory of change

A rationale for the planned, causal chain of actions that predict and explain how a professional learning program works—that is, the central processes or drivers by which change occurs, and the program's underlying assumptions upon which the rationale is based; a participatory planning process to identify the goals and conditions to achieve them; often depicted graphically.

Time-series design

An evaluation and analysis method over time intervals in which repeated measures of a key variable are taken and compared over time.

T-tests

A statistical process for testing the significance of the difference between the means of two outcomes.

Unit of analysis

The entity in an evaluation study that is being analyzed; in professional learning evaluations it may be individual or clusters of teachers or students, such as at a particular grade level, schools, school systems, or larger groups.

Univariate analysis

The analysis of a single variable often measured by a change in a pretest and posttest score.

Use

The intended way in which stakeholders will use the evaluation such as making decisions about future funding, continuation of the program, staffing, or the like.

User

Stakeholders, policy makers, or decision makers who will use information produced from the evaluation to take further actions related to the professional learning program.

Utilization-focused evaluation

An approach to evaluation developed by Michael Quinn Patton (1997) that places significant emphasis on the intended use of the evaluation.

Value

The political or social contextual criteria influencing decisions about merit or worth; that is, what one person, organization, or entity perceives as valuable may not be perceived as valuable to another one.

Variable

Concepts of interest in an evaluation, either independent (the circumstances, situation, condition, factor, or action being altered to produce changes in the dependent variable) or dependent (circumstances, situation, condition, factor, characteristics, or action expected to change and is dependent on the independent variable); in evaluations of professional learning, professional learning is the independent variable and changes in educator KASABs and client KASABs are the dependent variables.

Worth

The extrinsic value of a program to those outside the program, such as the larger community or society.

References

Administration of Children, Youth, and Families, U.S. Department of Health and Human Services. (n.d.). *A program manager's guide to evaluation.* Retrieved December 21, 2006, from www.acf.hhs.gov/programs/opre/other_resrch/ pm_guide_eval/ index.html

American Evaluation Association. (2004). *Guiding principles for evaluators.* Retrieved from www.eval.org/Publications/GuidingPrinciplesPrintable.asp

Bauer, S. (2014, August 13). Building values-based, results-based leaders. *Stanford Social Innovation Review.* https://ssir.org/articles/entry/building_values_based_ results_driven_leaders

Bennett, C. (1975). Up the hierarchy. *Journal of Extension, 13*(2), 7–12.

Bennett, C. (1979). *Reflective appraisal of programs.* Ithaca, NY: Cornell University Media Services.

Bennett, C. (1982). *Analyzing impacts of extension programs.* Washington, DC: U.S. Department of Agriculture.

Bradley, J., Munger, L., & Hord, S. (2015). First focus on outcomes when planning change, improved student learning is the ultimate goal. *JSD, 36*(4), 44–52.

Brinkerhoff, R. O. (2003). *The success case method: Find out quickly what's working and what's not.* San Francisco, CA: Berret-Koehler.

Bryk, A. S, Gomez, L. M., Grunow, A., & LeMahieu, P. G. (2015). *Learning to improve: How America's schools can get better at getting better.* Boston, MA: Harvard Education Publishing.

Bryson, J. M., & Patton, M. Q. (2015). Analyzing and engaging stakeholders. In K. Newcomer, H. Hatry, & J. Wholey (Eds.), *Handbook of practical program evaluation* (4th ed., pp. 36–61). Hoboken, NJ: John Wiley & Sons.

Chen, H. (1990). *Theory-driven evaluations.* Newbury Park, CA: Sage.

Chen, H.-T. (2005). *Practical program evaluation: Theory-driven evaluation and the integrated evaluation perspective.* Thousand Oaks, CA: Sage.

Chen, H.-T. (2015). *Practical program evaluation: Theory-driven evaluation and the integrated evaluation perspective* (2nd ed.). Thousand Oaks, CA: Sage.

Connell, J., & Klem, A. (2000). You can get there from here: Using a theory of change approach to plan urban education reform. *Journal of Educational and Psychological Consultation, 11*(1), 93–120.

Connell, J., & Kubisch, A. (1998). Applying a theory of change approach to evaluating comprehensive community initiatives. In K. Fulbright-Anderson, A. Kubisch, & J. Connell (Eds.), *New approaches to evaluating community initiatives* (Vol. 2). Washington, DC: Aspen Institute. Retrieved from www.aspeninstitute.org/site/c .huLWJeMRKpH/b.613709/k.B547/Applying_a_Theory_of_Change_Approach_

to_the_Evaluation_of_Comprehensive_Community_Initiatives_Progress_
Prospects_and_Problems.htm

Creswell, J. (2002). *Educational research: Planning, conducting, and evaluating quantitative and qualitative research.* Upper Saddle River, NJ: Pearson Education.

Darling-Hammond, L., Wei, R. C., Andree, A., Richardson, N., & Orphanos, S. (2009). *Professional learning in the learning profession: A status report on teacher development in the United States and abroad.* Palo Alto, CA: National Staff Development Council and The School Redesign Network, Stanford University.

Deming, E. (1994). *The new economics for industry, business, education* (2nd ed.). Cambridge, MA: The MIT Press.

Desimone, L. M. (2009). Improving impact studies of teachers' professional development: Toward better conceptualizations and measures. *Educational Researcher, 38*(3), 181–199.

Desimone, L. M., & Garet, M. S. (2015). Best practices in teachers' professional development in the United States. *Psychology, Society and Education, 7*(3), 252–263.

Desimone, L. M., Porter, A. C., Garet, M. S., Yoon, K., & Birman, B. F. (2002). Effects of professional development on teachers' instruction: Results from a three-year longitudinal study. *Educational Evaluation and Policy Analysis, 24*(2), 81–112.

Echevarria, J., & Graves, A. (2003). The sheltered instruction observation protocol (SIOP). *Sheltered content instruction: Teaching English-language learners with diverse abilities* (p. 56). Boston, MA: Allyn & Bacon.

Elementary and Secondary School Act of 1965, Pub. L. No 89-10 §10 Stat. 2362.

ESSA Consolidated Plan Template. (2016).

Every Student Succeeds Act (ESSA) of 2015, Pub. L. No 114-95 §114 Stat. 1177 (2015–2016). (1177-295).

Fournier, D. M. (2005). Evaluation. In S. Mathison (Ed.), *Encyclopedia of evaluation* (pp. 139–140). Thousand Oaks, CA: Sage.

Fullan, M. (2001). *The new meaning of educational change* (3rd ed.). New York, NY: Teachers College Press.

Funnell, S. C., & Rogers, P. J. (2011). *Purposeful program theory: Effective use of theories of change and logic models.* Hoboken, NJ: John Wiley & Sons.

Garet, M. S., Cronen, S., Eaton, M., Kurki, A., Ludwig, M., Jones, W., & Sztejnberg, L. (2008). *The impact of two professional development interventions on early reading instruction and achievement* (NCEE 2008-4030). Washington, DC: National Center for Education Evaluation and Regional Assistance, Institute of Education Sciences, U.S. Department of Education. Retrieved from http://ies.ed.gov/ncee

Garet, M. S., Porter, A. C., Desimone, L., Birman, B. F., & Yoon, K. S. (2001). What makes professional development effective? Results from a national sample of teachers. *American Educational Research Journal, 38*(4), 915–945.

Garet, M., Wayne, A., Stancavage, F., Taylor, J., Walters, K., Song, M., . . . Doolittle, F. (2010). *Middle School Mathematics Professional Development Impact Study: Findings after the first year of implementation* (NCEE 2010-4009). Washington, DC: National Center for Education Evaluation and Regional Assistance, Institute of Education Sciences, U.S. Department of Education. Retrieved from https://ies.ed.gov/ncee/pubs/20104009/pdf/20104010.pdf

Goodrick, D., & Rogers, P. J. (2015). Qualitative data analysis. In *Handbook of practical program evaluation* (4th ed., pp. 561–595). Hoboken, NJ: John Wiley & Sons.

Grob, G. F. (2015a). Providing recommendations, suggestions, and options for improvement. In K. E. Newcomer, H. P. Hatry, & J. S. Wholey (Eds.), *Handbook of practical program evaluation* (4th ed., pp. 725–738). Hoboken, NJ: John Wiley & Sons.

Grob, G. F. (2015b). Writing for impact. In K. Newcomer, H. Hatry, & J. Wholey (Eds.), *Handbook of practical program evaluation* (4th ed., pp. 739–764). Hoboken, NJ: John Wiley & Sons.

Guba, E. G. (1978). *Toward a methodology of naturalistic inquiry in educational evaluations.* Los Angeles: University of California.

Guerra-Lopez, I. (2008). *Performance evaluation: Proven approach for improving program and organizational performance.* San Francisco, CA: Jossey-Bass.

Guskey, T. (2000). *Evaluating professional development.* Thousand Oaks, CA: Corwin.

Hall, G. E., & Hord, S. M. (2015). *Implementing change: Patterns, principles, and potholes* (4th ed.). Boston, MA: Pearson.

Hanssen, C., Lawrenz, F., & Dunet, D. (2008). Concurrent meta-evaluations: A critique. *American Journal of Evaluation, 22*(2), 211–228.

Harper, B., & Millman, N. B. (2016). One-to-one technology classrooms: A review of the literature from 2004 through 2014. *Journal of Research on Technology in Education, 48*(2), 129–142.

Haslam, M. B. (2010). *Teacher professional development evaluation guide.* Oxford, OH: National Staff Development Council. https://learningforward.org/docs/pdf/evaluationguide.pdf

Hatry, H. P., & Newcomer, K. E. (2015). Pitfalls in evaluation. In K. E. Newcomer, H. P. Hatry, & J. S. Wholey (Eds.), *Handbook of practical program evaluation* (4th ed., pp. 701–724). Hoboken, NJ: John Wiley & Sons.

Hirsh, S., & Killion, J. (2007). *The learning educator: A new era in professional learning.* Oxford, OH: NSDC.

Hood, S., Hopson, R. K., & Kirkhart, K. E. (2015). Culturally responsive evaluation. In K. E. Newcomer, H. P. Hatry, & J. S. Wholey (Eds.), *Handbook of practical program evaluation* (4th ed., pp. 281–317). Hoboken, NJ: John Wiley & Sons.

House, E. (1990). Research news and comments: Trends in evaluation. *Educational Researcher, 19,* 24–28.

Jackson, C. K., & Bruegmann. E. (2009, July). *Teaching students and teaching each other: The importance of peer learning for teachers.* Cambridge, MA: National Bureau of Economic Research, Working Paper No. 15202.

Johnson, M., & Wilkerson, S. (2016). *MNPS IC Map for Collaborative Inquiry.* www.mnpscollaboration.org

Joyce, B., & Showers, B. (1995). *Student achievement through staff development* (2nd ed.). White Plains, NY: Longman.

Joyce, B., & Showers, B. (2002). *Student achievement through staff development* (3rd ed.). White Plains, NY: Longman.

Katz, S., & Dack, L. A. (2013). *Intentional interruptions: Breaking down learning barriers to transform professional practice.* Thousand Oaks, CA: Corwin.

Killion, J. (1999). *What works in the middle: Results-based staff development.* Oxford, OH: National Staff Development Council.

Killion, J. (2001). School district audit [Unpublished].

Killion, J. (2003). 8 smooth steps: Solid footwork makes evaluation of staff development a song. *JSD, 24*(4), 15–26.

Killion, J. (2013). *Comprehensive professional learning system: A workbook for states and districts.* Oxford, OH: Learning Forward.

Killion, J. (2015). *The feedback process: Transforming feedback for professional learning.* Oxford, OH: Learning Forward.

Killion, J., & Harrison, C. (2016). 5 core roles for central office learning leaders. *JSD, 37*(4), 44–51.

Killion, J., Harrison, C., Bryan, C., & Clifton, H. (2015). *Coaching matters.* Oxford, OH: Learning Forward.

Killion, J., & Roy, P. (2009). *Becoming a learning school.* Oxford, OH: National Staff Development Council.

Kipling, R. (1942). *The elephant's child and other just so stories.* Garden City, NY: The Junior Literary Guild and Garden City Publishing Company.

Kirkpatrick, D. L. (1998a). Great ideas revisited. In D. L. Kirkpatrick (Ed.), *Another look at evaluating training programs* (pp. 3–8). Alexandria, VA: American Society for Training & Development.

Kirkpatrick, D. L. (1998b). Evaluating training programs: Evidence vs. proof. In D. L. Kirkpatrick (Ed.), *Another look at evaluating training programs* (pp. 9–11). Alexandria, VA: American Society for Training & Development.

Kirkpatrick, D. L., & Kirkpatrick, J. D. (2006). *Evaluating training programs: The four levels* (3rd ed.). San Francisco, CA: Berrett-Koehler.

Kirkpatrick, J. D., & Kirkpatrick, W. K. (2016). *Kirkpatrick's four levels of training evaluation.* Alexandria, VA: ATD Press.

Learning Forward. (n.d.a). *Definition of professional development.* Oxford, OH: Author. https://learningforward.org/who-we-are/professional-learning-definition#.Ucmq6o7qOV8

Learning Forward. (n.d.b). *PD redesign principles.* Oxford, OH: Author. Retrieved from https://learningforward.org/learning-opportunities/Redesign-PD/redesignpd-principles

Learning Forward. (2011). *Standards for professional learning.* Oxford, OH: Author.

Learning Forward. (2012). *Standards assessment inventory.* Oxford, OH: Author. Retrieved from https://learningforward.org/consulting/sai

Learning Forward. (2014). Professional learning drives Common Core and educator evaluation. Oxford, OH: Author. Retrieved from https://learningforward.org/docs/default-source/publicationssection/Knowledge-Brief/kb-feb14-common-core-eval.pdf?sfvrsn=2

Mathison, S. (2005). *Encyclopedia of evaluation.* Thousand Oaks, CA: Sage.

McLaughlin, J. A., & Jordan, G. B. (2015). Exploratory evaluation. In K. E. Newcomer, H. P. Hatry, & J. S. Wholey (Eds.), *Handbook of practical program evaluation* (4th ed., pp. 88–107). Hoboken, NJ: John Wiley & Sons.

Mertens, D. M., & Wilson, A. T. (2012). *Program evaluation theory and practice: A comprehensive guide.* New York, NY: Guilford.

Mizell, H. (2003). Facilitator 10: Refreshments 8: Evaluation 0. *JSD, 24*(4), 10–13.

Morse, J. M. (1994). *Critical issues in qualitative research methods.* Newbury Park, CA: Sage.

Newcomer, K. E., Hatry, H. P., & Wholey, J. S. (2015). Planning and designing useful evaluations. In *Handbook of practical program evaluation* (4th ed., pp. 7–36). Hoboken, NJ: John Wiley & Sons.

Patton, M. Q. (1997). *Utilization-focused evaluation* (3rd ed.). Thousand Oaks, CA: Sage.

Patton, M. Q. (2005). Utilization-focused evaluation. In S. Mathison (Ed.), *Encyclopedia of evaluation* (pp. 429–433). Thousand Oaks, CA: Sage.

Patton, M. Q. (2008). *Utilization-focused evaluation* (4th ed.) Thousand Oaks, CA: Sage.

Patton, M. Q. (2015). *Qualitative research & evaluation methods* (4th ed.). Thousand Oaks, CA: Sage.

Phillips, J. (1997). *Return on investment in training and performance improvement programs.* Houston, TX: Gulf Publishing.

Poister, T. H. (2015). Performance measurement. In K. E. Newcomer, H. P. Hatry, & J. S. Wholey (Eds.), *Handbook of practical program evaluation* (4th ed., pp. 108–136). Hoboken, NJ: John Wiley & Sons.

Popham, W. J. (2001, September 19). Standardized achievement tests: Misnamed and misleading. *Education Week, 21*(3), 46.

Posavac, E. (2016). *Program evaluation: Methods and case studies.* London: Routledge Taylor and Francis Group.

Rossi, P., Freeman, H., & Lipsey, M. (2003). *Evaluation: A systematic approach* (7th ed.). Thousand Oaks, CA: Sage.

Scriven, M. (1991). *Evaluation thesaurus* (4th ed.). Newbury Park, CA: Edgepress.

Scriven, M. (1993). *Hard-won lessons in program evaluation. New directions for program evaluation*, No. 58. San Francisco, CA: Jossey-Bass.

Scriven, M. (2009). Metaevaluation revisited. *Journal of Multidisciplinary Evaluation*, *6*(11), iii–viii.

Spaulding, D. T. (2008). *Program evaluation in practice: Core concepts and examples for discussion*. San Francisco, CA: Jossey-Bass.

Stufflebeam, D. (2001, Spring). *Evaluation models: New directions for evaluation* (No. 89). San Francisco, CA: Jossey-Bass.

Stufflebeam, D. L. (2007). Program evaluations metaevaluation checklist. https://wmich .edu/sites/default/files/attachments/u350/2014/program_metaeval_short.pdf

Stufflebeam, D. L., & Shinkfield, A. J. (2007). *Evaluation theory models and applications*. San Francisco, CA: Jossey-Bass.

Supovitz, J. A., Mayer, D. P., & Kahle, J. B. (2000). Promoting inquiry-based instructional practice: The longitudinal impact of professional development in the context of systemic reform. *Educational Policy*, *14*(3), 331–356.

Supovitz, J. A., & Turner, H. M. (2000). The effects of professional development on science teaching practices and classroom culture. *Journal of Research in Science Teaching*, *37*(9), 963–980.

Taplin, D. H., & Clark, H. (2012). *Theory of change basics: A primer on theory of change*. New York, NY: ActKnowledge.

Taylor, M. J. (2001, September 9). Personal communication.

Timperley, H., & Alton-Lee, A. (2008). Reframing teacher professional learning: An alternative policy approach to strengthening valued outcomes for diverse learners. *Review of Research in Education*, *32* (pp. 328–369). Washington, DC: Sage.

U.S. Department of Education. (2016, September 16). *Non-regulatory guidance: Using evidence to strengthen education investments*. Washington, DC: Author. https:// www2.ed.gov/policy/elsec/leg/essa/guidanceuseseinvestment.pdf

Wayman, J. C., Wilkerson, S. B., Cho, V., Mandinach, E. B., & Supovitz, J. A. (2016). *Guide to using the Teacher Data Use Survey* (REL 2017–166). Washington, DC: U.S. Department of Education, Institute of Education Sciences, National Center for Education Evaluation and Regional Assistance, Regional Educational Laboratory Appalachia. https://ies.ed.gov/ncee/edlabs/projects/project.asp?projectID=2461

Weiss, C. H. (1998). *Evaluation* (2nd ed.). Upper Saddle River, NJ: Prentice Hall.

Wholey, J. S. (2015). Exploratory evaluation. In K. E. Newcomer, H. E. Hatry, & J. Wholey (Eds.), *Handbook of practical program evaluation* (4th ed., pp. 88–107). San Francisco, CA: Jossey-Bass.

Wilkerson, S., & Johnson. M. (2016). *MNPS (Team or Coach) Focus Group Protocol*. Created for Metropolitan Nashville Public Schools under REL Appalachia 2011–2016 contract. www.mnpscollaboration.org

Yarbrough, D. B., Shulha, L. M., Hopson, R. K., & Caruthers, F. A. (2011). *The program evaluation standards: A guide for evaluators and evaluation users* (3rd ed.). Thousand Oaks, CA: Sage.

Yoon, K. S., Duncan, T., Lee, S. W.-Y., Scarloss, B., & Shapley, K. L. (2007). *Reviewing the evidence on how teacher professional development affects student achievement. Issues and Answers Report*, REL 2007-No. 033. Washington, DC: U.S. Department of Education, Institute of Education Sciences, National Center for Education Evaluation and Regional Assistance, Regional Educational Laboratory Southwest. Available at http://ies.ed.gov/ncee/edlabs

Index

::

CORWIN
A SAGE Publishing Company

Helping educators make the greatest impact

CORWIN HAS ONE MISSION: to enhance education through intentional professional learning.

We build long-term relationships with our authors, educators, clients, and associations who partner with us to develop and continuously improve the best evidence-based practices that establish and support lifelong learning.

THE PROFESSIONAL LEARNING ASSOCIATION

Learning Forward is a nonprofit, international membership association of learning educators committed to one vision in K–12 education: Excellent teaching and learning every day. To realize that vision, Learning Forward pursues its mission to build the capacity of leaders to establish and sustain highly effective professional learning. Information about membership, services, and products is available from www .learningforward.org.

Solutions you want. Experts you trust. Results you need.

Author Consulting

On-site professional learning with sustainable results! Let us help you design a professional learning plan to meet the unique needs of your school or district. www.corwin.com/pd

Institutes

Corwin Institutes provide collaborative learning experiences that equip your team with tools and action plans ready for immediate implementation. www.corwin.com/institutes

eCourses

Practical, flexible online professional learning designed to let you go at your own pace. www.corwin.com/ecourses

Read2Earn

Did you know you can earn graduate credit for reading this book? Find out how: www.corwin.com/read2earn

Contact an account manager at (800) 831-6640 or visit **www.corwin.com** for more information.